PENGUIN TRUE CRIME

THE POISONED LIFE OF MRS MAYBRICK

Bernard Ryan, Jr, is a native of Albion, New York, and a graduate of Kent School and Princeton University. He has published two books for parents on the child's first year of school and a book on advertising and on journalism. For many years he was a Creative Supervisor with the New York advertising agency Batten, Barton, Durstine & Osborn. Since 1983 he has served on the staff of the American Association of Advertising Agencies, where he is Senior Vice-President for Public Affairs. He and his wife Jean live in Wilton, Connecticut, and have two daughters and one grandson.

The Rt Hon. The Lord Havers of St Edmundsbury was educated at Westminster and Corpus Christi, Cambridge, and was called to the Bar in 1948. In 1965 he became Chairman of the West Suffolk Quarter Sessions. He was returned as MP for Wimbledon in June 1970 and was appointed Solicitor-General in 1972. After a period as Shadow Attorney-General from 1974 to 1979, he was made Attorney-General under the Thatcher Government. In 1987 he became the Lord High Chancellor of Great Britain. He is co-author of two earlier books on famous cases, *The Royal Baccarat Scandal* and *Tragedy in Three Voices*.

D1347779

The Poisoned Life
of
Mrs Maybrick

BERNARD RYAN

with

THE RT HON. THE LORD HAVERS, QC, MP

Foreword by
Lord Russell of Killowen

PENGUIN BOOKS

PENGUIN BOOKS

Published by the Penguin Group
27 Wrights Lane, London w8 5tz, England
Viking Penguin Inc., 40 West 23rd Street, New York, New York 10010, USA
Penguin Books Australia Ltd, Ringwood, Victoria, Australia
Penguin Books Canada Ltd, 2801 John Street, Markham, Ontario, Canada l3r 1b4
Penguin Books (NZ) Ltd, 182–190 Wairau Road, Auckland 10, New Zealand

Penguin Books Ltd, Registered Offices: Harmondsworth, Middlesex, England

First published by William Kimber & Co. 1977
Published in Penguin Books 1989
1 3 5 7 9 10 8 6 4 2

Printed and bound in Great Britain by
Richard Clay Ltd, Bungay, Suffolk

For Jean, Nora Louise, and Barbara Ann

and to the memories of three who loved the courtroom:

my father, Bernard Ryan
lawyer and Judge of the New York State Court of Claims

my brother, William Fitts Ryan
lawyer and Member of the Congress of the United States

and my grandfather, William Cochran Fitts
lawyer and Attorney General of the State of Alabama
and Assistant Attorney General of the United States.

B.R.

Contents

PART THREE
AFTER THE TRIAL

List of Illustrations

Between pages 148 and 149

Foreword

by

LORD RUSSELL OF KILLOWEN

Lord of Appeal

This absorbing book is the first that I have read on the Maybrick case. My qualification for writing this note is limited to the fact that Sir Charles Russell QC, who unsuccessfully defended Mrs Maybrick, was my grandfather. Perhaps the oddest thing about the case is the ground upon which the Home Secretary recommended a reprieve from the death sentence, a ground with which the trial judge, Mr Justice Stephen, is said to have concurred. The finding of guilty of wilful murder by the jury meant that in their view there was no reasonable doubt of that guilt: the Home Secretary said in terms that there *was* a reasonable doubt thereof: this could only mean that he considered that the conviction was wrong and that the accused ought to have been found not guilty, which must have meant her freedom. But the Home Secretary did not free her: he found her guilty of an unsuccessful attempt to murder and in effect sentenced her to life imprisonment for that attempt – a crime with which she had never been charged, and of which it would not have been open to the jury on the indictment to find her guilty. Couple this with a summing up to the jury the defects of which forecast the ultimate total mental collapse of an outstanding judge, and the Maybrick case must be rated a most unhappy example of both the administration of the criminal law and the exercise of executive discretion.

In spite of the conversation between my grandfather and the son of the trial judge reported in this book, I would be surprised if the former thought that Mrs Maybrick was guilty even of the Home Secretary's afterthought of attempted murder. I do not speak from any internal family knowledge or tradition: but I think it improbable that my grandfather was moved, when he was Lord Chief Justice, to visit Mrs Maybrick in prison merely because of illogicality in the Home Secretary's grounds.

Preface

by

THE RT HON. THE LORD HAVERS, QC, MP

The trial in 1889 of Mrs Maybrick, for the murder of her husband by poison, played a major part in influencing changes in English criminal law. The modern reader who is unacquainted with our law as it was then framed and administered may be astonished at the strides towards greater justice that have been made since those days. It may be a shock to him that in this comparatively recent era the defendant, on such a grave charge, was not allowed to give evidence. It may be even more surprising to know that there was no Court of Appeal to which the verdict could be referred on any ground whatsoever. The extent to which newspapers could take up partisan and changing attitudes which could easily sway a jury is yet another contrast to the present time.

So quite apart from its fascinating human elements, this trial has been of the keenest interest to me in my profession of lawyer in tracing the reforms it sparked off. Accordingly, I was glad to accept the invitation of the publishers, to whom Bernard Ryan had submitted his manuscript, to collaborate with the author in finalising the presentation of the legal aspects of Florence Maybrick's tragic story and to add an account, designed for the general reader, of its impact on English law.

Introduction

If you drive northward along Route 7 on the western edge of Connecticut from Danbury to Kent, you travel one of the world's loveliest broad valleys, between low hills that are more mound than mountain. If, as you cross the muddy Housatonic River to Gaylordsville, you leave Route 7 and turn right, then immediately left, and follow a narrow and winding back road north again to South Kent, you will begin to climb over the mound that lies on the eastern side of the valley. And if after a little less than a mile you turn left again, just after the cemetery, leaving the narrow and winding back road, you will climb more steeply than before on a lane more narrow and winding. When the rutted lane straightens, and after it seems that all farmhouses must be forgotten and you wonder why the road continues at all, you will pass on your left a ramshackle ruin of a tiny cottage, all overgrown with vines and underbrush.

You will realise almost immediately that, although it is now deep in the woods, this cottage must once have commanded a magnificent view of the Housatonic Valley. When you examine it in detail, you will find that the small ruin has some unusual portals. They are small – very small. Large enough only for an animal the size of a cat to come and go. There are several such openings. They lead from a little front porch or stoop by way of a tunnel through a woodbox into a tiny turnaround of a hallway, thence into what was once a primitive kitchen without running water.

In this cabin, long ago, there came to an end the life of an elderly derelict person known in the neighbourhood up and down the road as 'the cat woman'. Beyond the fact that she kept house for an uncountable number of cats – perhaps 75, perhaps 100 – nothing seemed to be known of her past, her origins, or her life. Yet once the world on both sides of the Atlantic Ocean had echoed her name and rallied to save her from execution by hanging.

Her name was Mrs Maybrick. This is the story of her life. Though it begins nearly two decades before the twentieth century, it offers surprising parallels to life in the 1970s. One is the controversial question of the procurement and use of habit-forming drugs. Another is that of sexual morality and permissive codes. A third is the question of holding an accused person incommunicado and the handling of court trials and appeal from a verdict, including the right of the defendant to testify on his own behalf. Still another is trial by newspaper, while a fifth is that of capital punishment and of inhuman penal conditions. Then there is the fascinating setting, so strange even to imagine in the domestic households of today, in which servants outnumbered family and were privy to every daily event, whether trivial or important.

The story of Mrs Maybrick is, like all great unsolved mysteries, proof that the truth is stranger than fiction. Its setting, too – including such minor yet key details as postal service, telegrams and trains that moved almost with the speed of lightning – seems to be stranger than the imagination could create.

BERNARD RYAN

PART ONE

Before the Trial

I

'To Miss Chandler!'
'To Mr Maybrick!'
'Long Life!'
'Good Health!'

The ship's captain rang a small bell at his table to attract attention. The two hundred and twenty first-class passengers in the dining-saloon of the liner *Britannic* interrupted their supper conversations to listen.

'It is my pleasure to inform you that we have made the Atlantic crossing in the usual excellent time upon which the White Star Line prides itself,' he began. 'We have moved at a steady sixteen knots, and we shall land in Liverpool in the morning. It has been, I think, as speedy a crossing as can be managed by any steamer in service in this remarkable year, 1881.'

He paused and looked across the room, his eyes seeming to search for a particular table. 'Customarily,' he went on, 'I propose a toast to Her Majesty, and often I accept a toast to the ship and her performance. But this evening I wish to offer first another toast. For events have moved swiftly aboard the *Britannic* since we sailed from New York seven days ago. I think perhaps most of you know to what – or should I say, to whom – I allude.'

The captain picked up his wine glass and held it in mid-air. 'I raise my glass to the health of two who met aboard this ship only seven days ago – I believe it was at tea at table 14 as we steamed from New York harbour – and who informed me this very afternoon of their intention to be married in July. To the long life and good health, then, of Miss Chandler – and Mr Maybrick.'

'Hear, hear!'
'To Miss Chandler!'
'To Mr Maybrick!'
'Long life!'
'Good health!'

The dining-saloon rang with good wishes that quickly subsided into a general buzz of excitement. Miss Chandler and Mr Maybrick engaged! After only one short week together aboard ship! How exciting to see love blossom in such blushing young cheeks as Miss Chandler's! But – Mr Maybrick? (Here voices dropped to whispers, fans came fluttering before faces as ladies leaned toward each other to compare notes.) Mr Maybrick's cheeks were – well, rather pasty – his figure a bit settled. Was it not a May–September romance? Perhaps May–October? Might one not observe that the prosperous-looking Mr Maybrick was considerably the elder of the very young, though clearly cosmopolitan, Miss Chandler?

If others were concerned over the difference in the ages of the couple, Miss Chandler was not. She found James Maybrick a handsome gentleman who cut the figure of a well-established English businessman. She had liked him at once, perhaps because he flattered her by noting what he called her 'charming self-possession in travelling alone' and realised that she was, like himself, an experienced ocean traveller. She smiled as she recalled his saying that he could tell, from her genteel manner of speaking and soft voice, that she came either from an upper-class English background with a strong continental influence or from one of the Southern states of America.

She really could claim no one city as home, she had replied. She was a native of Mobile, Alabama. But she had divided her formative years between London, Paris, and other European cities, and New York, where she had just now been visiting her grandmother. She knew Liverpool, she added. She had attended the Grand National at Aintree last year. And wasn't it a shame, she said, her large, penetrating eyes searching the rather pale face of the English gentleman, that they had missed the race this year? It had been run only two weeks ago. Did Mr Maybrick happen to know which horse had won?

On the common ground of horsemanship they had found mutual interest. Riding was, indeed, Miss Chandler's special pastime. She had indulged in it to her heart's content when she lived in Cologne with her stepfather, the Baron von Roques, a cavalry officer in the Eighth Cuirassier Regiment of the German Army.

At the card tables in the saloon and on the iron promenade deck where the brisk sea air refreshed their appetites, Maybrick and Miss Chandler had developed their interest in each other. He was impressed by her independence and confidence as a sea traveller. She had first crossed the ocean more than fifteen years ago, and had recrossed it any number of times since then.

Soon Maybrick asked Miss Chandler's first name. It was Florence

Elizabeth, she said, adding that she was the fifth generation in her family to bear the name, Elizabeth. The remark brought up the subject of ancestry, and Florence Elizabeth Chandler obliged with a knowledge of genealogy such as only a heritage-conscious Southern upbringing was likely to produce.

She was the great-great-granddaughter of the Reverend Benjamin Thurston, a Harvard College graduate who had married the sister of the founders of the boys' preparatory schools, the Phillips Academies at Exeter and Andover. Their daughter Elizabeth had married an Ingraham of Portland, Maine – a family that included the first Episcopal bishop of Illinois as well as Salmon P. Chase, Lincoln's Secretary of the Treasury and more recently Chief Justice of the United States. Chase, Miss Chandler reminded Mr Maybrick, had presided over the impeachment of President Johnson in 1868. A daughter of the Ingraham union had married Darius Blake Holbrook, originator of the Illinois Central Railroad and owner of much of the real estate of Cairo, Illinois. Their daughter, Caroline Elizabeth, had married William G. Chandler, nephew of a former justice of the United States Supreme Court who had later been Assistant Secretary of State for the Confederacy. Florence Elizabeth was the daughter of that union.

Her father had died in 1863, and her mother had taken the girl and her older brother, Holbrook St John, abroad to be educated. There her mother had remarried, survived a second husband, and taken yet a third, the Baron von Roques. Florence's brother was now pursuing medical studies in Europe. She herself, having grown up partly in Europe and partly in America and always under the instruction of tutors and governesses, had been considered too delicate for college life and now spent her time travelling, visiting friends, or with her mother, the Baroness. Altogether, Miss Chandler's background did not fail to impress Mr Maybrick. His shipboard friend and dining companion was unquestionably of the American aristocracy.

As for Florence Chandler, she was more susceptible than most young ladies of her age to the charms of an older English gentleman. Having grown up among the adults of several countries, she was receptive to Maybrick's maturity and courtliness. His solid, if not stocky, frame and fine clothes, his self-assurance and debonair ways, appealed to her more strongly than the often supercilious airs of the cosmopolitan young men she knew. She enjoyed winning from him at euchre and losing to him in the return match, and when they played four hands she soon decided she would rather be his partner than his opponent.

After the first few days, rough seas worried those who had not pre-

viously voyaged abroad. Maybrick calmed them with assurance gained
from a number of ocean crossings. He had sailed aboard Brunel's levia-
than, the *Great Eastern*, and he regaled his fellow passengers with des-
criptions of shipboard life within her empty saloons and unbooked cabins.

If some of those travelling in first class found this fellow Maybrick a
bore, Florence Chandler was not one of them. If some noticed that a
pasty complexion and a flabby figure went with the hand that was so
liberal with gratuity and wager, they were either too stuffy or too well-
bred to bring such matters to the attention of the self-possessed young
lady who travelled alone.

To complete the picture, there was Maybrick's business. He made it
plain that his cotton brokerage required frequent trips between Norfolk,
Virginia and his home office in Liverpool and that it prospered. Surely
Miss Chandler knew, he ventured, that Norfolk was surpassed as a cotton
port only by New Orleans and Galveston? He did not hesitate to add
that Liverpool was the destination of as many as a quarter million bales
of cotton yearly – and left it to his audience to guess how many sales
were arranged by the Maybrick firm. Obviously, James Maybrick made
money and spent it, whether on fine cigars and an extra bottle of wine
aboard ship or at the race track ashore – where, he also made plain, he
enjoyed the expensive sport of wagering.

As the *Britannic* steamed across the Atlantic, it had become clear to all
in first class that Mr Maybrick and Miss Chandler were spending a great
deal of time together. Some questioned the propriety of a middle-aged
bachelor paying so much attention to an unchaperoned young female.
Some were shocked at the mere idea of a single young lady travelling
alone. Others, charmed by the discovery of a shipboard romance, were
titillated by the sight of the couple strolling the promenade deck or
sitting down together to enjoy the ship's concert.

If questions of propriety or of a difference in age bothered the first-
class passengers, they did not bother the couple. Maybrick approved of
the way Miss Chandler liked to dance and to ride. Her card-playing
challenged him. Her sweet round face and pale complexion, her soft
auburn hair pulled back and up to give perch to a tiny hat and attention
to tiny ears – these told him of style and maturity.

Florence Chandler liked this man. She was impressed with his experience of ocean travel and his knowledge of the cotton market. She
was proud to have him escort her from the dinner table to the ladies'
saloon, where coffee was served, before he went off to his cigar and
brandy with the men. She was pleased that he approved of her appearance. But, sometimes, when Mr Maybrick studied her from across the

card table, she worried that her complexion might not please him.

If others aboard ship were concerned about the difference in their ages, Florence Chandler was not. She came from the American South, where young ladies were adept at flirting with men considerably their seniors. She also hailed from a sophisticated international set in which her French and German were fluent in conversations with older men. She felt perfectly at home with maturity.

She was also at home with impulse. Her mother's incessant travels had made Florence used to sudden departures and arrivals. Her mother's romances had often left her to her own devices and forced independence upon her. Although she was young, it never occurred to her not to make up her own mind. She crossed the Atlantic alone, came and went as she pleased, and relied in blind faith upon things working themselves out for the best.

And so there went ashore at Liverpool, on the morning after the captain's announcement, a prospective groom who was forty-two years old and his intended bride, who was scarcely eighteen.

Maybrick turned to his business in Liverpool. Florence Chandler went on to meet her mother in Paris. Here the Baroness von Roques was enjoying an active social season, separated, by mutual agreement, from the Baron. She greeted the news of her daughter's engagement with approval. She had brought up Florence to act independently, without the counsel of others. She was pleased that Florence had made such a good choice. Obviously this Mr Maybrick would be able to provide the home and servants due a young lady who was to the manner born.

Florence would be married in London, of course, in St James's Church, Piccadilly. The Baroness and her daughter hurried to London to see about the arrangements, and shortly Florence was able to write to James Maybrick that she had set the date at St James's for 27th July.

In Liverpool, James Maybrick let it be known that his long period of bachelordom was drawing to a close. Among the first he told was his younger brother, Edwin, who was a prosperous cotton broker like himself. Word of Maybrick's engagement spread through Liverpool society.

The news had a devastating effect on a family of sisters named Janion. Two were married, but two were spinsters who had long hoped that one or the other of them would become the wife of James Maybrick. They held this hope particularly because James had maintained his friendship with the Janion family even though he had once been engaged to one of them – the one who was now Mrs Briggs – and the wedding date had been set before he broke the engagement. All four were keenly disappointed to learn that James had fallen in love with an American – especially so, since an eight-day shipboard romance was to take him to the altar.

Meanwhile, in Manchester, Maybrick's elder brother, Thomas, who was a well-to-do shipping agent, learned the news. Shortly after that Maybrick went down to London to break the news to his brother Michael. He was particularly anxious to let Michael know of the engagement himself, for though this brother was third in the family in order of birth, he was much admired and looked-up-to by the others. He was the policy-maker on family affairs, probably because of his immense financial and public success, under the name of Stephen Adams, as the composer and author of many popular songs.

Maybrick's fourth brother, William, who lived in Liverpool, scarcely seemed interested to learn of the proposed marriage.

There was someone else to whom the news of James Maybrick's forthcoming marriage came as a shock. This person was known neither to Florence Chandler nor to the Janion sisters nor to the Maybrick brothers. She dwelt in Liverpool, but she lived permanently outside the Maybrick and Janion social circle. Despite the social inequality, she felt that Maybrick's proposal of marriage should have come to her, for he had long promised that some day they would be wed. Her claim seemed just, for she had already borne him three children.

The bride wore satin and lace. From a simple V neckline with lace collar, a tightly-laced bodice stretched smoothly to Florence Chandler's tiny waist. Below, the ivory satin was pleated to the floor. The slight train was a sweep of unpleated satin rounded from hip to hip by a horse-shoe of lace and satin ruffles. Pointed elbow-length sleeves were edged with lace, and Florence wore openwork mittens of fine silk that matched the ivory satin of her dress. She carried a bouquet of white columbine and lilies of the valley and a broad fan of muslin trimmed with ivory lace on sticks of genuine ivory. Her stockings were embroidered with a single spray of flowers, in ivory silk, and Florence was pleased to be wearing the first of the newly-stylish pointed toe slippers in ivory satin.

James Maybrick wore satin, too. His waistcoat, with eight double-breasted buttons of ivory, was of white satin, embroidered with silver-threaded roses and lilies of the valley. His cutaway coat was lined with cream-coloured and elaborately quilted satin. He wore a fine linen shirt and satin Ascot necktie with embroidered ends.

To witness the ceremony and rejoice in the event came friends of the Baroness von Roques from France and Germany and London. The brothers Maybrick gathered, and the sisters Janion came down from

Liverpool. Holbrook Chandler took leave from his medical studies in Paris to give his sister in marriage to the Liverpool cotton broker. Absent was Florence's second step-father, the Baron von Roques.

The society columns, which gave ample coverage to this important wedding at St James's Church, assured their readers of the bride's heritage with a full report on members of her family, from her father, the Mobile banker who had died when she was an infant as a result of 'worriment over the outcome of the war', back to her many illustrious ancestors. She was, so far as London readers might know, an American heiress.

II

'I frequently tell Jim I hate him'

The wedding trip took them to Brazil. When the bride and groom returned, they rented a house in Liverpool from Maybrick's old friend, Mrs Briggs. Here the brothers Maybrick and the sisters Janion were frequent callers. The married Janions, Mrs Briggs and Mrs Martha Hughes (each of whom happened to be separated from her husband), found Florence Chandler Maybrick to be a naive young bride. She had the Southern gift of gab. Following her visitors' lead in discussing family matters, she disclosed that the Chandlers had fared no better than others in the South in salvaging material wealth from the war. But, she added, she and her mother and brother were the inheritors of some two and a half million acres of land spread over a vast area in the adjoining states of Virginia, Kentucky and West Virginia. This, however, was almost entirely wilderness and produced little income. But, as her mother always said, what counted was not what you had but who you were.

It was true, the Maybrick brothers learned: James's bride had an income of only a few hundred dollars a year at best. Not that they expected James to depend on his bride's dowry, but if he was going to import a wife from America, he might have found a rich one. Like their friends the Janion sisters, they were not over impressed with the idea that American culture, name and background outweighed the advantages of wealth. The eldest brother, Thomas Maybrick, who dined frequently with James and Florence when his business brought him the twenty miles from Manchester to Liverpool, was cordial enough. But Edwin and Michael openly expressed their disdain. They considered Florence to be beneath them. Their resentment, combined with the jealousy of the Janion sisters, subjected Florence to much criticism, of which she was aware of only a small part.

If she did not recognize the jealousy and resentment around her, Florence was aware of a sense of uneasiness. She had moved as a foreign-

22

er into an established, close-knit circle, bringing with her memories of the sunny dispositions of her Southern relatives and the open warmth of her mother's continental friends. She attributed the coldness she felt surrounding her more to Liverpool's and the Maybricks' business-like attitude than to herself. She concentrated on making a comfortable home for her husband, with whom she was much in love.

By late autumn, Mrs Briggs and Mrs Hughes noticed a growing change in Florence's appearance. They took it upon themselves to tell Florence that ladies in her condition simply were not seen on the street. Wasn't it time now for her to remain in seclusion at home?

Florence resented their presumption. She knew that any self-respecting expectant mother kept herself out of public sight. She had been about to retire from trips to Church Street or St George's, but didn't know why these meddling Janion sisters had to tell her what to do. Oh well. When the baby came, things would be different. They wouldn't be forever butting into her business.

James Chandler Maybrick was born on 24th March 1882. To celebrate his arrival, James Maybrick promised his wife that they would move to Norfolk as soon as she was well recovered from the birth. Maybrick did not go so far as to say that his business had been handicapped by his absence from the Norfolk Cotton Exchange during the trading this season, but the move was based on business needs.

Norfolk was prospering. From Virginia, the Carolinas, and Georgia, new railways hurried cotton to the port city. The rail freight cost was low and the voyage from Norfolk to Europe was several days shorter than from ports farther South. Gathered in Norfolk, during the market season from September to March, were about one hundred brokers who represented spinners in Liverpool, Manchester, and Bremen. They accounted for the shipping of more than half a million bales of cotton yearly – an amount worth roughly fourteen million dollars.

James Maybrick was one of these. His business day began shortly after eight o'clock in the office of one of the members of the Norfolk Cotton Exchange. Here, at a rolltop desk provided by his host, Maybrick went through his mail. By 8.30 he went down to the Exchange floor, where the Liverpool market quotations were on the board and a cable from Liverpool gave him orders for cotton his firm had sold to English manufacturers. After noting prices and exchanging pleasantries with the lively crowd of exporters, brokers and buyers on the Exchange floor, Maybrick and his exporter friend walked a short distance to the cotton warehouses. The exporter bought for him such lots as he selected. Back they went to the Exchange, to check on the course of prices, then again to the firm's office to book space aboard a vessel that promised the best time of delivery in Liverpool.

Like his fellow businessmen, Maybrick walked home for dinner, the heavy meal of the day, at one o'clock. Offices were closed, and it was customary for a businessman to enjoy a nap before returning to the job. Around three, Maybrick could be found again at his desk, getting off cables to Liverpool, arranging his financing, checking on shipments. Between four and five he went down with other members of the Exchange to one of the many clubs nearby, where congenial company shared a few drinks. Once more he returned to his desk to write his own correspondence by hand, and toward seven o'clock he walked home for supper.

Such, as far as Florence Maybrick knew, was her husband's routine six days a week. After supper they entertained other couples at cards or went out to play cards or to the theatre. Cotton brokers such as Maybrick were considered men of standing. They were welcomed in Norfolk's active social circles.

If Florence Maybrick had followed James on almost any morning of the week, she would have discovered that he did not go directly to his office. He made a brief detour to one of the apothecary shops on Main Street. On certain evenings when correspondence kept him late, she had no way of knowing that his outgoing mail for Liverpool included financial support for his fatherless children. Had she gone round to the flat where her husband had resided during the cotton market from 1877 until 1881, she might have learned from Nicholas Bateson, with whom Maybrick had shared the quarters, the reason for his regular visits to the drug-store. She might also have heard the name of an American woman, Mary Hogwood, whose acquaintance with her husband's habits was even more intimate than Bateson's.

But Florence Maybrick had no reason to be suspicious. A wife did not presume to question a husband's coming and going any more than she would have questioned the decisions he made on the floor of the Exchange. A key to the relationship could be seen when *The Times* arrived from London with the news that the Married Women's Property Act had been passed. Gladstone had established the right of a wife to do what she liked with her own money without consulting her husband. Snorted Maybrick, 'Preposterous'.

Maybrick's many Atlantic crossings and his business connections in Norfolk and Liverpool had led to many friendships among men of the sea. They stopped in now and then at his Norfolk office. The Maybricks had been living in Norfolk for more than a year when Master Mariner

John Fleming, of Halifax, Ontario, visited the office one day. Maybrick was preparing some food. The sea captain saw him add some grey powder to the dish.

'You would be horrified, I dare say,' said the cotton broker, 'if you knew what this is – it is arsenic.'

Fleming was indeed horrified, and said so.

'We all take some poison more or less,' Maybrick went on grandly. 'For instance, I am now taking arsenic enough to kill you. I take this arsenic once in a while because I find it strengthens me.'

Maybrick's morning calls at the drugstore continued. If his wife noticed how frequently he started the day by rubbing the backs of his hands, complaining of poor circulation, she did not presume to ask what caused his complaint – any more than she presumed to argue with him when he learned from his *Times* that in London the Rational Dress Society was promoting the wearing of a gymnastic tunic and the abandonment of the corset by ladies engaged in games. Croquet, the popular sport of his youth, was no longer active enough for ladies? 'They must now be seen on the tennis and badminton court?' said Maybrick, 'and improperly attired? Ridiculous.'

Before New Year's Day, 1884, James Maybrick announced that at the end of the market in March they would pack their things and return to Liverpool. He reminded Florence of the gala day a few weeks earlier when the New River Railway completed its line into the Pocahontas coal mining region. All Norfolk had come down to Water Street to see the first carload of Pocahontas coal hauled to the waterfront. This event, Maybrick declared with authority, marked the beginning of Norfolk's decline as a cotton port. While it was a fact that in the current year, 1883, nearly sixty vessels had sailed from Norfolk for Liverpool, it was a more significant fact that twice that number had sailed for other foreign ports. Some had predicted years ago that Norfolk would become America's greatest coaling station. The proximity of abundant coal fields in Virginia, Kentucky and West Virginia, combined with Mr McCullough's foresightedness in developing the Granby Street piers and wharves and rail terminals, now brought that day nearer. Maybrick would have to concentrate his business in Liverpool, where by cable he could buy almost simultaneously from exporters in a number of other American cities.

Florence Maybrick went ashore in Liverpool a mature and confident woman. She took up the management of her home with an authority affirmed by two years of busy social and domestic life, and she moved immediately into prominence in Liverpool society. She and James were seen at public events in St George's Hall, at the best private dinner parties, and at the races at Birkenhead and Wirral across the Mersey.

They had been back in Liverpool only a short time when in 1884 the city went agog over a sensational murder case. The newspapers outdid each other in providing colourful details of how two lower class women, a Mrs Higgins and a Mrs Flanagan, had obtained arsenic by soaking it out of flypapers, and had then poisoned a number of persons. The women were tried and convicted.

In April 1885, Florence Maybrick received word that her brother, Holbrook St John Chandler, had died of tuberculosis in Paris. Old friends in America and in Europe were notified by card :

Fell Asleep in God

At his residence, 37 bis nee [*rue*] du Colisée, after a lingering ill-ness, Holbrook St John Chandler, student at the Paris Faculty of Medicine, only son of William G. Chandler, Ala., USA, deceased, grandson of Darius H. Holbrook, of New York, deceased.

Distant friends and relatives, pray for a peaceful rest.

Baron Adolf von Roques, Baroness Caroline Holbrook von Roques, James Maybrick, Mrs Daniel Chandler, John L. Chandler and family, Heywood Stannard and family, Rev. John A. P. Ingraham and family, Hon. John A. Campbell and family.

The funeral services will take place at the American Episcopal Church, rue Bayard 17, on Wednesday, April 15, at 2 o'clock.

The inhumation at Pansy Cemetery.

Those who received the announcement could note that, while the estranged Baron and Baroness were each listed, the names Florence Chandler Maybrick or Mrs James Maybrick were absent.

Maybrick's cotton brokerage flourished. He maintained a fine office in the Knowsley Buildings, off Tithebarn Street. As a member of the Liverpool Cotton Exchange, he appeared daily on the exchange floor – except when business took him to London. It was the railway age. Service was frequent and fast between such cities as Liverpool, Manchester, Birmingham and London. Men like Maybrick thought nothing of stepping aboard the London, Midland and Scottish to go up to London for the day. Maybrick in particular thought nothing of staying overnight. Frequently he stayed two or three days at a time.

Soon after the Maybricks returned to Liverpool, James consulted Dr Arthur Hopper. He had been taking quinine, he said, for the effects of malaria contracted in the swampy climate of Norfolk. But quinine did not agree with him. The doctor suggested arsenic, and Maybrick mentioned that he knew the drug as an antiperiodic. The doctor also prescribed the nerve tonics, nux vomica and phosphoric acid.

The business decline of 1886 had little effect on Maybrick's earning power. Only foodstuffs made a greater volume of British imports than raw cotton, and raw cotton was Maybrick's livelihood. He continued to prosper.

His personal routine was disrupted in 1886. A cousin of his had been employed for two years by a wholesale drug business in Liverpool, and Maybrick had made it a habit to visit him regularly. Each time, they strolled together through the warehouse full of drugs. Whether because of the recession or for some other reason, the cousin was discharged in 1886. Maybrick went personally to plead with his employer. But he was unsuccessful in getting the man reinstated.

A second child was expected in June. Anticipating the addition, Florence and James rented a large home called Battlecrease House, in the Liverpool suburb of Aigburth. Here the growing city was reaching out to where wealthy merchants from Bold and Dale Streets had long maintained homes in quiet seclusion. In this house the staff became larger than the family it served. A cook ruled in the kitchen and a housemaid took charge of the linens, doing the cleaning and sewing and waiting on table. A parlourmaid answered the door, supervised the setting of the table, and saw to Mrs Maybrick's personal linens and clothing, made the beds and kept the upstairs rooms tidy, and did any needlework required in her mistress's wardrobe. In the nursery above reigned a nurse who had full charge of the feeding, bathing and general care of young James, and who looked forward to the arrival of an infant to care for. Already she was busy making the layette. In addition, a man was in charge of the grounds and stable.

Mrs Briggs and Mrs Hughes, as old and intimate friends, still came and went as they pleased, but by now Florence was as accustomed to their unannounced appearance as she was to the presence of the servants. She had proved herself to be a devoted wife, a capable mother, and a popular hostess, and the atmosphere of resentment which she had known as a bride had largely disappeared.

On 20th June 1886, in Battlecrease House, Dr Hopper brought Gladys Evelyn Maybrick into the world. In six generations on her mother's side of the family, she was the first girl not to be baptized Elizabeth. Her mother recovered quickly from the birth, anxious to be out again in Liverpool society. Then, as the summer ended, Florence Maybrick was alarmed to learn that an epidemic of Scarlatina was raging through Liverpool. By mid-September every hospital was filled. Also called Black Scarlet Fever, the disease seemed to attack more boys than girls, and twice as many children under five as older. New cases averaged two hundred and fifty a month, and by the end of the year Liverpool counted more than two hundred deaths from Scarlatina.

Early the next year, as the epidemic continued, five-year-old James was stricken. His father immediately packed up the baby girl and the nursemaid and sought refuge in Wales, while Florence stayed home with the boy. Dismissing all servants except the cook, she isolated herself and her patient in one bedroom. There she nursed her son through his illness. She had hung a heavy curtain outside the door, and before it the cook set each meal on the floor. For six weeks the siege continued, with Florence washing the dishes within the room before putting them outside the door.

James recovered. His father and sister and nurse came home and life at Battlecrease House went on as before – with one important exception.

It was an exception known only to two people within the house, and possibly to one other in Liverpool, but it was vital. For Florence Maybrick had learned of her husband's mistress. She learned that he was the father of three children born out of wedlock before his marriage, and that he had sired two more children by the same woman since he and Florence had been married.

So Florence Maybrick found herself the victim of the prevailing Victorian double standard of sexual conduct. Somewhere in Liverpool, she now knew, there was a woman who loved her pompous husband as much as she did, a woman who depended on him and had been willing to continue to bear his children after he had married another.

Florence had many acquaintances, but no intimate confidante. Her mother, a woman of considerable experience in matrimonial problems, was far away in Europe. With no intimate friend or relation to consult, she did what she had done when a shipboard romance brought a proposal of marriage. She consulted only her own self-reliance about what to do. James had another woman to sleep with in Liverpool? Very well – his wife would no longer sleep with him.

No one outside the Maybrick household – and, indeed, no one except James and Florence Maybrick within it – was aware that anything was amiss. The couple's busy social life continued. James continued to spend

frequent evenings 'at the club' and to travel often to London for a day
or two 'on business'. But Florence could no longer feel sure of just where
he was or what he was doing.

One day in 1888, Dr Arthur Hopper, who had delivered Mrs Maybrick's daughter a year or so earlier, received a visit from her. She said
she wanted to consult him about her husband. For some time he had had
a habit of 'taking a strong medicine which had a bad influence on him.
He always seemed worse after each dose.' Florence added that her husband insisted that she was not to be concerned with what he did. Would
Dr Hopper, she pleaded, please look into the matter? Would he, in fact,
remonstrate with James about it?

The doctor reassured Mrs Maybrick and promised to see what he could
find out. The next time he paid a professional call at Battlecrease House,
to treat Maybrick for a slight dyspepsia and nervousness, he took the
opportunity to look around his patient's dressing room for the strong
medicine, or any sign of it. But he found nothing, and he said nothing
to Maybrick.

He also refrained from saying anything to Mrs Maybrick about a
noticeable increase in the frequency of her husband's complaints. Though
Maybrick had consulted him occasionally since his query about quinine
in 1884, his visits now occurred weekly in the summer and autumn of
1888. The doctor, confidently recognising the symptoms of hypochondria,
was only slightly dismayed to learn that his patient had consumed a
bottle of bromide of potassium in half the time prescribed. He warned
Maybrick not to be so free with medicines.

In November, a Liverpool doctor noted for skill in treating nervous
dyspepsia received James Maybrick as a patient. As Maybrick complained of ceaseless headaches over a period of three months, of a numbness of the left leg and hand after smoking heavily or taking too much
wine, and of various skin eruptions, Dr J. Drysdale asked what medicine
he had been taking.

Maybrick mentioned nitro-hydrochloric acid, strychnine, hydrate of
potash, and several other drugs. Dr Drysdale, who saw Maybrick three
times in November and twice in December, entered a complete account
of his patient's remedies in his diary, noting that Maybrick seemed to be
quite knowledgeable about medicines.

In the same year, a practising apothecary named Edwin Garnett
Heaton, who was nearing retirement after thirty-seven years in business
in Liverpool, observed a change in a prescription which he had been
refilling almost daily for a year and a half. The prescription was for a

'pick-me-up' or tonic, a medicine required by many gentlemen of the Cotton Exchange to relieve the effects of over-indulgence. In this instance, for a Mr Maybrick, the prescription had regularly called for four drops of liquor arsenicalis. Now the dosage was increased to seven drops, and Heaton observed that his customer stopped in at least twice a day and sometimes as often as five times a day. In addition, when Maybrick was going out of town, he often had as many as eight to sixteen doses made up in advance. Curious about his customer's habit, Heaton asked him about it. Maybrick's reply was that he was taking the arsenic for its aphrodisiacal qualities.

In December 1888, Florence and James Maybrick entertained at a small dinner party at home. Among the guests was one of James's friends. His name was Alfred Brierley. He came of an excellent Lancashire family and was the wealthy senior partner of Brierley and Wood, cotton brokers who maintained offices in New Orleans and Liverpool. Tall, bearded and handsome, Brierley was a thirty-eight-year-old bachelor. Florence found him charming. She invited him to Battlecrease House frequently through the winter, and she and James were often joined by Brierley when they went out for the evening.

The domestic problem between husband and wife that had been simmering quietly for nearly two years came to the boil on the last day of 1888. Florence and James quarrelled, and, she wrote her mother in Paris on December 31st:

> In his fury, he tore up his will this morning, as he had made me sole legatee and trustee for the children in it. Now, he proposes to settle everything he can on the children alone, allowing me only the one-third by law! I am sure it matters little to me, as long as the children are provided for. My own income will do for me alone. A pleasant way of commencing the New Year!

One evening early in 1889, Florence and James came home earlier than expected. As they entered Battlecrease House, Florence heard cries coming from the nursery. She rushed upstairs to find the two-year-old, Gladys, screaming in the dark, while her brother bravely tried to find matches to strike a light. After calming the children, Mrs Maybrick sought their nurse, who had been given strict orders never to leave them alone. The woman, Alice Yapp, was in the kitchen, enjoying a social evening with the staff. All were well beyond earshot from the third floor nursery. Mrs Maybrick severely reprimanded Nurse Yapp.

The reprimand was not quickly forgotten. Nurse Yapp complained within a day or two to Mrs Briggs, who made it a point to befriend her and to censure Florence. On lesser occasions, Nurse Yapp did her own censuring of her mistress, behind her back. Often she joined Alice Grant, wife of the gardener, in criticising Mrs Maybrick as 'an old cat, always sticking indoors', for her domestic habit of spending long hours in the sitting room reading or sketching. That a pet cat was Mrs Maybrick's constant companion merely added to the ridicule.

In January 1889, a man named Valentine Charles Blake searched the membership of the Liverpool Cotton Exchange for someone who might invest in a project of his. Introduced to James Maybrick, he explained that he was developing a substitute for cotton. Maybrick was curious and asked for details. Blake explained that his basic material was ramie, a perennial plant in Asia which had a strong and lustrous fibre that could be spun and woven. Wouldn't Mr Maybrick help him place it on the Liverpool market?

Maybrick asked what chemicals were used to process the fabric. Blake remarked that arsenic was one. Maybrick asked Blake whether he had heard of the Styrian peasants, who ate arsenic so regularly that their tolerance for it was high. He also spoke of De Quincey's *Confessions of an Opium-Eater*. De Quincey, he said, had been able to take as much as 900 drops of laudanum in a day. Arsenic meant much the same to him, said Maybrick.

'It is meat and liquor to me,' he said, adding, 'I don't tell everybody. I take it when I can get it, but the doctors won't put any into my medicine except now and then. That only tantalises me.'

They talked further, and at last Maybrick said, 'Since you use arsenic, can you let me have some? I find a difficulty in getting it here.'

The inventor agreed to supply the broker with what arsenic he had on hand, in return for Maybrick's assistance in marketing the ramie product. A month later, when they met again, Blake gave Maybrick 150 grains of arsenic in three separate paper packets. Some was white and some, mixed with charcoal, was black.

During the winter, Alfred Brierley had become a frequent dinner guest at Battlecrease House. As March came, he often joined James and Florence Maybrick as they went round the Lancashire countryside attending the early spring race meets. Soon he had become their constant companion.

Returning toward Liverpool one evening, the party decided to stop overnight at the Palace Hotel in Birkenhead, across the Mersey from Liverpool. The Maybricks had with them not only Brierley but a couple named Samuelson. After dinner, Charles and Christina Samuelson sat down to play cards with James and Florence Maybrick. The men were winning, and the ladies were annoyed with their luck. When Charles Samuelson took still another hand, his wife snapped, 'I hate you!' To relieve the tension, Florence Maybrick turned to Samuelson and said, 'You mustn't pay any attention to your wife. I frequently tell Jim I hate him, without meaning a word of it.'

At about this time, Florence Maybrick was beginning to realise that the opposite of hatred was being expressed by her attractive friend Alfred Brierley. He seized whatever opportunities arose to be with her. More and more, he turned up when James Maybrick was absent from home. Soon he made an intimation that he could offer Florence more than the companionship he now supplied.

Florence needed little encouragement to be interested in Brierley. She found herself susceptible to his gentlemanly charm. Alfred Brierley was younger than Jim Maybrick. He was taller. He was more handsome. And he was something that Jim had never been : in a word, the word most descriptive of the debonair Englishman of the time, he was dashing. As for her husband, he was often disagreeable. He seldom paid Florence the kind of attention that had originally won her. He was usually a bore. He was almost always pompous. And he annoyed her by seeming not to be distressed that for nearly two years now she had not permitted him to sleep with her. He was apparently satisfied with his continuing arrangements with the mother of his five nameless children in Liverpool.

Florence was aware that the world would censure her husband very lightly, if at all, for maintaining a mistress. She was also aware that for her to indulge in extramarital passion would be an unforgivable sin. In recent months, she knew, there had been considerable public discussion on the failure of marriage – so much discussion, in fact, that she had become aware of the lack of intelligence of such divorce laws as existed. But above all she was aware of her increasing pleasure in the companionship of Alfred Brierley. She found herself ready to make whatever arrangements were needed to fill her own emotional needs. She discussed the pros and cons with no one before deciding what to do.

On day early in March, Dr Richard Humphreys, a general practitioner in Aigburth, was summoned to Battlecrease House. He had often attended the Maybrick children, and he found one of them suffering from a minor illness. During the visit, he casually asked Mrs Maybrick about her husband's health. She said that Maybrick had a habit of taking some white powder. She thought perhaps it was strychnine, she said, and asked the doctor what was likely to be the result. Dr Humphreys told her that if it was strychnine and if he took a large enough dose he would die. He then thought a moment, looked at her over the top of his gold-rimmed spectacles, and added laughingly, 'Well, if he should ever die suddenly, call me, and I can say you have had some conversation with me about it.'

On 7th March, Dr Drysdale received his first visit from James Maybrick since 10th December. Maybrick said that he had been better during the interval, but had never had more than two days without a headache. He complained of a little 'creeping' sensation, but said he had no aggravation after eating. He added that the numbness of his left leg and hand continued.

In London, about 12th March, Michael Maybrick received a letter from his sister-in-law. Florence was concerned because her husband seemed to be in the habit of taking some pernicious drug which regularly had a bad effect on him. She had tried to reason with him about it, but he refused to discuss it.

Michael brought up the subject when James came down to London the following Saturday night. 'What is it with reference to those white powders I am told about?' he said. 'I am told you take a certain powder.'

James looked at him. 'Whoever told you that, it is a damned lie.'

Michael did not pursue the subject.

While James Maybrick was absent in London, Alfred Brierley and Florence Maybrick met. Brierley professed his love for Florence, and asked her to go away with him. Yielding at last to emotions that had not been stirred in twenty-four months, Florence admitted that she returned his love. She made it clear that she would not be afraid to let the deed follow the word. With her usual determination, she told her lover as they parted that she would make all necessary arrangements.

III

'Such a scandal will be all over town tomorrow'

The small hotel known as Flatman's consisted of adjoining buildings around the corner from each other on Henrietta Street and Chapel Place in Cavendish Square in London. Its proprietor opened a telegram on the morning of the 16th March 1889, and learned that a Mrs James Maybrick of Liverpool wished to reserve rooms for a London visit the following week. The wire mentioned her sister, Mrs Thomas Maybrick. Mr Flatman wrote back immediately to say that he would reserve rooms for Mrs Maybrick and her sister.

By return mail, Mr Flatman received a letter from Mrs Maybrick. It was only Mr and Mrs T. Maybrick who were coming. Mrs Maybrick added that she had taken it upon herself to make the arrangements for Mrs T. Maybrick, as she was a young lady without much experience in such matters.

Still another letter from Mrs Maybrick on Tuesday, 19th March, made it very clear that she was ordering a bedroom and sitting room for Mr and Mrs Thomas Maybrick. She added that while Mrs Maybrick would arrive on Thursday her husband could not possibly arrive until Friday.

Mr Flatman turned to his room clerk, a stoop-shouldered, obsequious man named Alfred Schweisso, who functioned also as waiter when room service was demanded. They agreed that Number 9 bedroom and Number 16 sitting room, which adjoined each other in the Henrietta Street part of the hotel, would do nicely for Mr and Mrs Maybrick. Mr Flatman filed the letters and telegram.

Two others in London received letters from Florence Maybrick. Each was a distant cousin. The first, Miss Margaret Baillie, was advised that Florence would be coming up from Liverpool and would like to stop with her for a few days. The second, a young man named John Baillie Knight, learned that his Cousin Florence would be stopping alone at Flatman's Hotel on the night of Thursday, the 21st. Since she disliked dining alone in London, would he escort her to dinner?

At Battlecrease House, Florence Maybrick asked Nurse Yapp to forward any mail to the Grand Hotel in London. She told her husband that an aunt was to undergo an operation, and that she had asked Florence to stay with her for a week or so during her first days of recuperation.

Early in the afternoon of 21st March, Schweisso was on duty at the desk at Flatman's. A woman arrived alone and registered in the names of Mr and Mrs Thomas Maybrick. Schweisso carried her dressing case and portmanteau to the rooms that had been reserved. It was Flatman's best suite, he said. He asked her if everything was in order.

'Everything is fine,' she said, adding, 'My husband will not arrive until later, but tonight another gentleman will call. When he does, send him up.'

Accepting half a crown, Schweisso bowed his way out of the room.

At about six-thirty, a young gentleman inquired at the desk for Mrs Maybrick, and was sent up to her suite. Within a few minutes they came down together, went into the street, and disappeared into a cab.

During the evening, a tall, bearded and handsome gentleman arrived at Flatman's adjoining building, around the corner in Chapel Place. He took a bedroom and small dining room.

When Alfred Schweisso went to bed that night, he noticed that Mrs Maybrick's key was still in its box at the desk. She had not returned to her suite. But when he served breakfast for one in the sitting room next morning, he saw that a tall, bearded gentleman had joined the guest in Flatman's best suite.

On Saturday morning, Schweisso was again summoned to serve breakfast, this time for two. When he entered the sitting room, the tall, bearded gentleman, in his dressing gown, took the breakfast tray. Through an open bedroom door, Schweisso could see Mrs Maybrick lying in bed. Schweisso took no other meals to the suite on Friday or Saturday.

Again on Sunday morning, Schweisso took breakfast to the suite. That afternoon at about one o'clock, the couple stopped by the desk to check out. Schweisso said he was surprised to see them leaving, for the rooms had been reserved for one week. The gentleman said something about having received a telegram from his brother. He paid the bill in full: two pounds, thirteen shillings.

As they parted in London on Sunday, 24th March, Florence Maybrick and Alfred Brierley agreed that they would make sure the high tide of their passion had been reached and passed. They would not meet again in London or any other place away from home. Nor would they correspond, unless Florence 'got into some complications as a consequence of our journey,' in which case she was to let Brierley know.

That afternoon, Florence arrived at the home of Miss Baillie. She told her cousin she had come from a weekend visit at the Grand Hotel.

Next day in Liverpool, Nurse Yapp received a telegram from Mrs Maybrick, asking the nurse now to forward any mail to the Baillies' rather than to the Grand Hotel.

Later that week, Florence Maybrick had dinner with her brother-in-law, Michael Maybrick. On another day, she was taken by Miss Baillie to see her cousin's solicitors, Markby and Stewart. And on Thursday, the 28th, she again boarded the LMS train and sped northwestward across England. She carried more luggage than the portmanteau and dressing case she had brought, for the London shops had been full of irresistible new accessories – silk and velvet bags with beetle-wing embroidery of iridescent green spangles, something she had not yet seen at Lewis's or Nusbaum's in Liverpool; a matinee bag of leather, fitted with scent bottle, opera glass and biscuit case; and the new parasols, which, she discovered, were longer and slimmer than last year's.

Florence was anxious to get home, not only because she had not seen her children for a week but because the Grand National would be run next day. It was specifically for her appearance at Aintree that she had bought the matinee bag and a new silk parasol.

Watching the Grand National from an omnibus chartered for the occasion was a party of friends that included James and Florence Maybrick, three of the Janion sisters, Christina Samuelson, and several others. They were soon joined by one who had not planned to be with them but who happened to see them there – Alfred Brierley.

Word had gone round that the Prince of Wales, with a large retinue, was in the grandstand. His presence reflected a new and unusual meeting of royalty and society. It showed the influence of the 'Marlborough House set', a witty group from the highest social circle who had been adopted by the middle-aged prince.

Brierley, in the spirit of the occasion, went off, bought grandstand tickets for everybody, and returned to hand them out cheerily. Mrs Briggs and Mrs Hughes, determined to have a look at his Royal Highness and the 'Marlborough Boys', hurried away. Mrs Samuelson accepted the escort of two gentlemen. Alfred Brierley asked Florence Maybrick if she would like to see the Prince. She took his arm and under her new parasol they strolled toward the grandstand.

Maybrick was left alone with Miss Gertrude Janion, who had for a long time been smitten with Brierley.

When Florence and Alfred returned, Maybrick scolded his wife loudly for being away too long. He was sullen and glowering. The others, returning shortly, could feel the anger hanging in the air. Just before the omnibus started toward Liverpool, Florence Maybrick said to Christina Samuelson, 'I will give it to him hot and heavy for speaking to me like that in public.'

At seven that evening in Battlecrease House, Nurse Yapp pursued her normal routine, getting James and Gladys ready for supper and bed. Arriving home, Mrs Maybrick came into the nursery to see the children. Mr Maybrick reached home ten minutes later, and his wife was still in the nursery when he came up. Striding into the room and ignoring his wife, he took Gladys on his knee and began to play with her. Mrs Maybrick, without a word, got up and left the room.

A few minutes later, the housemaid Bessie Brierley, climbing the stairs with the children's supper, heard the voices of her master and mistress shouting angrily as she passed their bedroom.

When the children had had their supper, Nurse Yapp came out onto the landing. She heard her master's voice from the bedroom, saying, 'Such a scandal will be all over town tomorrow. Florie, I never thought it would come to this.'

Bessie Brierley in the kitchen answered the bedroom bell. She hurried to the bedroom door, and Maybrick told her to go for a cab at once. She hastened into the street to call a cab.

Cook Humphreys, wondering what all the commotion was about, bustled into the front hall in time to see Bessie Brierley rush down the stairs and out the door. She was followed by Mr Maybrick, stamping his feet and waving his handkerchief over his head. Mrs Maybrick was close behind him, still wearing her hat and fur cape. She was out of breath. Her eyes were red and filled with tears, and the cook noticed that the button-holes of her dress were torn. Maybrick turned to his wife. She was not to go away wearing the cape, he shouted. As an afterthought, he roared that he had bought it for her to go up to London in.

The cook, asserting the authority that went with her position, said, 'Oh, master, please don't go on like this, the neighbours will hear you.'

'Leave me alone,' said Maybrick. 'You don't know anything about it.'

The cook persisted. 'Don't send the mistress away tonight. Where can she go? Let her stay until morning.'

Maybrick turned on his wife, shouting, 'By heavens, Florie, if you cross this doorstep you shall never enter this house again.' With that, he fell exhausted across the oak settle in the hall.

Bessie Brierley came in from the street. The cab was waiting.

Nurse Yapp stepped close to Mrs Maybrick and asked her to go up to the nursery to see the baby. Mrs Maybrick did not move. The nurse put her arm around her mistress's waist and led her up the stairs.

Bessie Brierley ordered the cabman to drive away.

Nurse Yapp took her mistress to a dressing-room off the nursery, next door to the nurse's own bedroom. There she made a bed, and there Mrs Maybrick spent the night.

At half-past eleven, when Mrs Maybrick had fallen asleep, Nurse Yapp went to Maybrick, who was still up. She told him that Mrs Maybrick had gone to bed in her room. 'Very well,' he said.

When Mrs Maybrick awoke next morning, she had a black eye.

For once, Florence Maybrick decided to seek advice. She had no one to turn to except the woman who had been given so much freedom of the house by her husband – Matilda Briggs. She went to Mrs Briggs first thing Saturday morning and told her about the quarrel. She said that, with this treatment added to the fact that her husband was supporting another woman, she was ready to seek a separation.

Mrs Briggs first suggested that they see Dr Arthur Hopper. As the family physician, the doctor enjoyed James's confidence and might be able to reason with him.

Dr Hopper examined Mrs Maybrick's black eye, and observed that she was distraught. Her husband had dragged her around the bedroom and beaten her, she said. She added that her feeling against him was so strong that she could not bear him even to come near her. She intended to see if a separation could be arranged.

The doctor tried to persuade his patient not to seek a separation. When she seemed calm, he sent her home with Mrs Briggs and promised to stop in at Battlecrease House shortly and speak to Maybrick.

On the way home, Mrs Briggs said that perhaps, after all, Florence should see a lawyer and ascertain her legal rights. They stopped in to see her solicitor, Mr Donnison.

In the afternoon, Dr Hopper came to Battlecrease House. First he saw the Maybricks separately. Maybrick described how his wife had annoyed him at Aintree by walking off with another gentleman. Then Mrs Maybrick told the doctor about her repugnance for her husband, and revealed that she had accumulated considerable debts. She was afraid they might stand in the way of a reconciliation. Dr Hopper advised her to make a clean breast of her debts and ask her husband's forgiveness for them.

Next the doctor met with the Maybricks together. Florence told her husband about her debts. Maybrick made light of them and promised to pay them all. The doctor departed from Battlecrease House under the impression that he had indeed effected a reconciliation.

Whatever the doctor's impression, the cook, Elizabeth Humphreys, found the dissension continuing on Sunday. It began when Mrs Briggs arrived, apparently to stay at the house. The cook soon heard both Maybricks and Mrs Briggs quarrelling and shouting. The mistress said something about never having invited any one to the house without Mr Maybrick's knowledge.

At six, the housemaid took tea to Mrs Maybrick and found her lying in a faint on the sofa. She called Elizabeth Humphreys, who thought her mistress was dead. They shook her, and called the master. Mr Maybrick and Mrs Briggs hurried upstairs together, and Maybrick came into the room crying, 'Bunny, Bunny, here's your hubby.' He immediately sent the cook to fetch Dr Richard Humphreys from nearby Garston.

Mrs Maybrick did not recover consciousness for another two hours. The frightened servants spent the night fetching the doctor, for every time he went away Mr Maybrick wanted him back. He made four or five visits that night.

A frequent visitor to the kitchen was Mrs Briggs. She kept coming to the cook for beer, repeating that she was quite put out about the quarrel and must have something to keep her up. In one appearance, at about nine o'clock, she was half undressed and was wearing a gown of Mrs Maybrick's which was much too small for her. Doctor Humphreys, seeing her thus attired as he came in on one of his visits, asked Cook Humphreys who that woman was.

Mrs Maybrick stayed in bed, ill, for almost a week.

In London, on the first day of April, Miss Margaret Baillie, with whom Florence Maybrick had stayed, looked through her mail. She was surprised to see that a letter she had addressed only three days ago to Cousin Florence at Battlecrease House, Aigburth, Liverpool, had been returned. She decided to write again.

Mary Cadwallader, the housemaid, received some special instructions that week. Mr Maybrick told her she was not to take any letters up to the mistress until he had seen them, adding that, 'Your mistress sees all my letters, and there is no reason why I should not see hers.'

The maid asked him if she should keep the letters that came for Mrs

Maybrick while he was at the office, and he answered, 'Certainly not.'

For a few days he looked at all letters the maid showed him before they went up to the bedroom, but did not open them. Then he changed, declining to look at them, and the maid took them without delay to Mrs Maybrick.

On 6th April, in his office, Alfred Brierley received a message from Mrs Maybrick. She wanted to see him without delay.

When they met, Brierley was shocked to see that Florence had a bruised and discoloured eye.

She wanted not merely to see Brierley. She wanted Brierley quite literally to see her – to see her black eye, to hear in detail how Jim had beaten her after the Grand National. She told Brierley the quarrel went on all that night.

In seeing Brierley, Florence had no particular plan in mind. She counted on something happening – on Brierley's taking some action, on his offering to go away with her permanently, on some solution or other presenting itself. She was disappointed to find that Brierley offered no action, no protection, no solution.

In London, at about this time, Florence Maybrick's cousin, Miss Baillie, was again surprised. Her morning mail included her second letter addressed to Battlecrease House. Like the first, it had been 'forwarded back' to her. But hadn't Cousin Florence said, as she was leaving, that she was going home? Certainly she had mentioned the Grand Hotel. Had Florence said she had come from there after spending the weekend – or had she said she was going there next?

At the Palatine Club in Liverpool, Sir James Poole was just coming out of the underwriters' room. Sir James was an authoritative businessman who wore a Vandyke beard and had served as mayor of the city. He ran into James Maybrick and some other club members, and during a casual conversation someone mentioned that it was becoming a common custom nowadays to take poisonous medicines.

James Maybrick responded with his usual impetuosity. 'Why,' he said, 'I take poisonous medicines!'

Sir James turned to him. 'How horrid!' he said. 'Don't you know, my dear friend, that the more you take of these things, the more you require, and you will go on till they carry you off?'

Maybrick grunted, shrugged his shoulders, and went on his way.

In Paris, the Baroness von Roques opened a letter from her cousin, Miss Baillie. Miss Baillie wondered about Florence, who had visited her toward the end of March. Since then, she had written several letters to Florence in Liverpool. Each had been returned. Remembering that Florence had said she had stayed at the Grand Hotel, she thought that perhaps Florence had returned there, and so had made inquiries. But the Grand Hotel denied that Florence had been registered. Miss Baillie was concerned. Did the Baroness know anything of Florence's whereabouts?

The Baroness replied reassuringly. She had heard from her daughter quite recently, from Liverpool, and all was well. Perhaps some oversight among the servants at Battlecrease House had caused the letters to be returned.

IV

'Thank God, Mrs Briggs, you have come,
for the mistress is poisoning the master.'

On Saturday, 13th April, James Maybrick boarded the train for London. For two weeks, when not preoccupied with business matters, he had been fulfilling his agreement to settle his wife's debts. He had paid several Liverpool creditors, and now he was going to see a London money-lender to whom she was in debt. He planned to spend the weekend with his brother Michael.

In London that day, Miss Margaret Baillie sat down at her writing desk. 'My dear Florie,' she wrote as she began trying to clear up a mystery :

> You can't understand the state of anxiety we were in about you on this day fortnight. You left us for home on Thursday, and the inference would be that when you left you warned your servants of your coming, and that they would not forward any more letters. Those that arrived on Thursday might be accounted for, but they came on Friday and Saturday morning, and letters written to you were returned here. What could we think but that you were not at home?

At Michael Maybrick's apartment in Wellington Mansions, Regent's Park, James complained to his brother of his persistent symptoms : pains in the head and numbness of the limbs. Michael recommended his doctor, Charles Fuller, a member of the Royal College of Surgeons who prac-tised nearby in Alwyn Street.

The doctor learned that Maybrick was apprehensive of being para-lysed, and spent over an hour on a thorough examination. At last he told his patient that he could find very little the matter with him, but that all the symptons might be attributed to indigestion. Certainly there was no fear of paralysis.

Maybrick seemed cheered by Dr Fuller's reassuring diagnosis, and accepted two prescriptions, one an aperient and the other a tonic, with liver pills known as Plummer's pills. The doctor told Maybrick to see him again in a week.

In Liverpool, the Sunday mail had brought Florence Maybrick the 'My dear Florie' letter from her cousin Margaret Baillie. She read it in dismay.

> ... What could we think but that you were not at home? I suggested that you might have returned to your hotel, and Harriet went there, and asked if you were there. She found that you had not been staying there. This added more perplexity to our feelings, and there was nothing I could think of but to write to your mother. Happily she was able to say that she had heard of you twice since your return here, and therefore had no anxiety. It was only at her special request that I told her afterwards the cause of our alarm. The forwarding of the letters was quite an innocent thing. When you were with your friend it did not matter where you were living, but you expressly stated that it was at the Grand Hotel, and this want of accuracy, you see, misled us. We are plain people, and accustomed to believe what is told us. – I am, dear Florie, yours truly,
>
> Margaret Baillie

Florence Maybrick slowly folded the letter. Absentmindedly she put it into the drawer of her dressing table as she pondered the fact that it was no longer a secret that she had not stayed at the Grand Hotel. She wondered if Jim had called on the Baillie sisters during his weekend in London.

Her husband's return brought Florence neither remonstrance nor reassurance. He went daily to his office, took one Plummer's pill every night, and on the weekend announced another trip to London.

Michael Maybrick was out of town this time, so James stayed in a hotel. He saw Dr Fuller again on Sunday. Noticing that the dyspeptic symptoms had partially disappeared, the doctor wrote a new prescription which substituted compound sulphur lozenges for the Plummer's pills, with a little sweet spirits of nitre added. He gave Maybrick a third prescription, for a stomach and nerve tonic.

Maybrick said he had been taking a pill prescribed for his brother. The doctor asked him to describe it, and he recognised a mild aperient containing powdered rhubarb, extract of aloes, and extract of camomile flowers. It was not a pill he had prescribed for Michael Maybrick. He asked his patient if he had been taking any other medicine. Maybrick said the pill had been the only one.

Maybrick waited until his return to Liverpool on Monday to get the prescriptions filled. He stopped at the chemists Clay and Abraham. When the two prescriptions had been filled, he took one bottle home, the other to his office.

Another chemist received a share of the Maybrick family trade at about this time. A short walk from Battlecrease House in Aigburth, Thomas Symington Wokes recognised Mrs Maybrick when she came into his shop toward the end of April. She asked for flypapers, remarking that flies were beginning to be troublesome in the kitchen. Wokes sold her a dozen for sixpence, and, though the Maybricks maintained an account with the shop, she paid cash. The chemist rolled up the flypapers in a cylinder and sent his boy round to Battlecrease House with the package.

Florence Maybrick hurried home ahead of the boy, and, determined to get a letter off to Paris, sat down at her writing desk. To her mother, she wrote,

> We are asked to a *bal masque* which, being given in Liverpool and the people provincials, I hardly think likely to be a success . . . we are requested to come in 'dominoes and masks', and I should like to know how the former is made and if the latter are not procurable in gauze instead of *papier mache*. I think I read something of the kind in an article about the *bal masque* at the Opera in Paris.

Florence had more than one reason to be pleased that week. Not only was there a *bal masque* to look forward to, but Edwin Maybrick had arrived in Liverpool on Thursday, 25th April. He had been in America since the previous August. Of all her husband's brothers, he was Florence's favourite. She invited him to dinner on Friday, and to stay with them as often as he could.

On the day of his brother's arrival, Maybrick was preoccupied with drawing a will to replace the one he had torn up on New Year's Eve :

Liverpool, 25th April 1889

In case I die before having made a regular and proper will in legal form, I wish this to be taken as my last will and testament. I leave all my worldly possessions, of what kind or description, including furniture, pictures, linen, and plate, life insurances, cash, shares, property – in fact, everything I possess, in trust with my brothers Michael Maybrick and Thomas Maybrick for my two children, James Chandler Maybrick and Gladys Evelyn Maybrick. The furniture I desire to remain intact, and to be used in furnishing a home which can be shared by my widow and children, but the furniture is to be the children's. I further desire that all moneys be invested in the names of the above trustees (Michael and Thomas Maybrick), and the income used for the children's benefit and education. My widow will have for her portion of my estate the policies on my life, say, £500 with the Scottish Widows' Fund and £2,000 with the Mutual Reserve Fund Life Association of New York, both policies being in her name. The interest on this £2,500 together with the £125 a year which she receives from her New York property, will make a provision of about £125* a year, a sum which, although small, will yet be the means of keeping her respectable. It is also my desire that my widow shall live under the same roof with the children so long as she remains my widow.

Witness my hand and seal this
twenty-fifth day of April, 1889,　　　　James Maybrick

Signed by the testator in the presence of us, who, at his request and in the presence of each other, have hereunto affixed our names as witnesses, Geo. R. Davidson, Ge. Smith.

George Davidson was a close friend of Maybrick's who was a frequent visitor at Battlecrease House. George Smith was the bookkeeper in the cotton broker's office.

On Friday morning at eight thirty, the housemaid answered the door and received a small pasteboard box addressed to Mr Maybrick from London. By its shape, she judged it to contain a bottle of medicine.

Later that morning, Brierley noticed a small sponge basin in her master and mistress's bedroom. Though Mrs Maybrick was in the room, she glanced into the basin and saw that some flypapers seemed to be soaking in water. As she came into the kitchen that afternoon, she found Nurse Yapp and Alice Grant, the gardener's wife, making a joke about flypapers and the Flanagan case. Bessie Brierley remarked that she had seen flypapers soaking in the mistress's bedroom. Nurse Yapp immediately betook herself to the room and found a washbasin covered with a towel. Beneath the towel lay another towel on a plate. She lifted the plate and found a basin containing several flypapers soaking in a small amount of liquid.

*Maybrick apparently was not aware of the error in addition represented by this figure.

That evening, Edwin Maybrick came for dinner. He observed that his brother seemed to be in his usual good health.

But when he came down to breakfast on Saturday morning, Maybrick complained to Cook Humphreys of numbness in his limbs. Before leaving for his office, he vomited. Brierley heard him say his feet and legs were dead to the knees. At the door he told Cadwallader he had taken an overdose of the medicine that had come from London the day before.

After he had gone, Mrs Maybrick said to Nurse Yapp, 'Master has taken an overdose of medicine. It is strychnine, and is very very dangerous. He is very ill.'

Nurse Yapp asked what medicine it was.

'Some that was prescribed by a doctor in London,' said her mistress.

Maybrick came into his office in the Knowsley Buildings sometime between ten-thirty and eleven o'clock. George Smith thought he looked unwell, and his clerk, Thomas Lowry, heard him complain of stiffness in his limbs.

Despite his complaints, Maybrick was determined to attend the races across the river at Wirral that afternoon. He left the office before one o'clock. On the way to the races, he saw his brother Edwin briefly.

It was a miserable day. Rain and dampness contributed to Maybrick's discomfort. He felt dazed. His legs were stiff. He was on horseback, and he had difficulty riding. When William Thomson, a racetrack friend, greeted him, Maybrick said that he was not well. Thomson agreed that he did not look well.

'You don't seem to be able to keep your horse,' he called out as Maybrick rode off.

Maybrick trotted back again and remarked that he had taken a 'double dose' that morning. Thomson observed that his friend seemed to be shaking in the saddle.

Mr and Mrs Morden Rigg ran into their old friend Jim Maybrick at the Wirral races. They had known him in America, and Rigg remembered Maybrick as a man who was always taking all sorts of medicines. They were not surprised to hear Maybrick say that he had taken an overdose of strychnine that morning.

By the end of the afternoon, Maybrick's clothing was wet through. But he insisted upon dining with a friend, a Mr Hobson, on the Cheshire side of the Mersey. During dinner, his hand became so unsteady that he upset his wineglass, and he was embarrassed by the thought that Hobson might think him drunk. He got home so late the servants had all gone to bed.

The servants were up and about their duties early next morning when the household was shaken by the violent ringing of the bedroom bell. Nurse Yapp, helping the children dress in the night nursery, ignored the bell, as it was not her duty. Next thing she knew, Mrs Maybrick was at the night nursery door. Would Yapp please go into the bedroom and stay with the master? Nurse Yapp went down, and found Mr Maybrick lying on the bed in his dressing-gown.

In the kitchen, Cook Humphreys had just noticed that the master's boots, standing in the corner, were soaked through. Mrs Maybrick hurried in.

'Humphreys,' she said, 'I want some mustard and water immediately. Master has taken another dose of that horrid medicine.'

The cook handed her mistress a cup of water with mustard in it. Mrs Maybrick stirred it with her finger as she started upstairs again.

Nurse Yapp saw her mistress return to the room with the cup in her hand.

'Do take this mustard and water,' Mrs Maybrick said to the master. 'It will remove the brandy, and make you sick again, if nothing else.'

The cook fixed a second cup and hurried up the stairs, meeting her mistress on the landing. Mrs Maybrick took the cup into the room, and the cook heard her master vomiting.

Soon Mrs Maybrick asked Cadwallader to fetch Dr Humphreys, the children's doctor, who was the only physician nearby.

When the doctor arrived, Mrs Maybrick spoke to him about the white powder she had described to him in March. She said her husband's present illness was probably due to some bad brandy taken at the races, and told him she had administered the mustard and water emetic.

The doctor found Maybrick in bed. The patient said his current symptoms had come from a cup of strong tea that morning. He added that he had had a headache for almost a year, and that he felt great stiffness in his limbs. He described the incident of spilling the wine at dinner the night before, and showed the doctor the prescription he had received in London from Dr Fuller.

Remembering Mrs Maybrick's concern about a white powder, the doctor asked Maybrick about the effects of strychnine and nux vomica upon himself.

'Humphreys,' said the patient, 'I think I know a great deal of medicine, I cannot stand strychnine and nux vomica at all.' Maybrick added that Dr Fuller's prescription contained nux vomica and it caused the stiffness in his limbs.

The doctor decided the trouble was indigestion. He prescribed dilute prussic acid and recommended discontinuing Dr Fuller's prescription.

Edwin Maybrick arrived soon after the doctor had left. Jim told Edwin about his miserable day at the races, and complained of numbness in his legs and hands.

Edwin joined Mrs Maybrick downstairs for noonday dinner. Maybrick did not appear. They dined on ox-tail soup. James Maybrick, left alone upstairs, found the strength to compose a rambling letter describing his illness to his brother Michael in London. The doctors, he said, were unable to diagnose his complaint. 'This time,' he said, 'Dr Fuller cannot say that I am suffering from a violent attack of indigestion.' He added that if he should die he would be perfectly willing to let his body be dissected for scientific purposes.

Edwin Maybrick decided to stay at Battlecrease House that night. In the evening, when his brother was resting quietly upstairs, he and his sister-in-law sat talking for an hour. The bedroom bell then rang, and Florence went upstairs. Edwin followed, and found Jim lying in bed. He complained that he had almost lost the use of both legs and his right hand, and asked Edwin to rub them.

Mrs Maybrick dispatched Cadwallader to get Dr Humphreys again. She then joined Edwin in rubbing her husband's limbs.

The doctor arrived at about ten o'clock. He himself rubbed Maybrick's legs, and the stiffness disappeared. The doctor suspected that the cause might have been his patient's mental attitude, based on what Maybrick had said of his knowledge of nux vomica. Dr Humphreys stayed half an hour, prescribed bromide of potassium and tincture of henbane, and departed, promising to call again in the morning.

Monday morning found Maybrick improved. His brother Edwin thought so, and went off to attend to business in Liverpool. Dr Humphreys thought so, and observed that his patient's worst symptom was a badly furred tongue, which he attributed to indigestion. The doctor decided that Maybrick was a chronic dyspeptic, and wrote out a diet for him. It prescribed coffee, toast and bacon for breakfast, Revalenta food, Du Barry's food and beef tea for luncheon, and alternate meals of fish and bacon for dinner. He also prescribed Seymour's preparation of papaine and iridin, one teaspoonful three times a day. The papaine was a vegetable digestive, and the iridin a slight laxative to act on the liver.

In the kitchen, Mrs Maybrick handed the cook an unopened tin of Du Barry's food. She asked the cook to prepare the food, and gave her a brown jug in which the master would take it to his office. When the jug was ready, the cook turned it over to Cadwallader for delivery to Mr Maybrick.

At the office, the bookkeeper, Smith and the clerk, Lowry saw their employer come in at noonday. Each thought he looked unwell.

In Cressington, a suburb only a few minutes' walk from Battlecrease House, a druggist named Christopher Hanson recognised Mrs James Maybrick, a customer whom he had known for more than two years. She gave him a slip of paper listing the ingredients of a lotion, and said she would wait while he made it up. The ingredients were tincture of benzoin and elderflowers. It was not a doctor's prescription.

Mrs Maybrick glanced around the chemist's shop, and presently she asked for some of the flypapers she saw near the door. She ordered two dozen and paid one shilling for them, taking them with her along with the lotion.

The 30th April was the day of the *bal masque*. Maybrick came down to breakfast, and Humphreys fixed him bread and milk. Shortly Cadwallader brought the dish back to the kitchen, saying that Mr Maybrick had asked if the cook had sweetened it. He had eaten hardly any. The cook remarked that she had put in only a pinch of salt. She poked her finger into the soft bread, then licked it. The food had indeed been sweetened.

Maybrick appeared at his office at mid-day, but stayed only half an hour. In that time, George Smith observed that the broker did not look well. Thomas Lowry was sent out with letters to mail, and Maybrick gave him a parcel containing Du Barry's food, Revalenta Arabica, to take to Battlecrease House.

Edwin came by in the evening. He found his brother 'out of sorts' and at the suggestion of both Jim and Florence he escorted his sister-in-law to the fancy-dress ball. He thought Jim did not seem seriously ill.

Edwin slept at Battlecrease House that night.

Next day was 1st May. Maybrick was off early to the office, leaving his brother Edwin behind at Battlecrease House. When George Smith greeted him, Maybrick said that he was feeling 'very seedy'.

Florence Maybrick asked Edwin if he planned to go down to Jim's office. If so, would he be good enough to take his brother's lunch to him? He did not mind, and as he left she gave him a brown paper parcel to carry.

At the office, James told Edwin he felt unwell. He immediately dispatched his clerk, Tom Lowry, to buy a saucepan, a basin, and a spoon.

When Lowry returned, Maybrick opened the parcel and took out a brown jug. He poured a sort of gruel into the saucepan, heated it over the fire, then poured it into the basin and ate it. He seemed none too pleased. 'The cook has put some of that damned sherry into it,' he said, 'and she knows I don't like it.'

Little business was conducted that afternoon, for Maybrick and his brother were soon joined by an old friend, Captain Irving, of the White Star Line, whose ship, the *Germanic*, had just berthed.

In the course of conversation, James remarked that he had been unwell after eating lunch, and that he believed his sickness was due to bad wine in the soup sent by his wife. The captain saw James pick up a glass, fill it partly with water from a decanter, then pull from his breast pocket a small packet. He emptied it into the glass, then drank it.

Edwin asked him what he had put into the glass.

'Oh, some prescription that Clay and Abraham made up for me,' said Jim.

It seemed to the captain that his friend felt better after taking the prescription.

Toward five o'clock, the Maybrick brothers and the captain walked to the Central Station and took a train to Grassendale. From that station they walked to Battlecrease House. Mrs Maybrick greeted them, and then they sat down to supper. James was served with soup and fish, and seemed not only to enjoy them greatly but to show no sign of illness.

Dr Humphreys looked in. He found his patient much better: the tongue was cleaner, the headache gone. He advised him to continue his present treatment.

Next day, Maybrick again went to his office, but he came home, feeling ill, after lunch. On 3rd May he stayed in bed, and Cadwallader again hurried to fetch Dr Humphreys. The doctor found Maybrick in the morning room on the ground floor. His wife was with him. Maybrick remarked that he did not think the doctor's medicine agreed with him.

Mrs Maybrick spoke up. 'You always say the same thing about anybody's medicine after you have taken it two or three days.'

The doctor examined his patient. 'Your tongue is certainly not so clean as it ought to be,' he said. 'But otherwise I cannot see any difference. My advice is to go on the same for two or three weeks. The medicine cannot disagree with you, as it tends more to assist your digestion than anything else.'

Maybrick wondered if it would do him good to have a Turkish bath. The doctor said he thought it would.

Soon after Dr Humphreys had gone, Maybrick decided he felt better, went to his office, stayed only a short time, went home again. Mrs Maybrick put him to bed with a hot water bottle. By late afternoon, he again felt better. He decided to see about that Turkish bath the doctor had approved. As he walked through the neighbourhood, he passed Dr Humphreys, who was making his rounds. He said only, 'Good afternoon', to the doctor.

Maybrick came home and took to his bed again. By late evening, he was in great pain. Each thigh ached from the hip to the knee. Florence and Edwin tried rubbing his legs with turpentine. It did little good. Despite the late hour, they called Dr Humphreys. He examined the patient, pressing his hands along his legs, and found that there was no pain from pressure : It was a gnawing pain, running down the great sciatic nerve through the rear of the hip and knee joints.

To alleviate the pain, the doctor administered a suppository containing a quarter of a grain of morphia. Fortunately, there was no need to awaken a chemist to supply the drug. The capsules were already in the house, having been prescribed for Mrs Maybrick at some earlier time.

Maybrick slept little that night, and by Saturday morning (it was now 4th May) he was sick again and vomiting. Dr Humphreys was summoned early. He assured patient and wife that vomiting was a common result of the administration of morphia. He advised Maybrick not to try to eat or drink anything. If he was thirsty, he could gargle with water or suck a damp cloth. To help stop the vomiting, the patient was to sip ipeca-cuanha wine in very small doses.

Dr Humphreys also brought a bottle of Valentine's meat juice to the house that day. The cook used the beef essence to strengthen stock soup.

When she answered the front door later in the day, she found the boy from one of the chemists's shops. He handed her some medicine, and she took it up to Mr Maybrick's bedroom. Then she saw Mrs Maybrick in the morning room downstairs and told her she had taken the medicine upstairs.

'Why did you do that?' said Mrs Maybrick. 'I have told all the rest but you not to take anything to the room unless I see it.'

Later, the cook asked how the master was. Mrs Maybrick said he was no better. She added, holding up thumb and forefinger so they almost touched, that if he had taken that much more of his medicine he would have been a dead man. She said she had thrown the medicine down the sink.

Sunday brought little improvement. Maybrick's spells of vomiting continued. Dr Humphreys found the patient's throat red and his tongue furred. Again he prescribed prussic acid, noting that a supply was on hand from his previous prescription. He told Maybrick to take Valentine's beef juice for sustenance, and to wash his mouth with Condy's fluid.

During the afternoon, Edwin Maybrick came out from Liverpool to see how his brother was coming along. While he was there, Florence Maybrick stepped out of Battlecrease House long enough to dispatch a telegram.

Dr Humphreys returned Sunday evening. He found no change and repeated that, if Maybrick was thirsty, he could have a wet towel put to his mouth.

After the doctor had gone, James asked his brother Edwin to stay overnight. Some time during the evening, James and Florence and Edwin decided that the patient would be more comfortable in Florence's room, which was next door to James's and was larger and airier than his. They moved him to her bed.

Later that evening, Elizabeth Humphreys came into the room. Mr Maybrick called the cook to him, saying he was very sick and wanted a drink of something. Would she get him some lemonade, with a little sugar in it? He added, 'I want you to make it as you would for any poor man dying of thirst.'

Mrs Maybrick offered him some lemon juice, but he said he did not want lemon juice in a glass, but lemonade from the kitchen.

'You cannot have it except as a gargle,' she said.

The cook asked the master if he would like anything – lemonade, lemon jelly, barley water?

Mrs Maybrick said it was no use making anything, for he could not take it except as a gargle.

The cook went down to the kitchen and made lemonade. When she returned with it, she handed it directly to Mr Maybrick. Mrs Maybrick took the glass from his hand. 'You can't have it, dear,' she said, 'except as a gargle.'

'Very well,' said Mr Maybrick.

It seemed to the cook that Mr Maybrick looked very wistfully at the glass as his wife took it from him.

Dr Humphreys was back at Battlecrease House at eight-thirty on Monday morning, 6th May. He learned that the Valentine's meat juice had made Maybrick vomit. The doctor now prescribed Fowler's solution, which contained white arsenic. He put four drops into five tablespoons of water in a wineglass at Maybrick's bedside. The patient was to have a few drops in less than half a teaspoonful of water every hour.

On this Monday, in Liverpool, Alfred Brierley wrote to Florence

Maybrick. They were concerned that Maybrick might be trying by means of advertisements to discover what had occurred in London at the end of March.

My dear Florie, I suppose now you have gone I am safe in writing to you. I don't quite understand what you mean in your last about explaining my line of action. You know I could not write, and was willing to meet you, although it would have been very dangerous. Most certainly your telegram yesterday was a staggerer, and it looks as if the result was certain, but as yet I cannot find an advertisement in any London paper.

I should like to see you, but at present dare not move, and we had better perhaps not meet until late in the autumn. I am going to try and get away for about a fortnight. Supposing the rooms are found, I think both you and I would be better away, as the man's memory would be doubted after three months. I will write and tell you when I go. I cannot trust myself at present to write about my feelings on this unhappy business, but I do hope that some time hence I shall be able to show you that I do not quite deserve the strictures contained in your last two letters. And now, dear, 'Goodbye', hoping we shall meet in the autumn. I will write to you about sending letters just before I go.

A.B.

Brierley posted his letter in Liverpool as soon as he had written it, confident that his dear Florie would have it in Aigburth that afternoon.

A late-afternoon mail delivery brought the letter to Battlecrease House, and Cadwallader delivered it promptly to Mrs Maybrick.

In the evening, Dr Humphreys made his now customary call. Since Maybrick had vomited a number of times during the day, the doctor recommended the application of a 'blister' to the patient's stomach, thinking it would put an end to his vomiting. He also examined two samples of the vomit which had been held for him. One was greenish and bilious-looking, the other yellowish.

On Tuesday morning, 7th May, Dr Humphreys found his patient cheery. 'Humphreys,' he said, 'I am quite a different man altogether today, after you put on that blister last night.'

The doctor learned that Maybrick had had only three doses of the medicine he had made from Fowler's solution, because it hurt his throat. Dr Humphreys threw the remaining medicine into the slop basin on the washstand in the bedroom.

The patient's good cheer was shortlived. As the morning went on he felt worse. Seeing no improvement, his wife decided to ask Edwin Maybrick for help. Edwin, she felt, could be counted on more than any other Maybrick brother.

The great staircase in Battlecrease House was a busy thoroughfare. Some member of the household was always going up or down. As Nurse Alice Yapp hurried down from the nursery, toward mid-day on Tuesday, she saw Mrs Maybrick on the landing outside the bedroom door. She noticed that her mistress seemed to be pouring something out of one medicine bottle and into another.

In Liverpool early Tuesday afternoon, Edwin Maybrick received a telegram from his sister-in-law. It suggested that Edwin send for his friend Dr McCheyne, a well-known medical man. Edwin went to see Dr McCheyne, who told him he did not make house calls. Edwin then telephoned a prominent Rodney Street practitioner, Dr William Carter.

At the Royal Southern Hospital, Dr Carter was called to the telephone. A man whose voice he did not know asked him if he could go at once to No 6, Riversdale Road, Aigburth, to see a gentleman in consultation with Dr Humphreys. Dr Carter said that he would be busy for some hours seeing patients. He agreed to meet Dr Humphreys at Battlecrease House at five-thirty.

A telegram also came to Mrs Matilda Briggs that afternoon from Michael Maybrick, in London. It asked her to go to Battlecrease House and see about his brother. Mrs Briggs consulted her sister, Mrs Hughes, and they decided to go first thing in the morning.

Edwin Maybrick caught the 4.45 train from Liverpool to Grassendale, and hurried to Riversdale Road to meet the doctors. Dr Carter found lying in bed a rather fair-complexioned man about fifty years old, of slight but muscular build. The patient said he had been suffering so severely from vomiting that he had not been able to keep down a drop of water all day. Now he had a sensation of a hair in his throat.

The doctor remarked that, despite Maybrick's badly furred tongue, his breath was quite sweet. A young woman sitting at the window said, 'That is so. His breath is quite sweet, though his tongue is so bad.' The doctor wonder who the young lady was. They had not been introduced.

The doctor proceeded to examine his patient. On raising his night-shirt, he unwittingly caused him pain by rubbing a freshly blistered area on his stomach, but he caused no pain when he pressed other parts of the abdomen. Maybrick was extremely restless during the examination, rolling and tossing, and occasionally kicking off the bedclothes.

In the bathroom the doctors examined a bowel movement which had been kept for them. It was copious and loose. Dr Carter observed that it looked like that of typhoid fever. Samples of the patient's vomit were in the bathroom, too, and Dr Carter examined these.

Mrs Maybrick had followed them into the bathroom. She suggested to Dr Carter that her husband's constitution might have been injured by dietary indiscretions before their marriage. It was then that the doctor realized that the young woman was the patient's wife.

The doctors consulted. Dr Carter concluded that Maybrick was suffering from acute dyspepsia. Together they prescribed a careful diet. To quiet Maybrick's restlessness they prescribed very small doses of antipyrin. This drug would relieve his painful throat, too. To produce a flow of saliva and relieve him from the sensation of a hair in his throat, they prescribed a small dose of tincture of jaborandi. Diluted chlorodyne was prescribed to relieve the taste of foulness in Maybrick's mouth. Chicken broth and milk were prescribed to give him nourishment, with Neave's food and lime water at longer intervals.

It was Dr Humphreys's opinion, shared by Dr Carter, that Maybrick was going on very favourably and would be well in a few days. The doctors departed. That night, Maybrick was weak and vomiting. He had pain in his bowels. He complained constantly about his throat. He said he had difficulty swallowing.

On Wednesday morning, 8th May, Nurse Yapp passed Mrs Maybrick on the stair and asked how the master was. 'About the same,' said Mrs Maybrick.

As her mistress went into the bedroom, Nurse Yapp heard Mr Maybrick ask his wife to rub his hands. 'You are always wanting your hands rubbed,' was Mrs Maybrick's reply. 'It does you no good.'

Edwin Maybrick was up early on Wednesday and saw his brother before leaving for Liverpool. James asked Edwin what he thought about sending for a nurse.

Edwin said he would ask the doctor. Florence said she had thought of sending to Hale for Mrs Howell, who had attended her when Bobo and Gladys were born. Jim knew her and liked her.

Edwin left shortly for business in Liverpool.

When Dr Humphreys arrived, Mrs Maybrick said that she was very tired, and asked him to telegraph to Mrs Howell, explaining that the woman knew her husband and the household.

Florence Maybrick was tired, and she was upset. Her husband was unable to get in or out of bed without help, and he had told her that morning that he thought he was going to die. At 9.30 she sent off a four-word telegram to her mother in Paris. It said, 'Jim very ill again.' Then she asked Mary Cadwallader to help her, and together they bathed Mr Maybrick. When they had finished, the maid saw her mistress give him some medicine.

At about this time, Nurse Yapp glanced out of the nursery window and saw Mrs Briggs and Mrs Hughes approaching in the street below. She hurried downstairs. In the yard, she beckoned to the arriving callers. They went to her, and she said, 'Thank God, Mrs Briggs, you have come, for the mistress is poisoning the master. For goodness sake go and see him for yourselves.'

Mrs Hughes said this was an awful accusation. Nurse Yapp told the ladies about the flypapers she had seen soaking, and said that Mrs Maybrick had tampered with food intended for Mr Maybrick. She then ushered the sisters into the house through the back door, up the back staircase, and into the invalid's room.

In the morning room, Mrs Maybrick realised she could hear voices coming from her husband's room above. She hurried up the stairs and found Mrs Briggs and Mrs Hughes there. More than a little annoyed, she told them her husband was not to be disturbed and must have absolute rest and quiet. She said that if they would come downstairs, she would tell them what was the matter with Jim in five minutes. Mrs Briggs said that they had come because they had received a telegram from Michael Maybrick. The ladies then went down to the morning room.

There they discussed the need for a nurse. Mrs Maybrick said she could nurse her husband herself. She said that was also the doctor's opinion. But the conversation ended with Mrs Briggs writing out a telegram to the Nurses' Institution in Liverpool. Mrs Maybrick gave her money to pay for the wire. The sisters left Battlecrease House toward noon, headed for the telegraph office.

In Liverpool, Edwin Maybrick left his office to call on Dr William Carter and ask what he thought of James's condition. The doctor assured him that, though Mr Maybrick's brother was very ill, he trusted he would recover.

When Edwin returned to his office, he found a telegram from Florence. It said, 'Jim worse again; have wired for a nurse.' He decided to catch the 12.40 train to Aigburth. On the way to the station he stopped and telegraphed his brother Michael in London to come down to Liverpool.

In London early that afternoon, Michael Maybrick received two telegrams. One, from his brother Edwin, asked him to come to Liverpool. The other, from Mrs Briggs, said, 'Come at once; strange things going on here.'

When Edwin Maybrick reached Battlecrease House, he was met in the yard by Mrs Briggs and Mrs Hughes. They spoke to him briefly, and he set off at once for Liverpool again, his destination the Nurses' Institution.

In Battlecrease House, meanwhile, Florence Maybrick found a moment after luncheon when she could sit down at her desk. She took a sheet of her mother's stationery, mongrammed with a crown and the initial R. Busy as she was and tired as she found herself from nursing her husband, she felt a compulsion to write a certain letter. Picking up a pencil, she hastily began scribbling.

At the Nurses' Institution, Edwin Maybrick asked that a nurse be sent to Battlecrease House to tend his brother. He learned that in response to a telegram Nurse Ellen Ann Gore had been dispatched only a short time earlier. He hurried back to Riversdale Road in Aigburth.

Nurse Gore arrived at Battlecrease House at 2.15. The cook took her immediately to the bedroom of a man who seemed very ill indeed. He told the nurse his feet and legs were very cold, and that he had been vomiting before she arrived. He added that the doctors did not know what was the matter with him, but believed it was something wrong with his liver and stomach.

In a moment, Mrs Maybrick came into the room and cleared the bedside table of its medicines, leaving only some photographs and books and a packet containing a powder she knew her husband to be in the habit of taking. Then she went to the lavatory and got some medicine from the medicine chest there. She told the nurse to give some to Mr Maybrick. The nurse did so.

Toward three o'clock, Mrs Maybrick finished writing her letter. Knowing that Nurse Yapp would be taking the children for a walk, she went down to the garden gate. There she saw Nurse Yapp in the roadway. She called the nurse to her, handed her the letter, and asked her to put it in the mail in time for the 3.45 post. She did not know that earlier in the day Nurse Yapp had intercepted Mrs Briggs in the yard and told her, 'The mistress is poisoning the master.' As mistress of the household, she assumed that the nurse would follow her order.

It was nearly five o'clock when Edwin Maybrick returned to Battlecrease House from his needless trip to the Nurses' Institution in Liverpool. As he approached, he saw Nurse Yapp in the driveway. She said she wanted to tell him something. They went to a seat in the garden, out of sight of the house.

There Nurse Yapp said that her mistress had given her a letter to post, and that she had handed it to the baby, Gladys, to carry on the way to the post office. As they crossed the road in front of the post office, she said,

Gladys had dropped the letter, and the envelope had been muddied. The nurse had gone into the post office and obtained a clean envelope. As she transferred the letter to the clean envelope, certain words caught her eye, and she then read the letter. She decided not to mail it, and now she handed it to Mr Maybrick.

The letter was addressed to A. Brierley, Esq, 60, Huskisson Street, Liverpool.

Wednesday

Dearest,

Your letter under cover to John K. came to hand just after I had written to you on Monday. I did not expect to hear from you so soon, and had delayed in giving him the necessary instructions. Since my return I have been nursing M. day and night. *He is sick unto death!* The doctors held a consultation yesterday, and now all depends upon how long his strength will hold out! Both my brothers-in-law are here, and we are terribly anxious. I cannot answer your letter fully today, my darling, but relieve your mind of all *fear of discovery* now and in the future. M. has been delirious since Sunday, and I know now that he is *perfectly ignorant* of everything, even *to the name of the street*, and also *that he has not been making any inquiries whatever!* The tale he told me was a pure fabrication, and only intended to frighten the truth out of me. In fact, *he believes* my statement, although he will not *admit it*. You need not therefore go abroad on that account, dearest; but, in any case, please don't *leave England until I have seen you once again!* You must feel that those two letters of mine were written under circumstances which must even excuse their injustice in your eyes. Do you suppose that I could act as I am doing if I really felt and meant what I inferred then? If you wish to write to me about anything do so *now*, as all the letters pass through my hands at present. Excuse this scrawl, my own darling, but I dare not leave the room for a moment, and I do not know when I shall be able to write to you again. In haste, yours ever,

Florie

It was the words, 'my own darling', said Nurse Yapp, which caught her eye and caused her to read the letter.

Night had fallen in the sickroom. Nurse Gore wanted to give her patient a little of the nourishing beef juice. Not finding the medicine glass, she asked Mrs Maybrick for it. The mistress said she had seen it in the bed-

room. The nurse looked again in the bedroom, then went into the lavatory. There she found Mrs Maybrick mixing medicine in the glass she
wanted. The mistress said she had added water to the medicine because
it burned Mr Maybrick's throat. The nurse threw the mixture down the
sink and poured the meat juice into the glass.

At seven o'clock, Dr Humphreys came in. He was surprised to see
Nurse Gore there from the Nurses' Institution, as he had anticipated
seeing Mrs Howell from Hale. He found no change in his patient.

It was nearly nine o'clock when Michael Maybrick got off the train at
the Edge Hill station. His brother Edwin met him with a cab, and they
set off for Battlecrease House. On the way, Edwin told Michael about
the letter given to him by Nurse Yapp. When they reached the house,
Edwin showed him the letter. Michael read it and said, 'The woman is
an adulteress.' They went upstairs.

Michael was shocked to see the state his brother was in. He seemed only
semi-conscious.

Mrs Maybrick left Edwin and Michael with their brother and went
downstairs. Soon Michael came down. He told her that he had strong
suspicions of the case.

She asked him what he meant.

He said that his suspicions were that Jim had not been properly attended to, and that he ought to have had a professional nurse and a second
doctor earlier.

Florence said that she had nursed Jim alone up to that point. Who, she
asked, had a greater right to nurse him than his own wife?

Michael agreed with her, but said that he was not satisfied and that
he intended to see Dr Humphreys at once. He left the house immediately.

While Michael was gone, Edwin Maybrick spoke to Nurse Gore. He
told her that he would hold her responsible for all foods and all medicines
given to his brother, and that no one was to attend to him at all except
his nurse. Edwin gave her a fresh, unopened bottle of Valentine's meat
juice.

It was ten thirty when Michael reached Dr Humphreys's house. He
introduced himself, and asked about his brother's prospects. The doctor
reviewed the case at some length, and at last he said, 'I am not satisfied
with your brother, and I will tell you why. Your brother tells me he is
going to die.'

Michael suggested to the doctor that there might be some basis for
suspecting foul play. He told him about the flypapers and Nurse Yapp's
suspicions.

Michael returned to Battlecrease House, and slept in a room on the top floor. Florence Maybrick slept in the dressing room next to her own room, where she could be close to her husband. Nurse Gore stayed up all night with the patient, who was restless and complained of almost continuous straining in the bowels and of the feeling of a hair in his throat.

When Edwin Maybrick looked in on his brother first thing in the morning on Thursday, 9th May, Jim seemed better. Edwin repeated to Nurse Gore his orders that she alone was to tend the patient. Then he set off for Liverpool to arrange for a continuing schedule of nurses.

Dr Humphreys came in early, and Nurse Gore reported on her patient's condition of tenesmus, or straining of the bowels. To give relief, the doctor made and introduced an opium suppository. His impression was that his patient was worse.

Nurse Gore had been on duty for nearly twenty-one hours when, as a result of Edwin Maybrick's arrangements, Nurse Margaret Jane Callery arrived. She found a patient who was very much exhausted, and who complained of a burning sensation in his throat and of pains in the abdomen. Nurse Gore told her about Mr Edwin Maybrick's orders that only the nurses were to tend the patient. She pointed out the fresh, unopened bottle of Valentine's meat juice which Mr Edwin had supplied the night before.

In the butler's pantry, Mary Cadwallader moved a tray that had not been used for some time. Behind it she found five or six flypapers. She recalled the talk when Bessie Brierley had seen flypapers soaking in the mistress's bedroom, and she remembered some things Alice Yapp had said the day before. She took the flypapers into the kitchen and burned them. When Cook Humphreys noticed the smell of the burning flypapers, the housemaid remarked that she had thought it best to burn them before a policeman arrived.

Dr William Carter went out to Battlecrease House again on Friday afternoon. He found Dr Humphreys there. He was introduced to Mr Michael Maybrick, who abruptly said, 'Now what is the matter with my brother, Dr Carter?'

The doctor had had no chance to see the patient or consult with his colleague, so he repeated the opinion he had formed on Tuesday : that Mr Maybrick was suffering from acute dyspepsia.

'But what is the cause of it ?' said Michael.

'That is by no means clear to us,' said Dr Carter. 'The conclusion we formed was that your brother must have committed a grave error of diet by taking some irritant food or drink, or both.'

Michael turned sharply to Dr Humphreys and asked if he had informed Dr Carter of the subject of their conversation last night.

Dr Humphreys said he had informed Dr Carter of nothing.

Michael Maybrick seemed to be greatly excited. Dr Carter asked him the reason.

'God forbid that I should unjustly suspect anyone,' said Michael, 'but do you not think if I have serious grounds for fearing that all may not be right, that it is my duty to say so to you?'

The doctors agreed that it was his duty.

Michael then told them that as late as the middle of April the patient had been able to eat any ordinary food at Michael's house, that he had been subject to sick attacks soon after returning home, that others had noticed this contrast between the condition of health away from home and at home, that there was a most serious estrangement between Mr and Mrs Maybrick, that Mrs Maybrick was known to have been unfaithful, and that just before his illness began she was known to have procured many flypapers.

When Michael had finished, the doctors consulted. They decided to surround the patient with absolute safeguards that would prevent any one from tampering with him. They wanted to keep their minds free from unjust suspicion, they agreed, but had to confess that they could explain the illness only by a hypothesis for which they had no evidence. They agreed that, if what Michael was hinting at were true, it would clear up much that had been obscure.

Michael rejoined them, and they went in to see the patient.

Dr Carter was distressed to learn of Maybrick's loose bowels and night-long straining. Until now, the symptoms had been consistent with either an irritant poison or dyspepsia. But the continuous bowel straining was unusual under the hypothesis he had formed. He tried to examine the lower bowel, but caused Maybrick such extreme pain that he had to give up.

Dr Carter reported his findings to Michael Maybrick and Dr Humphreys. He learned that, before he arrived, the doctor had ordered bismuth, which was astringent and would act as a stomach sedative. They agreed to give double doses if the symptoms continued, and, if necessary, to add diluted brandy.

As they were leaving, Michael gave Dr Carter a bottle of Neave's food to take back to his office for analysis. At the same time, Dr Humphreys took samples of the patient's urine and faeces which they had examined in the bathroom.

In his office, Dr Humphreys performed an analysis, known as Reinsch's test, learned in his medical school days. He boiled a tablespoonful of the faeces in copper with a little hydrochloric acid, looking for a deposit of antimony, arsenic, or mercury on the copper. He found no deposit. A test of the urine was equally negative.

Toward dinnertime that evening, Mrs Maybrick stepped out of the bedroom just as Cook Humphreys came upstairs to ask about dinner plans. She followed the cook downstairs. There was something she had to say. The cook was the only member of the household she could talk to. She hesitated, lingered, and at last spoke. 'Well, Humphreys,' she said, 'I am to blame for all this.'

It seemed to the cook that Mrs Maybrick was very much upset. 'You? To blame? In what way, mistress?'

'For not getting proper nurses and other doctors.' She had said enough to break the dyke, and now she felt the tears beginning to flow. She hurried into the servant's hall and began to cry. She hoped the cook would not follow, but she did. Despite herself, the words poured out with the tears. 'My position isn't worth anything in this house,' she sobbed. 'I'm not even allowed to go into the master's bedroom and give him his medicine.'

'There,' said Cook Humphreys, hoping to comfort her mistress. 'Well, I'd rather be in my own shoes than yours, if I may say so, Mrs Maybrick.'

'It's Mr Michael,' Mrs Maybrick went on. She was not thinking about what she was saying, or to whom she was saying it. It just had to be said. She could not contain herself any longer. 'Mr Michael has always had a spite against me, ever since my marriage. Do you know – if he went out of the house, I wouldn't let him in again. If I could, I'd turn every one of you out of the house.'

'Have I ever done anything to you?' asked the cook.

'No,' said Mrs Maybrick. She wiped her eyes and thought a moment. Already she regretted the outburst. It wouldn't help matters any for Humphreys to see her mistress break down. She shouldn't have said anything.

The cook said she was sorry for the state of affairs.

'Oh, never mind,' said Mrs Maybrick. She turned and went upstairs, as exasperated with herself as with what Humphreys called the state of affairs.

Dr Carter reached his office in Liverpool and immediately analysed the Neave's food which Michael Maybrick had given him. He felt intensely relieved when he could find nothing wrong with it.

At eleven that night, Nurse Gore returned and Nurse Callery went off duty. Mrs Maybrick came into the sickroom just after Nurse Gore arrived. Within a few minutes, the nurse picked up the bottle of Valentine's meat juice which she had pointed out to Nurse Callery in the morning. It was a small, onion-shaped bottle, dark brown in colour. It contained, she knew, about 1,100 grains or nine teaspoonfuls of the liquid, made in America. The bottle had not been opened before. She measured two spoonfuls into some water in the medicine glass. The meat juice looked like a rich brown sherry. She tasted the mixture to see if it was all right, and put the bottle on a small table near the bedroom window.

Mrs Maybrick said that Mr Maybrick had had the meat juice before, and that it had made him sick. The nurse ignored the remark and gave him the food.

Soon Mrs Maybrick rang for Cadwallader and asked her to bring her a cup of tea. The maid went downstairs but, as she was busy, asked Bessie Brierley to take the tea up to the mistress. Brierley knocked at the sick-room door. Mrs Maybrick was in the little dressing room, through the bedroom. The maid took the tea in, passing Nurse Gore, who was sitting on the edge of the bed, rubbing the master's hands. In the semi-darkness on the far side of the room she saw Mr Michael Maybrick pick up a small bottle from the washstand and put it in his pocket. He then walked out of the room.

Every quarter hour, the nurse gave her patient a sip or two of champagne. Some time before midnight, she cleaned his tongue with glycerine and borax. Mrs Maybrick got the glycerine for her from her room.

At midnight, Maybrick was drowsy, and he shortly fell asleep. The nurse saw Mrs Maybrick get up and go toward the dressing-room. As she passed the table near the window, she picked up the bottle of Valentine's meat juice. She went into the room and closed the door. She stayed in the room for about two minutes. When she came back, she stood beside the table near the window and asked the nurse to get some ice to put into the water to bathe Mr Maybrick's head.

The nurse said that Mr Maybrick was asleep, and that she would get the ice when he awoke.

While Mrs Maybrick was talking, she held the bottle to her left side, away from the nurse, as if her hand were in her pocket. Then, as she raised her right hand, her left hand put the bottle on the table. She then went back into the dressing room to lie down, telling the nurse to call her if Mr Maybrick awoke.

He slept for nearly three quarters of an hour, and woke with a choking sensation in his throat. Mrs Maybrick came into the room, and Nurse Gore saw her pick up the meat juice bottle from the table and move it to the washstand. The nurse then went to get the ice, which was in the lavatory on the stair landing.

In the early morning on Friday, 10th May, Dr Humphreys found his patient weaker than the day before. His pulse was more rapid. Maybrick himself seemed greatly depressed by his condition. When Nurse Callery returned to duty at eleven o'clock, Nurse Gore told her how Mrs Maybrick had taken the bottle of meat juice from the room for a few minutes at midnight. She had not afterward fed Mr Maybrick any of it, she said, and she now suggested that Nurse Callery pour off a sample from this bottle and keep it in reserve. She handed Nurse Callery an empty medicine bottle for the purpose. Meantime, Nurse Gore said, she was going in to Liverpool to consult the Lady Superintendent at the Nurses' Institution.

As Nurse Gore left, Nurse Callery, alerted to the need for vigilance, gathered all the medicine bottles in the sickroom and put them on a small table.

As Ellen Gore went downstairs, she saw Mr Michael Maybrick. She told him she was suspicious of a bottle of brandy that was in the sickroom. Michael went up and removed the brandy, which was among the medicines on a small table by the window. The bottle was half full.

Soon it was time for the patient to have his dose of bismuth. Nurse Callery fixed the medicine in a glass, but Mr Maybrick refused it. Mrs Maybrick tried to persuade him to take the medicine.

He again refused, and said, 'Don't give me the wrong medicine again.'

'What are you talking about?' said Mrs Maybrick. 'You never had the wrong medicine.'

In Liverpool, Nurse Ellen Gore reached the Nurses' Institution and asked to see the Lady Superintendent. She was with her only a few minutes, and then hurried back to the station to catch the 1.35 train for Aigburth.

Nurse Callery was surprised to see Ellen Gore return to the sickroom. She was more surprised to learn that the matron of the Nurses' Institution had ordered Nurse Gore to see the sample of meat juice was thrown away.

Michael Maybrick was approached by Nurse Gore when she went off duty. He listened as she told him about Mrs Maybrick taking the bottle of meat juice from the room at midnight. He then went to the sickroom and found the bottle among the others on the small table. It was half full. He removed it, then went for a walk in the garden.

Florence Maybrick went down to the garden to get some fresh air, and found Michael there. They talked about Jim's illness, and she asked why Michael had not brought Dr Fuller from London.

Michael said he believed that Dr Carter fully understood the case. It was, he said, rather late in the day to send for Dr Fuller.

Soon after they went indoors, Michael was coming up the stairs when he saw Florence outside the door of the sickroom. She seemed to be pouring medicine from one bottle to another. 'Florie,' he said, 'how dare you tamper with the medicine?

She said that there was so much sediment in the smaller bottle that it was impossible to dissolve it, so she was putting it into the larger bottle so it could be shaken more easily.

Michael said he was much annoyed, and that he would have the prescription made up fresh. He summoned one of the maids and sent her to the chemist's.

Dr Humphreys arrived at four o'clock, followed almost immediately by Dr Carter. Michael Maybrick handed Dr Carter the bottles of brandy and of meat juice and asked him to test them. They then went up to see the patient.

Maybrick said he was better. But his pulse was quicker than in the morning, and the fingers of his right hand were entirely white and blood-less. He said he had again had a restless night, and asked for something to make him sleep.

The doctors were not satisfied with their patient. They ordered cocaine applied to his throat externally, to relieve the pain there. Since he had vomited once during the day and seemed unable to take anything but brandy and champagne, they ordered a nutrient suppository which would supplement his nutrition if it could be retained. They prescribed also a thirty-grain dose of sulphonal, a white, tasteless, odourless hypnotic powder which would produce sleep.

As they completed their consultation, the doctors agreed that Mr Michael Maybrick's suggestion of the day before might be justified. There might indeed be cause for suspicion.

Nurse Wilson, a large woman as fat as Nurse Gore was thin, relieved Nurse Callery of duty. Mrs Maybrick was at the bedside most of the time. The nurse could not hear everything the patient and his wife said, but at about six o'clock she heard Mr Maybrick exclaim, 'Oh, Bunny, Bunny, how could you do it? I did not think it of you.' She particularly noticed what he said because he repeated it twice.

'You silly old darling,' said Mrs Maybrick. 'Don't trouble your head about things.'

In the kitchen at seven o'clock, Elizabeth Humphreys had dinner ready when the front doorbell rang. Thomas Lowry and George Smith, from

Mr Maybrick's office, said they had some papers for Mr Maybrick. Mr Michael and Mr Edwin took the papers up to the sickroom.

The servants were waiting to serve dinner. Presently they heard Mr Maybrick shouting out, in a voice that could be heard all over the house, 'Oh, Lord! If I am to die, why am I to be worried like this? Let me die properly.'

The cook and the maid went into the hall and looked up the staircase. They saw Mr Edwin come out of the bedroom with a paper in his hand. They hurried back into the kitchen, where Alice Yapp told them that the brothers had been trying to get the master to sign a will. Mr Maybrick had made a new will, she said, after the quarrel on the day of the Grand National, but Mr Michael and Mr Edwin could not find it. Now they were trying to get one signed.

During the evening, Maybrick began to have periods of delirium.

The cook was still in the kitchen at nine o'clock when Mrs Maybrick came in. She asked for a sandwich and a glass of milk, and ate them there. As she was leaving, she asked the cook to get some soup and a sandwich ready for the night. She thanked Humphreys for her kindness to her, and kissed her.

The cook asked how the master was, and Mrs Maybrick said he had inflammation now and was sinking very fast. There was, she said, no hope.

It seemed to the cook that her mistress was very much distressed.

Dr Humphreys returned at 10.30 p.m. He felt the patient's pulse. It was so fast it was almost uncountable. He was steadily becoming weaker. The doctor told Mr Michael Maybrick that he anticipated fatal results, suggesting that a solicitor might be seen as to James Maybrick's affairs.

At eleven o'clock, Nurse Ellen Gore relieved Nurse Wilson.

It was after eleven o'clock that night when Dr Carter completed his day of calls on patients. He stepped into his workroom and turned to the bottles of brandy and meat juice given to him that afternoon by Mr Michael Maybrick.

He poured a small amount of the brandy into a test tube, added hydrochloric acid, and brought the liquid to a boil. He introduced a piece of copper foil. When he examined the foil, he found no trace of any metallic substance.

Next he tried the meat juice. Using a few drops of the juice, he repeated the test. When he put a piece of copper foil into the test tube, he immediately got a deposit in crystalline form on the copper.

The doctor was cautious. He applied special tests to each of the reagents he was using, checking carefully to determine the purity of each. Then he performed the test again and again, using several drops of the meat juice each time until two teaspoonfuls had been used. The result was the same each time : a crystalline deposit on the copper. Since the effect of the test was to drive away everything except arsenic, Dr Carter could come to only one conclusion : the bottle of Valentine's meat juice contained arsenic.

The doctor now poured some of the meat juice onto a white plate and swished it around to see if he could find specks of white arsenic, soot, or antimony. He made one more test, on the assumption that the arsenic had probably been introduced in solution, to see if the specific gravity of the meat juice had been diminished. The test was inconclusive.

In the sickroom at Battlecrease House, Nurse Gore and Mrs Maybrick stayed up through the night. Maybrick seemed to be somewhere between sleep, consciousness and delirium. When awake and conscious, he was extremely weak.

At three in the morning, Florence Maybrick became alarmed. She went to Michael's room and told him matters were much worse. Then she hurried to Elizabeth Humphreys's room and asked the cook to send someone to fetch Mrs Briggs.

The two maids, Mary Cadwallader and Bessie Brierley, got up and went to Sefton Park.

The brothers went into the sickroom, and Nurse Gore told them that Mr Maybrick was very sick indeed.

'Is not this sad?' said Florence.

'What?' said Edwin.

'To see Jim suffer so,' she said, 'and not be able to relieve him.'

Nothing more was said.

In Sefton Park, the servants from Battlecrease House pounded at the door of Mrs Briggs's house until it was opened. Mrs Briggs recognised them, learned that she was urgently needed and that Mr Maybrick was dying, and said that she would have to bring her sister, Mrs Hughes, as she did not like to go out alone at that hour of the night.

At five o'clock, as the first morning light was beginning to enter the house, Mrs Maybrick woke Nurse Yapp and told her to awaken the children. Bobo and Gladys were brought sleepy-eyed into the sickroom to see their father.

Mrs Briggs and Mrs Hughes arrived with the dawn and went up to see James.

In the kitchen, Elizabeth Humphreys stirred about, getting breakfast. Mrs Maybrick came down. The cook made toast and tea for her and spoke sympathetically to her. As she was leaving, her mistress put her arms around her neck and kissed her.

Dr Humphreys arrived at his customary hour – eight thirty. He found the patient unable to swallow, and knew that Maybrick was dying. The doctor stayed at Battlecrease House through the morning. At eleven o'clock, Nurse Wilson returned to duty, relieving Nurse Gore.

Soon after eleven, exhaustion caught up with Florence Maybrick. She was so tired and weak that she lay down on the bed in the dressing room. Edwin and Michael went in and spoke to her, but she did not respond. She seemed to be partly asleep or semi-conscious. They left her alone.

At noon, Dr Carter arrived. He told Dr Humphreys and Mr Michael Maybrick the result of his test of the meat juice. He showed them the copper slips with the metallic deposit, and said that if things turned out as he feared they would, the matter must pass entirely out of their hands. However, said Dr Carter, he did not wish to do an injustice to anyone. He wanted to examine a new, unopened bottle of meat juice. It was just possible that some adulteration might have been accidentally introduced in the process of manufacture.

The doctor added that if this should not be the case, it would be his duty to hand the bottle of meat juice that had been given to him the day before to a skilled analyst. If the patient should die – and Dr Carter remarked that, from what Dr Humphreys had just told him of Mr Maybrick's present condition, this seemed almost certain – if the patient should die, he and Dr Humphreys would feel it impossible to give a certificate of death from natural causes. The case would then have to be referred to the Coroner.

They found the patient much worse. They wanted to examine his tongue, but had great difficulty getting him to understand their instructions. They found that he could not retain the nutrient suppositories. It was evident that he could not live, and that nothing more could be done for him.

The doctors were not told that Mrs Maybrick had collapsed and lay in a faint or swoon on the bed in the dressing room next door.

After lunch, Edwin Maybrick went into Liverpool for two hours. He notified his brother Thomas, in Manchester, that Jim was dying.

During the afternoon, the brothers spoke to Florence several times. She did not respond. Mrs Briggs and Mrs Hughes stayed at Battlecrease House all day. Thomas Maybrick joined Edwin and Michael late in the afternoon, and towards evening James Maybrick's close friend George Davidson came in.

Soon after eight in the evening, Dr Carter and Dr Humphreys, sensing the need for family privacy at the death-bed, withdrew from the sick-room. At 8.30, Nurse Gore returned to duty, relieving Nurse Wilson. At 8.40, when James Maybrick died, he was in the arms of his friend George Davidson, and his brothers and the Janion sisters, Mrs Briggs and Mrs Hughes, were at his bedside. His wife, Florence, lay quietly alone on the bed in the dressing room.

V

'Edwin has just said there were some
flypapers found. What were they for?'

An hour after James died, Michael Maybrick summoned Nurse Yapp and Bessie Brierley. He ordered the servants to begin searching the house. His instructions were vague yet sinister: They were to see what they could find. At the same time, he asked Nurse Yapp to pack the children's clothing, as they would be leaving Battlecrease House next day.

While Michael was instructing the servants, Edwin told Mrs Briggs and Mrs Hughes about Dr Carter's analysis of the meat juice and asked them to stay overnight at Battlecrease House.

While Yapp and Brierley were occupied, Humphreys and Cadwallader were in the kitchen. Alice Grant bustled in with the breath-taking information that a love letter of Mrs Maybrick's had been picked up.

Dr Carter went back to Liverpool. He took the bottle of Valentine's meat juice to an analytical chemist he knew, Mr Edward Davies, and asked him to test it. With the bottle, he gave Davies a handwritten note telling him what he had found. The chemist locked up the bottle in a cabinet and went to bed.

Edwin Maybrick went into the dressing room. Florence lay as she had lain for nearly twelve hours, fully dressed and semi-conscious. He carried her into the spare bedroom on the far side of the house, then asked Nurse Wilson to look after her.

Carrying out Mr Michael's orders, Brierley and Yapp went into the linen closet on the landing next to Mr and Mrs Maybrick's bedroom. The door was unlocked. The closet contained a trunk of Mrs Maybrick's in which the bedroom towels were kept.

They carried the trunk into the night nursery. Alice Yapp then went upstairs to get some of the children's clothes to pack in the trunk. Bessie Brierley went down to the kitchen.

When Alice Yapp came down again, Nurse Wilson followed her into the night nursery. She was standing beside the trunk when Nurse Yapp opened it.

Michael and Edwin Maybrick were in the breakfast room on the ground floor when Alice Yapp hurried to them at midnight. She was carrying a chocolate box and a small parcel wrapped in brown paper. She said the box and the parcel had been wrapped in a sheet which fell out of the tray of the trunk when she lifted the lid. She had opened both the box and the parcel, and she thought the gentlemen ought to see what was inside them.

Michael opened the chocolate box. In it were a packet, two bottles, and a handkerchief. The packet was labelled 'Poison.' On the other side he read, 'Arsenic.' The words, 'Poison for cats' were handwritten in red ink.

The bottles contained a white fluid. The brown paper parcel was partly open at one end, and a yellow power was almost running out of it.

For the first time, the brothers felt the need of legal advice. A solicitor, Mr A. G. Steel, lived next door. Edwin Maybrick went to see him.

The solicitor's advice was that they seal up any evidence and keep it in a safe place. They wrapped the chocolate box and the brown paper parcel together, then sealed the package with sealing wax. They then locked up the package in the wine cellar. Michael Maybrick kept the key.

In the spare bedroom, Florence Maybrick became aware of darkness and stillness. The bang of a closing door startled her, and it flashed through her mind that her husband was dead. Then she heard a voice. She opened her eyes. Edwin Maybrick was bending over her. He gripped her arms and shook her. 'I want your keys,' he said. 'Do you hear? Where are your keys?'

She tried to reply. But before she could gather her thoughts, she fainted again.

All those living in Battlecrease House, except Florence Maybrick, were up early on Sunday morning, 12th May. At breakfast, Edwin and Michael told Mrs Hughes and Mrs Briggs about the packet labelled poison. All wondered if that was the only poison in the house. They talked of the need to find Jim's will, which was probably in his safe, and Edwin said that he had been unable to get Florence to tell him where the keys to the safe were.

The brothers Maybrick and the sisters Janion rose from the breakfast table and set about searching for Jim's will, for the keys that might lead to the will, and for any further evidence that Battlecrease House contained arsenic.

As they left the table, Mrs Briggs went to the kitchen door and spoke to the servants. 'Mrs Maybrick is no longer mistress here,' she said.

The kitchen buzzed with excitement. The servants had overheard, or had learned quickly from those who went in and out of the breakfast room, the details of the suspicions now at large in the house. They discussed the probability of an investigation, and Alice Yapp said to Elizabeth Humphreys, 'I will tell all I know, if only to prevent Mrs Maybrick having the children.'

Upstairs, the search began in Mrs Maybrick's room, where the body of James Maybrick lay in the bed. After a moment or two, Edwin and Michael and Mrs Briggs moved into the dressing room beyond, which could be reached only through the bedroom. Mrs Hughes stayed in the bedroom, looking carefully into each drawer of Florence Maybrick's dressing table.

She felt something under the paper lining of the small middle drawer. Lifting the lining, she found three letters addressed to Mrs Maybrick and a slip of paper that seemed to contain a copy of a telegram. She took them to Michael Maybrick.

Her sister, meanwhile, had made her way to the far side of the bed on which Florence had often rested during her husband's illness and on which she had lain semi-conscious during the twenty-four-hour period in which he died. There in plain sight in the corner she saw two hatboxes standing one atop the other. She opened the top hatbox and saw a man's slouch hat, crown up, brim down. She lifted the hat and found beneath it a little blue wooden box. In it were several small bottles, including a partly full bottle of Valentine's meat juice.

Mrs Briggs took the little wooden box across the room and showed it to Michael Maybrick. He told her to put it back in the hatbox just as she had found it.

Now, in the lower hatbox, she found a tall silk hat, brim up, crown down. Lying in the crown of the hat was a small hat brush, and standing in the crown was a tumbler containing liquid. A piece of linen was soaking in the liquid.

Mrs Briggs showed the tumbler in the hat to the others and replaced the lid.

Edwin Maybrick at this time was busy examining a cupboard in the lower part of a fancy table. Far back in the corner of the cupboard he found a bottle standing upright with a handkerchief wrapped around it. He showed the bottle and handkerchief to the others, then put them back where he had found them.

Michael Maybrick now wanted the others to see one of the letters he had been reading. It was Alfred Brierley's letter expressing his concern that the London visit might be traced and saying that he was planning a trip to the Mediterranean.

When they had read the letter, all four left the room. Edwin Maybrick locked the door and pocketed the key.

While the rooms in Battlecrease House were being searched, Edward Davies unlocked a cabinet in his laboratory in Liverpool and took out the bottle of meat juice given to him the night before by Dr Carter. Using ten drops of the juice, he tried Reinsch's test and obtained a strong deposit of arsenic on a slip of copper. He then treated the copper in a glass tube, and obtained crystals of white arsenic. Then, to double check, he took another ten drops and put it in Marsh's apparatus. He obtained spots of arsenic. He passed the gas from Marsh's apparatus into nitrate of silver, and got a precipitate of silver, indicating the presence of arsenic. Finally, he used a testing method established by Fresenius and Van Babo and got a precipitate of sulphide of arsenic, soluble in ammonia.

When he had completed the fourth test, Davies was absolutely certain that the bottle of Valentine's meat juice handed him by Dr Carter contained arsenic.

The children's clothes were packed. With Nurse Yapp as escort, they went off to the home of Mrs Janion, mother of Mrs Briggs and Mrs Hughes, in Gateacre.

In the spare bedroom, Mrs Maybrick still lay in her clothes. Consciousness came and went. She became aware of the presence of Nurse Wilson. She knew that it was the Sabbath day. Then Michael Maybrick came into the room.

'Nurse,' he said, 'I am going up to London. Mrs Maybrick is no longer mistress of this house. As one of the executors I forbid you to allow her to leave this room. I hold you responsible in my absence.'

Toward evening, Mrs Maybrick said to the nurse, 'I wish to see my children.'

The nurse ignored her.

Mrs Maybrick's voice was weak. She thought perhaps the nurse had not heard her. 'Nurse,' she said again, 'I want to see my children.'

The nurse said, 'You cannot see Master James and Miss Gladys. Mr Michael Maybrick gave orders that they were to leave the house without seeing you.'

Mrs Maybrick fell back on her pillow. She felt dazed. Why should

Michael give such orders? she wondered. Why should her children be taken away from her?

In the evening, the police at Garston were notified of the death in Aigburth under suspicious circumstances of Mr James Maybrick. Inspector Baxendale was sent to Battlecrease House, where he questioned Michael and Edwin Maybrick, Mrs Briggs, and all the servants. (Michael Maybrick had been to London and back during the day.)

After viewing the body, the inspector asked to look into the dressing room. Mr Edwin unlocked the door, and they went in together. The inspector asked if the room had been searched. Mr Edwin said that it had. They talked about the search, and Mr Maybrick brought the hatboxes from the far corner to a table, where Inspector Baxendale looked through them. He then took possession of the hatboxes and of the bottle found in the back corner of the cabinet in the dressing room.

He was not given the sealed package that Edwin and Michael had locked in the wine cellar.

On Monday morning, 13th May, Mrs Maybrick lay ill in bed. Nurses Wilson and Gore had been kept on to care for her, and they had changed their patient's clothes, helped her get under the covers, and fed her – all with little sign of consciousness from her.

That morning, Dr Humphreys decided that, because arsenic had been found on the premises at Battlecrease House, he could not issue a certificate of death. He reported the death to the County Coroner, Mr S. Brighouse, who ordered a post mortem examination to be made by Dr Humphreys and Dr Carter.

Upon hearing that a death certificate had been refused, Isaac Bryning, superintendent of county police for the district, went to Battlecrease House. He talked with the Maybrick brothers, questioned the servants, and ordered his man to open the drains of the house. In his presence, Dr Humphreys took samples from the drains.

The post-mortem began at five in the afternoon. Maybrick's body lay on the bed in which he had died. Dr Carter and Dr Humphreys were joined by Dr Alexander Barron, who practised in Liverpool and was a member of the Royal College of Surgeons and a Professor of Pathology at University College. He had been asked to attend on Mrs Maybrick's behalf. Police Superintendent Bryning was also present.

Dr Barron and Dr Humphreys did most of the dissection. Dr Carter's only active role was to begin the procedure required for removing the brain. During the rest of the time, Dr Carter took notes as Dr Barron, usually, dictated them.

The doctors found Maybrick to be a man of well-developed frame and condition. Brain, lungs and heart seemed normal and were returned to the body after examination. There were, however, signs of inflammation throughout the alimentary canal. Towards the stomach, on the lower part of the mucous membrane, there appeared a yellow gelatinous quality with black patches. A small ulcer was found in the larynx, the upper edge of the epiglottis was eroded, and the rear of the voice box had red patches. Each end of the stomach was inflamed, and its lining showed small blood spots. Red inflammation appeared in the duodenum, with more red inflammation in the lower intestines and at the extremity of the bowels.

The doctors removed a number of parts of the viscera and put them into jars. The stomach, tied at each end, the intestines, the spleen and parts of the liver were all put into jars, sealed, and turned over to Inspector Baxendale.

Dr Barron, who had not attended the deceased, concluded that death was due to acute inflammation of the stomach, probably caused by some irritant poison.

In the evening, Michael Maybrick, who had returned from another day in London, unlocked the wine cellar and brought up the sealed package containing the chocolate box with its packet of 'Arsenic. Poison for cats' and its two bottles and handkerchief. He handed the package, unopened, to Inspector Baxendale.

On Tuesday, the inspector delivered to Edward Davies, a chemist of the Royal Institution Laboratory in Liverpool, the jars from the post mortem, the sealed parcel, several glass jars containing sediment from the drains, the bottles and tumbler from the hatboxes, the bedding in which Maybrick had died and a flannel shirt he had worn two or three days before death, and several other bottles and small parcels from Battlecrease House. The chemist set about testing each one for arsenic.

On that Tuesday morning, County Coroner Brighouse summoned a jury to the Aigburth Hotel and opened an inquest into the death of James Maybrick. To allow time for the chemical analysis, the coroner adjourned the hearing for a fortnight, but asked the members to come round to Battlecrease House to view the body.

Mrs Maybrick had not been informed that a jury had been called, and she was not represented at the inquest. She still lay in bed, weak and ill, in the spare bedroom. She heard nothing of the commotion as the curious jurymen mounted the stairs and moved into her bedroom to view the body of her husband.

The foreman of the jury was especially concerned. He had known the deceased, and after viewing the body he was disturbed and perplexed.

In her room, Mrs Maybrick was equally disturbed and perplexed. Michael Maybrick had come in and greeted her brusquely. 'I think you had better have counsel,' he said, adding that there were charges against her which he would not detail.

Despite her weakened condition, Florence Maybrick realised she was without help. She knew solicitors Richard and Arnold Cleaver of Liverpool. She asked Michael to send for them. She thought of friends in America, including her mother's New York lawyers, Roe and Macklin, and she wrote out several cablegrams and asked Michael to dispatch them. She also asked her brother-in-law to send word of her trouble to the Baroness von Roques in Paris.

During the morning, Edwin Maybrick went into the lavatory adjacent to the room in which his brother had died. There hung a dressing-gown of Florie's. One of the nurses said she had taken it out of the death room, and that Mrs Maybrick had worn it while tending Mr Maybrick. Edwin locked the gown into a cupboard.

Michael Maybrick went downstairs with the cablegrams Florence had written. Finding Inspector Baxendale there, he gave the inspector the three letters Mrs Hughes had found under the lining of the dressing table drawer. Looking over the cablegrams, he decided that one, addressed to Messrs Roe and Macklin in New York, should also be turned over to the police. The inspector said he did not think the cable was important, and put it in his pocket. Michael then went out and dispatched the remaining cables, paying for them himself, and instructed Messrs Cleaver and Arnold to act as Mrs Maybrick's solicitors.

Florence Maybrick looked up from her bed as Mrs Briggs came into the room. She told her visitor Michael had advised her to have counsel, and asked Mrs Briggs what she knew of this terrible business.

Why, said Mrs Briggs, there was arsenic found in a bottle of Valentine's meat juice, and Dr Humphreys had refused to sign a death certificate.

Instantly, a key turned in Florence Maybrick's mind. She knew how arsenic came to be in a bottle of meat juice, and she began to explain to Mrs Briggs. It was the Thursday night before Jim died, she said, and –

The bedroom door, which was only slightly ajar, was pushed open. 'You are not to say anything,' said a voice. It was Mrs Hughes. Florence was not sure whether she was speaking to her or to her sister.

Behind Mrs Hughes she saw a policeman. 'You are not to speak,' he said.

Then the door opened wide. Dr Humphreys came in. He said nothing, but took Mrs Maybrick's wrist and felt her pulse. In a moment he left the room.

Now the room filled with men. Her brothers-in-law and several strangers were there. They stood back from both sides of the bed. All stared at her. A police officer stepped forward. 'Mrs Maybrick,' he said, 'I am superintendent of the police, and I am about to say something to you. After I have said what I intend to say, if you reply be careful how you reply, because whatever you say may be used as evidence against you. Mrs Maybrick, you are in custody on suspicion of causing the death of your late husband, James Maybrick, on the eleventh instant.'

Florence Maybrick made no reply. As the men filed out of the room without a word, she felt weak again. In custody? On suspicion of causing Jim's death?

Mr Richard Cleaver and his brother Arnold hurried round to Battle-crease House. A policeman insisted that they obtain a permit to enter the house, and after some delay, they were shown in.

As they started up the stair to Mrs Maybrick's room, Mrs Hughes called after them, 'Go up and see her. She's the greatest liar on earth.'

Mrs Maybrick told the lawyers that Mrs Briggs said arsenic had been found in a bottle of Valentine's beef juice, and she then described what had happened in the sickroom on Thursday night. Early that evening, she said, her husband asked her to give him a powder which he was accustomed to taking. She refused. Later on, soon after Nurse Gore gave him some beef tea, he again begged her to put the powder in some food. The powder was, he said, in a pocket of his waistcoat, hanging in his bedroom. He implored her so piteously, she said, and she herself was so anxious and distraught, that at last she found the powder and, at midnight, took a bottle of Valentine's meat juice into the dressing room and put the powder into it. When she returned, he was asleep. She moved the bottle to the washstand, where she hoped he would not see it. Only today, she said, when Mrs Briggs told her of the accusation against her, did she realise that the powder was arsenic.

The lawyers wanted to ask the young widow particularly about such powders as her husband seemed to have carried in his waistcoat, but she was ill and exhausted. Very well. They would leave, until the coroner's inquest came to some conclusion, such investigation as would be needed in preparing her defence – if, indeed, the defence of Mrs Maybrick became necessary at all. They returned to their office.

Awaiting them there was a man named Dalgleish, who said he was foreman of the coroner's jury. He thought what he had to say was so important that he ought not to sit upon the jury. He had known the deceased, and could testify to a certain statement made by the deceased some time ago, as to the cause of his illness.

Mr Cleaver listened patiently. The foreman said he had run into Mr Maybrick before the Wirral races, and saw Maybrick take a packet of powder from his pocket. He asked what it was, and Maybrick said it was strychnine.

Mr Cleaver advised the jury foreman to tell the Coroner his story.

Again in the afternoon Mrs Briggs appeared in the spare bedroom at Battlecrease House. She listened as Florence said she wanted to get in touch with friends who would help her, but had no money for telegrams and stamps.

'Perhaps Mr Brierley will help you,' said Mrs Briggs.

Florence acted at once. While Mrs Briggs waited, she found paper and pencil. Mrs Briggs said that, if Florence wrote a letter to Mr Brierley, she would give it to the police. She suggested that Florence might better telegraph to him.

Florence sat down and wrote a short note. As she finished, she asked Mrs Briggs to read it. The letter was addressed to A. Brierley, 60 Huskisson Street.

> Battlecrease House, Aigburth
>
> I am writing you to give me every assistance in your power in my present fearful trouble. I am in custody, without any of my family with me, and without money. I have cabled to my solicitor in New York to come here at once. In the meantime send some money for present needs. The truth is known about my visit to London. Your last letter is at present in the hands of the police. Appearances may be against me, but, before God, I swear I am innocent.
>
> Florence E. Maybrick

Mrs Briggs finished reading and looked at Florence Maybrick. If Florence wished this to go, she said, she would hand it to the policeman at the door.

Florence again asked Mrs Briggs to post the letter for her. As Mrs Briggs left the room, she turned the letter over to the policeman on duty.

Mr Brighouse, the Coroner, listened to what his jury foreman had to say. Then he got in touch with the solicitor, Mr Steel, and with Superintendent Bryning. If you think Mr Dalgleish's statement is useful, he said to each, if you think it is evidence and the foreman ought to appear as a witness, I will discharge him.

Each said he thought the better course would be for the coroner to discharge the foreman. He did so.

As Tuesday evening drew in, Mrs Hughes and Mrs Briggs gathered their things and left Aigburth. They had been at Battlecrease House constantly since dawn on Saturday. Behind them they left Florence Maybrick a prisoner in her home.

On Wednesday morning, 15th May, readers of the *Liverpool Daily Post* saw the prominent headline, SUSPICIOUS DEATH OF A LIVERPOOL MERCHANT. Below, the reader's appetite for sensational news was fed by several paragraphs, under the heading, 'The Maybrick Mystery', which described the coroner's inquest and offered much conjecture about criminal proceedings. Though many of Maybrick's acquaintances could speak of his business life, it was mainly the gossip of servants that raised questions about the private life of the middle-aged Liverpudlian and his very young American wife. The situation was ripe for sensational press coverage.

At Battlecrease House that morning, however, little attention was paid to the newspapers. Nurses Wilson and Gore were still in attendance on a weak and distraught Mrs Maybrick, and a policeman stood guard in her room. Another was just outside the bedroom door, which was never permitted to be closed.

Edwin and Michael Maybrick came up to see her. They had been going through Jim's things, and they could not find a number of pieces of jewellery which they knew he owned. What did Florie know of them? Had she hidden them, or sold them to pay some of the debts she had incurred in her extravagant way?

She knew nothing. She remembered some of the jewels, but she did not know when she had last seen them. Perhaps two or three years ago – she wasn't sure. Had they looked everywhere? Weren't the jewels in his safe?

No, the brothers agreed firmly, the jewels were not in the house. What had Florence done with them?

In the afternoon, the *Daily Post*'s sensational story brought its first result.

Traffic in Riversdale Road increased noticeably as people decided to walk or ride past Number 6, where the man who was poisoned had lived. Through the crowd hurried a Liverpool dressmaker. He knocked hard at Number 6.

A policeman answered the door, and the dressmaker asked to see some representative of the family. Edwin Maybrick listened to his story, and the visitor presented Edwin with a bill for £10 for dresses he had made. In view of what he had read in the *Post* that morning, he thought it just as well to have the bill settled at once.

Edwin asked the dressmaker to wait. He went upstairs and showed the bill to Florence. Was this still another of the debts she had accumulated?

No, she said. She knew neither the dressmaker nor his shop.

Edwin went down again. The dressmaker insisted that his instructions had been to send the bill to Mr James Maybrick, Battlecrease House, Number 6, Riversdale Road. The bill was now some months overdue, and he wanted a settlement.

Edwin asked him to check his records as to what person the dresses had been made for, and the dressmaker departed.

That afternoon, Inspector Baxendale handed back to Michael Maybrick the cablegram which Florence had asked Michael to send to attorneys Roe and Macklin in New York. When he went out, Michael dispatched the cablegram.

Still a prisoner, and her strength still not recovered, Florence Maybrick lay in bed on Thursday morning, 16th May and wondered at the clamour of excited voices and footsteps she could hear. 'Nurse', she said, 'is anything the matter?'

'The funeral starts in an hour,' said Nurse Wilson.

'Whose funeral?' said Mrs Maybrick.

'Your husband's,' said the nurse. 'But for you – if your husband had died naturally – he would have been decently buried on Tuesday.'

Mrs Maybrick got out of bed and began dressing herself. Her hands were weak and fumbling. The nurse came towards her. 'Stand back,' said Mrs Maybrick. 'I'm going to see my husband before he is taken away.'

Mrs Maybrick pushed the nurse aside and went to the policeman at the door. 'I demand to see my husband,' she said. 'The law does not permit a person to be treated as guilty until she is proven so.'

The policeman hesitated, then said, 'Follow me.'

He led Mrs Maybrick to her bedroom. There she found the coffin, covered with white flowers, lying on the bed. She turned to the police-man and the nurse, and said, 'Leave me alone with the dead.'

They refused to leave her, and she knelt down at the bedside and at last yielded to the tears that had until then refused to flow.

When she was calm, she returned to the spare bedroom and sat near a window, still weeping quietly, until the nurse said, 'If you wish to see the last of the husband you have poisoned, you had better stand up. The funeral has started.'

Mrs Maybrick rose and, clutching the windowsill, watched as the coffin was borne into the hearse at the front gate. A large crowd stood silently watching. She stayed at the window until the hearse was out of sight. Then she fainted.

The Maybrick brothers were in full attendance at the funeral. Even William, who dwelt in Liverpool but had never entered Battlecrease House, came to say farewell to his brother. Nine carriages filled with relatives and friends followed the hearse to Anfield Cemetery, where a large crowd waited. New friends of the deceased, whom they knew only from the sensational newspaper accounts, they watched in silence and bitterness the final rites for the victim of an outrageous plot.

When she recovered from her fainting spell, Mrs Maybrick found herself again in bed. She asked why her mother had not been sent for. The nurses reported her question to Mr Michael after the funeral. When he went out he sent a telegram to the Baroness von Roques, in Paris: 'Florie ill, and in awful trouble. Do not delay.'

The Baroness did not delay. She was in London that night, and the LMS brought her down from London with the speed of lightning on Friday morning. By chance she ran into Michael Maybrick in the Liverpool station.

'Florie is very ill,' he said. 'Edwin will tell you everything. It is a case of murder, and there is a man in the case.'

The Baroness did not understand the remark, and Michael seemed to be in a hurry. She dashed for Aigburth and Battlecrease House. She found the street and yard crowded with people. They gave her the impression they were waiting for something.

Edwin Maybrick met her in the hall and took her into the morning room. 'Why didn't you send for me before?' she said. 'Why wasn't I allowed to come?'

'Florie didn't ask for you,' he said, 'and no one knew your address.'

The Baroness drew herself up with dignity. 'Everyone knew it,' she said. ' "Paris" would have found me.' She paused to study the effect upon

Edwin. 'Tell me what has happened. Michael told me you would explain. I must see Florie at once.'

Edwin looked at her. 'The police are in the house.'

'Police? Why?'

'I suppose you know it is said Jim was poisoned.'

'Poisoned by whom?'

Haltingly, Edwin told the Baroness of Michael's suspicions, and how the doctor thought something was wrong with Jim.

'What doctor?' asked the Baroness.

'Dr Carter,' said Edwin. 'And we thought Jim was not properly nursed. The nurse said Florie put something in the meat juice, and Michael gave the bottle to Dr Carter. He refused a certificate of death, and then the police came in.'

The Baroness was furious. 'Why not have sent for me? How could you deliver her up to the police in this way, and not a friend by her? Who has been here?'

'Mrs Briggs,' said Edwin, 'but she left on Wednesday. We had no idea matters would result in this way. I would rather cut my hand off than have had it so.'

'But the children,' said the Baroness. 'How could you ruin their future? Your suspicions alone are horrible, and for a girl like that, without father, brother, mother – you are doing her to death among you, and for what?'

'Oh,' said Edwin, 'I've been very fond of Florie. I would have stood by her, and I did until the letter to a man was found.'

'Letter to a man?' said the Baroness. 'What man? Do, Edwin, tell me a straight story.'

'Why, to the man Brierley,' he said. 'She wrote him a letter and it was found.'

'Who found it? You? And who is Brierley? When did she know him?'

'She met him this winter at some dances,' said Edwin, 'and she was always so quiet and domestic before, I would never have believed it of Florie, but this winter she was changed and would go out to dances – I wish I could meet Brierley.'

'Yes,' said the Baroness, nodding firmly, 'That is just about the best thing you could do. In my country and among the men I have known, they would have met Brierley instead of calling in the police.' She paused again to look Edwin over. 'But what about this letter,' she went on. 'Who found it?'

'Nurse.'

'Where? And if she found it, why didn't she give it back to her mistress?'

'She found it on the floor,' Edwin said. 'It fell from her dress when she fainted, and I carried her into the spare bedroom.'

'But how did you know it was to Brierley?'

'It was directed to him,' said Edwin.

The Baroness gave up in despair and went upstairs. She found two policemen in the hall. Through an open door, she saw her daughter lying on a sofa. She went in. Florence, she thought, looked deadly pale. A policeman was sitting in a chair near the sofa. As the Baroness started to kiss her daughter, a rather fat nurse moved between them. The Baroness pushed her aside and kissed Florence. She spoke to her in French. *'Pourquoi sont ces personnes ici?'*

The nurse said, 'You must speak only English.'

The policeman said, 'I warn you, madam, I shall write down what you say.' He drew paper and pencil from his pocket.

'Write as much as you like, my friend,' said the Baroness in English. 'I have nothing wrong to say. But it strikes me as very strange to see you in this room.'

'Mammy dear,' said Florence. 'The inspector is only doing his duty.'

'But what is the nurse for?' she asked. 'And the people outside? I consider it infamous. And Edwin seems to have lost his head. What on earth does it mean?'

Florence spoke quietly. 'They think I have poisoned Jim.'

'Poisoned Jim!' said the Baroness. 'Why, if he is poisoned, he poisoned himself. He made a perfect apothecary's shop of himself, as we all know.'

Florence sighed. 'Mamma, go into Liverpool, and see my solicitor, Mr Cleaver. He will explain everything. And please don't say anything.'

The Baroness found Edwin again, and tried to get further details. He told her only that an intrigue with a man had been discovered, and that they had wanted an excuse to send Florie home to her and keep the children. To clinch matters, they called in Dr Carter and mentioned their suspicions, and the doctor had declared he would not give a certificate of death.

When Michael Maybrick returned, the Baroness tried to discuss the case. Michael seemed quite agitated, and said that if the Baroness would prove her daughter mad and have her shut up they would drop the inquiry.

During this time, Sergeant Davenport, feeling the tedium of his duty outside Mrs Maybrick's room, wandered into the nearby linen closet.

Glancing around, he noticed a dressing case which belonged to the deposed mistress of the house. Within it he discovered a bottle containing a white powder and a bottle containing six white pills. The tray of a trunk lay on the floor, and on the tray stood a small round bottle, without a label, containing a small quantity of light liquid. The sergeant held the three bottles for Inspector Baxendale.

After dinner, Michael went up to London, and Edwin, excusing himself, said that he had to go out. The Baroness, alone in the room where they had told her to sleep, heard her daughter crying. She found her in hysterics, with two nurses holding her down in bed. 'If you will kindly sit down and let me hold her hand and soothe her,' said the Baroness, 'she will be quiet. As my child, I know how to help her.'

The nurses refused, and soon four policemen joined them in holding Florence down in bed. The Baroness was outraged. She was a large woman, and with all her strength she pulled the fat nurse away from the bed and ordered the men out. 'I know more of nursing than you do,' she shouted. 'These men have no right in a lady's room, and there is nothing to fear as to violence. If you will let me hold her hand and speak to her she will be calm.'

The fat nurse said insolently that she would put the Baroness out if she did not take care. She was in charge, and she would act as she thought best.

The Baroness gave up, overpowered by the situation. 'Better death than dishonour,' she exclaimed as she went to her bedroom.

On Saturday morning, the Baroness saw Edwin first thing. He repeated that Florie had swooned on Saturday a week ago in the room in which Jim was dying, and that he had picked her up and carried her into the spare bedroom, where she lay unconscious, neither moving nor speaking, until Monday. On Monday they had asked her if her mother should be sent for and she said no. 'In fact,' said Edwin, 'we all lost our heads.'

At ten o'clock, the Baroness saw a strange woman come upstairs and go into the nursery. She asked the nurse in Florence's room who it was, and learned that she was the children's nurse, Alice Yapp. The Baroness found the nurse gathering some of the children's clothes. 'Are you Bobo's and Gladys's nurse?' she asked.

'Yes,' said the nurse.

'How are the children?'

'Very well.'

'And where are they?'

'At Mrs Janion's.'

'You mean Gladys's godmother?' said the Baroness.

'Yes. In Halewood Road, Gateacre.'

'Are you the nurse who has been here so long?'

'Yes.'

'And are you the one who has caused additional trouble to that poor young thing by showing letters you find?'

'She wasn't a poor young thing then.'

'Well,' said the Baroness, 'you are an ungrateful, disloyal servant.'

She went back into the spare bedroom, told Florence the nurse was there to get clothes for the children, and said that if Florence would give her the name and address of her solicitor she would go into Liverpool. The thin nurse wrote out the name and address of Messrs Cleaver, solicitors, in Liverpool.

The Baroness started downstairs, then remembered something Edwin had said. She went back to her daughter. 'I have been trying to get something out of Edwin,' she said, 'but I understand nothing. Will you tell me, my dear, what this talk of flypapers means? Edwin has just said there were some flypapers found. What were they for?'

'Why, for cosmetics,' said Florence.

The Baroness looked at her daughter and, ignoring the nurse and the policeman in the room, spoke in French. '*Dis moi, vraiment, ma cherie, est-ce que tu as fait mal à ton mari?*'

'*Non, maman,*' said Florence, '*je te jure que je ne suis pas coupable. J'ai met dans le jus de la viande un poudre qu'il a demandé, mais il n'en buvait pas.*'

The nurse interrupted them, and the Baroness set off for Liverpool.

She had been in the office of Richard Cleaver for five minutes when a telegram was handed to him. Seeming surprised, he stood up. 'If you wish to see her before she is removed,' he said, 'you had best hurry.'

The solicitor brothers and the Baroness raced back to Battlecrease House. There several brusquely important men were waiting near the front gate. They hailed the Cleaver brothers when they stepped down from their cab. The Baroness hurried indoors, leaving the solicitors at the gate. They were informed that Superintendent Bryning had been to County Magistrates' Court at Islington that morning and consulted Mr Swift, one of the clerks to the justices. The police believed they had collected sufficient evidence to justify preferring a formal charge against Mrs Maybrick. It was deemed advisable to prefer it at her residence, without waiting until she was in a fit state to be taken to court. Colonel Bidwell, one of the county magistrates, and Mr Swift had come back to Battle-crease House with Superintendent Bryning, and Dr Hopper and Dr Humphreys had been called. All were now at the gate.

The Cleaver brothers listened intently as the superintendent disclosed the nature of the evidence against Mrs Maybrick, and immediately said they would offer no objection to a remand.

Inside Battlecrease House, the Baroness found that the number of police-men had more than tripled. Denied access to her daughter's room, she was forced to stay either in the morning room, or in the downstairs hall. After several minutes she saw Dr Hopper and Dr Humphreys come in and go upstairs.

The doctors came into the spare bedroom. They asked Mrs Maybrick how she was feeling, and took her pulse. Then they left, and she heard them go down the stair. In a moment there came the sound of many foot-steps on the stair. The room filled with men. Mrs Maybrick recognised her lawyers and Superintendent Bryning. Three other men (Colonel Bidwell, Mr Swift, and a representative of the press) were unknown to her. The superintendent stepped to the foot of the bed.

'This person is Mrs Maybrick, wife of the late Mr James Maybrick,' he said.

'She is charged with having caused his death by administering poison to him. I understand that her consent is given to a remand, and therefore I need not introduce nor give evidence.'

'You ask for a remand of eight days?' said Mr Swift.

'Yes,' said the superintendent, 'that is so.'

'I appear for the prisoner,' said Arnold Cleaver. 'I consent to a remand.'

'Very well,' said Colonel Bidwell, 'that is all.'

As the men came down, the Baroness asked Dr Hopper to explain what was happening. He said formal charges had been preferred and that Mrs Maybrick would be taken to jail. 'It is on your account they are removing her so soon,' he added.

The Baroness wanted to know whom to ask for permission to see her daughter, and was referred to the magistrate. She asked Colonel Bidwell if she could be allowed to say goodbye to her daughter. He refused.

Hadn't he a mother, said the Baroness, and couldn't he feel how she felt?

The Colonel seemed angered, and repeated that she would not be per-mitted to see Mrs Maybrick.

Hoping at least to see Florence as she was taken away, the Baroness hurried upstairs to the room where she had slept, which looked out towards the front gate.

In the spare bedroom, Nurse Gore, who was the thin one, told Mrs Maybrick she must get up and dress. The prisoner begged for her children to be sent for, to come say goodbye to her. The nurses and the policemen refused. She asked to be allowed to gather some clothing, and again was refused. As the policemen waited impatiently on the landing, the nurses hurriedly dressed her.

Escorted by nurses and policemen, Mrs Maybrick started down the stair. She seemed too weak to stand. One of the nurses seized the cloak and hat of the Baroness from a chair in the hall, and put them on the prisoner. The policeman settled her quickly into one of the hall armchairs, picked up the chair, and carried Mrs Maybrick out of Battlecrease House to a cab that was waiting in the drive. Dr Humphreys climbed into the cab after Nurse Wilson and Superintendent Bryning.

As the cab clattered down Riversdale Road, Florence Maybrick realised that her handbag containing her toilet articles had been left behind.

Upstairs, the Baroness von Roques watched the cab bearing her daughter until it was out of sight. Turning to the door of the room, she found it locked. She shook it, and a red-haired policeman opened it. She asked by whose orders he had locked her in, and he mumbled something she could not understand.

While Colonel Bidwell and his hastily convened Magistrates' Court were in the spare bedroom, a policeman stationed at the entrance of the drive turned away several tradesmen and others who tried to call.

Now one of these returned. He was the dressmaker who had presented his bill for £10 on the previous Wednesday. He was admitted to see Mr Thomas Maybrick, and he explained that he had traced the woman for whom he had made the dresses. She was not a resident of Battlecrease House. She dwelt in quite another part of Liverpool. But Mr James Maybrick of Battlecrease House, 6 Riversdale Road, Aigburth, had paid her bills a number of times in the past, and the estate of Mr Maybrick would be expected to settle the current debt.

Inspector Baxendale now called together Sergeant Davenport and the other policemen on duty. The sergeant was to be congratulated on finding the bottles of medicine yesterday in the linen closet. All the rooms of the house would now be unlocked and a thorough search made. All medicines or drugs that might be tested for the presence of poison were to be gathered. As for himself, the inspector was going to Mr Maybrick's office in Liverpool to see what he could find.

Edwin Maybrick went with him. They found twenty-eight bottles and pill boxes, a dozen of which were locked up in Maybrick's private desk. Those in the desk ranged from a bottle of liqueur brandy, vintage 1854, to prescription medicines from seven different apothecaries in Liverpool and London. Elsewhere in the office were still more prescription bottles, including belladonna and podophyllin, some empty and some containing as little as a drop or two of sediment. They took them all, with the jug in which Maybrick had last brought his special gruel from home and the pan and basin in which he had heated and served it, to Edward Davies at the Royal Institution Laboratory.

At Battlecrease House, the search was fruitful. From the sitting room came seven bottles of pills (two contained the notorious nux vomica, which James Maybrick said he could not tolerate) and other medicines. Nurse Yapp returned and joined the hunt. She brought down twenty-two items, ranging from paregoric to the late master's prescribed ipeca-cuanha wine. Mrs Maybrick's dressing room and bedroom yielded eight bottles, including one labelled 'C. Hanson, Cressington, Tincture of Benzoin, A. Elderflower Water.' The largest number, some fifty-one items, came from Mr Maybrick's dressing room. They ranged from small blue bottles containing prescriptions marked 'Poison' to an empty tooth paste pot, but most were prescription medicines. From the lavatory came another twenty-four bottles, ointments and powders.

When all was gathered, Inspector Baxendale was able to inspect bottles blue and green and clear, empty, partly empty, and full, containing liquids thin and thick, light and clear and dark and brown and red. He saw pills white and mint and 'anti-bilious' and tasteless 'phosphate'. He examined powders from white to violet, marked antipyrin and liquorice and for insects. He pored over castor oil, glycerine, pepsine, camomile flowers, carbolic acid, cod liver oil, condal water, borax, corn plasters, oil of mustard, acetic acid, zinc ointment, and several kinds of salve. He beheld an array of patent medicines that included Pond's Extract Ointment, Spirits of Nitre, Tincture of Arnica, Glycerine of Tanner, Rice's patent glycerine, Parrish's Syrup, Dinneford's Fluid Magnesia, Bynin Liquid Malt, McSymond's Hair Wash (marked 'Poison'), Sanitas Disinfecting Fluid, Cascara Cordial, Horsford's Acid Phosphate, Colman's mustard, Gordon's Extract, Parisian Polish, Vaseline, and Calvert's Tooth Paste. Altogether, the house yielded one hundred and seventeen items from twenty-nine apothecaries in Liverpool, Manchester, London and Wales.

It was a two hour drive to Walton Jail, a tall, gloomy building in the suburbs of Liverpool. When their cab arrived at the gates, Dr Humphreys gave Mrs Maybrick a few shillings, and she asked him to give her love to her mother. As a bell rang, the great iron gate swung open and the cab rolled into the prison grounds.

Mrs Maybrick was received by the governor. Then a female warder immediately led her away, weighed her, and took her valuables – a watch, two diamond rings, and a brooch. Next she was led into a hospital cell, where she sank to the floor unconscious.

With the dressmaker's information, Thomas and Michael Maybrick set off for a distant part of Liverpool. There they found a woman who readily admitted that James Maybrick had paid for dresses made for her, that jewels in her possession had been given to her by Jim as security for money she had loaned him, and that her five children were, in fact, the Maybrick brothers' nephews and nieces.

The Baroness von Roques asked Cadwallader to send for a cab, and took her leave of Battlecrease House. She went that night to the Aigburth Hotel, where she immediately began writing letters and sending telegrams and cables.

The Sabbath brought throngs of sightseers to Riversdale Road, where they waited hopefully to see the police or members of the family of poor Mr Maybrick go in or out. They waited in vain. They learned why on Monday morning. The *Liverpool Daily Post*, in a story headlined, EXTRAORDINARY MAGISTERIAL PROCEEDINGS, detailed Saturday morning's meeting of lawyers, doctors, and magistrates and revealed that the prisoner had been taken to Walton Jail. 'Owing to the hasty decision on the part of the police,' it said, 'the people in the neighbourhood were quite unaware of the serious aspect which the case had assumed, and there was a total absence of the usual crowd of sightseers.'

Those whose curiosity persisted did have something to see on Monday. Inspector Baxendale returned to Battlecrease House, gathered up the one hundred and seventeen bottles and other items and took them to the analyst, Davies, in Liverpool, where they joined the eighteen items delivered the day after the autopsy and the twenty-eight brought round from Maybrick's office on Saturday morning.

To add to his chores, the analyst sent for nine flypapers each from the shops of Hanson, the chemist in Cressington, and Wokes, the chemist in Aigburth. He would see whether arsenic could be obtained by soaking them.

While Mr Davies was sorting out the bottles and pillboxes, Inspector Baxendale went back to Battlecrease House and looked round once more. In a small drawer under a looking-glass in Maybrick's dressing room, he found still another box of corn plasters, another box of pills, a small bottle of white powder, a small green bottle of pills, and a small box of potash tablets.

The Baroness went to see the Cleaver brothers and advised them to get in touch with the New York law firm of Roe and Macklin, which had long represented the estate of Darius Holbrook. Alfred Roe and his partner would, she knew, thoroughly investigate Maybrick's habits during his residence in America.

By Tuesday morning, Florence Maybrick had become accustomed to the appalling stillness and the dim light which filtered through a dirty, barred window into the cell where she lay in bed. She had already begun to look for the morning visits of the prison governor, the doctor, and the chaplain, brief and formal as they were. But this morning, someone else was shown into her cell. It was Mr Richard Cleaver.

Mr Cleaver questioned her at length about the flypapers she had soaked. She explained that long ago she had had a prescription for a face wash containing arsenic. When she was planning to go to the *bal masque* on 30th April, she was bothered by a skin eruption and looked for the prescription. Not finding it, she remembered that schoolgirls she had known in Germany often soaked flypapers to get arsenic for cosmetic use, and so she tried the home remedy herself. If someone could search through her things at Battlecrease House, she added, surely the face wash prescription could be found.

Before leaving Mrs Maybrick, Mr Cleaver brought up the subject of legal fees. The prisoner assured him that, while she was without funds in prison and did not know what provisions would be found in her husband's will, her mother, the Baroness von Roques, would be able to answer any questions as to fees. Mrs Maybrick mentioned her cash box, which would be found in her room. Reassured, the solicitor arranged for Mrs Maybrick to use a cell that was set apart for prisoners who could afford to pay five shillings a week for the comfort of a table, an armchair, and a washstand. In addition, her food was to be sent in from a nearby hotel.

When he returned from Walton Jail, Mr Cleaver went to Battlecrease House and told Thomas and Michael Maybrick he would like to look through Mrs Maybrick's things. He particularly asked about her cash box. The brothers were firmly uncooperative. They gave the solicitor only a few small personal articles gathered from her room, including a Bible which had belonged to her father. Mrs Maybrick's cash box was not among them.

The lawyer visited Mrs Maybrick in her cell again on Thursday, 23rd May. She said she had mentioned to both Dr Humphreys and Mr Michael Maybrick that her husband was in the habit of taking a white powder, and she described how on the Thursday evening before he died he asked her for some of his powder.

'I told him the nurse would not permit me,' she said, 'and he suggested putting it into something. He was taking beef juice and milk. The milk jug was big, and so I took the beef juice into the dressing room. There was very little powder in the packet, about as much as would lie on a three-penny bit. I put it all in.'

While the prisoner and her lawyer were discussing the beef juice, the bottle itself was being handled again by Mr Davies. He had previously proved that arsenic was present. Now he determined that the amount was half a grain. Since its specific gravity was less than that of another sample of meat juice which did not contain arsenic, he believed the arsenic had been put in in solution. At the same time, he tested the bottle of meat juice in the hat box, and a bottle fresh from the importers. He found arsenic in neither. He reported this to Inspector Baxendale, adding that he had completed his analysis of the parts of the body removed at the autopsy. He had found no poison in the stomach or its contents. Certain of the other parts produced only faint but unweighable traces of poison.

A new cause for the curious to linger in Riversdale Road was found on Saturday morning. Vans drew into the drive, and moving men climbed the front steps. Thomas and Michael Maybrick had ordered all the furnishings removed, and everything – linens, housewares, silverware, books, clothing, pictures, draperies, carpets, and all the furniture – was packed up and carted off.

As the movers picked up the washstand in James Maybrick's bedroom, something was heard tumbling about in the drawer. They looked inside and found a pillbox. They gave it to Mr Edwin Maybrick as they carried the stand through the downstairs hall, and he paused to read the label.

TAYLOR BROTHERS
Pharmaceutical Chemists
Norfolk, Virginia

Iron, quinine, and arsenic, one
capsule every three or four hours;
to be taken after food.

Mr Maybrick

Edwin put the pillbox in his pocket.

By nightfall, he and his brothers saw Battlecrease House silent and empty of all Maybricks and Maybrick belongings, except for Mrs Maybrick's cash box and her dressing gown. They were locked in the linen closet.

On Sunday, 26th May, the Walton Jail doctor checked Mrs Maybrick's condition and issued a certificate that she could not be moved from the prison hospital without 'grave risk of serious consequences'. The hearing at the Magistrates' Court, which was scheduled for next day, would have to be postponed.

Since the remand approved by Colonel Bidwell on 18th May was valid for only eight days, the court of inquiry had to be called again. The men met in Mrs Maybrick's cell – Superintendent Bryning, Mr Cleaver, and the magistrate – and the superintendent again charged her : 'You are now charged with the murder of your husband, Mr James Maybrick, at Garston, on the eleventh of May.'

Mrs Maybrick did not reply. Her solicitor consented to another remand. He made no attempt to disrupt the proceedings on the technical point that James Maybrick had neither lived nor died in Garston. Battlecrease House stood within Aigburth, several hundred feet from the Garston line.

While Inspector Baxendale and the others were at Walton, the Coroner instructed the authorities at the cemetery at Anfield to open the grave of James Maybrick and prepare for exhumation of the body.

It was to Garston that all those involved in the case came on Tuesday morning, 28th May, to resume the Coroner's Inquest. The Coroner, seeking the largest public room available within the county, hired the old Police Court in Wellington Road, Garston, which could accommodate 500 people. The sensationalism of 'The Aigburth Mystery' brought some forty newspapermen to add to the nearly two dozen witnesses, half a dozen lawyers, and as many officials, plus fourteen jurymen, and an overflow crowd of spectators.

The first result of intensive efforts by the Baroness von Roques on her daughter's behalf could now be seen. Mr William Pickford appeared as Mrs Maybrick's counsel, instructed by the Cleavers. Pickford was a graduate of Liverpool College and of Oxford and for fifteen years he had been enjoying a lucrative practice as one of Liverpool's most prominent lawyers. As a barrister, as distinguished from a solicitor, he was entitled to appear in the higher courts of law. His experience included, as the newspapers did not fail to remind their readers, having defended Mrs Higgins and Mrs Flanagan in Liverpool's famous flypaper case.

Samuel Brighouse, the County Coroner, sat promptly at nine-thirty and addressed the jury. 'Gentlemen,' he said, 'you are summoned here to investigate the circumstances attending the death of the late Mr James Maybrick. Mrs Maybrick has been apprehended, charged with having caused the death of her husband, and it will be for you to say, after hearing all the evidence, whether you consider she is criminally responsible for the death of her husband. Generally after hearing the evidence, you will have to say how and by what means Mr Maybrick came by his death.'

Almost no one could hear the Coroner. The room was rightfully known as 'The Reading Room', for its acoustics were impossible. The journalists began scrambling from the tables assigned them to what they hoped would be better positions. Some squeezed between the ranks of policemen, others squatted close to the tables of counsel or leaned over the backs of the lawyers, a few knelt on the floor before the jury.

The lawyers, who sat in front, nodded approvingly. An inquest on the body was exactly what the investigation was supposed to be : It centred on the corpse. How and by what means Mr Maybrick came by his death was the question at hand. But neither the police nor the Coroner mentioned that Mr Davies's tests of the viscera had brought negative results, or that the Coroner had ordered the grave of James Maybrick to be opened.

Superintendent Bryning began to call the witnesses. Michael Maybrick told of the suspicions of Nurse Gore which caused him to remove the bottles of brandy and meat juice, of the finding of the powder marked 'Poison. Arsenic for cats' soon after his brother's death, and of the finding of letters and a telegram next day.

Nurse Alice Yapp described the quarrel after the Grand National, the flypapers soaking, the master's overdoses of medicine, the mistress pouring medicines, the letter dropped in the mud.

The Coroner produced the letter. The acoustics of the Reading Room were treated to absolute silence, for at long last the gossip of servants, the rumours of neighbours, the speculations of journalists were to be satisfied. Mrs Maybrick's famous letter to her lover, which had actually been read only by Edwin and Michael Maybrick, Nurse Yapp and the police, (not even the suspicious doctors and nurses and Mrs Briggs had had a chance to read it), was now to be read. The Coroner held the letter well in the light and slowly and loudly read every word. His listeners seemed to hold their collective breath throughout.

As he finished, the room buzzed with gasping reactions and the Coroner rapped on the dais for silence. The nurse concluded her testimony by telling how she found the chocolate box containing the packet marked 'Poison.'

Bessie Brierley was next, reciting the quarrel after the Grand National and describing the soaking flypapers. The chemists, Wokes and Hanson, appeared to say that Mrs Maybrick had bought flypapers from them. The cook, Elizabeth Humphreys, told of bread and milk tasting differently than she made it, of lemonade kept from her husband by Mrs Maybrick, of the mistress saying Mr Michael had had a spite against her since her marriage. Nurse Ellen Gore described Mrs Maybrick's furtive handling of the bottle of Valentine's meat juice. Nurse Callery testified to the patient's telling his wife she had given him the wrong medicine again. Nurse Wilson told of hearing the patient say, 'Oh, Bunny, Bunny, how could you do it? I did not think it of you.'

The last witness was Mrs Charles Samuelson, who remembered the conversation in Birkenhead when Mrs Maybrick said she hated her husband. She mentioned the quarrel at the Grand National when Mrs Maybrick said to her, 'I will give it to him hot and heavy for speaking to me like that in public.'

The Coroner adjourned the inquest until 5th June. Thus far, he had taken no evidence concerning the cause of death of James Maybrick.

While the inquest was being held in Garston, five workmen in the cemetery in Anfield dug through two feet of earth at the Maybrick family vault and exposed two heavy flagstones some six inches thick. Then, with cemetery officials, they waited through the evening at the gatehouse.

The cemetery was in a lonely neighbourhood, and the night was silent until ten minutes after eleven, when two carriages drove up to the gates. Inspector Baxendale came in and showed the necessary authority from the Home Secretary, and the carriages moved slowly through the cemetery with the gravediggers following.

When they stopped, Doctors Barron, Humphreys and Carter stepped down from one carriage, and Mr Baxendale and another police inspector from the other. At the grave, naphtha lamps cast a faint glow over the surrounding tombstones. The workmen pulled up the heavy flagstones and revealed a whitewashed brick vault which contained the remains of Maybrick and of his mother and father. The coffin was quickly raised, placed across two benches, and the lid unscrewed. One doctor held a lamp overhead. When the body was revealed, all agreed that it was remarkably well preserved.

Without removing the body from the coffin, Dr Barron went to work with his dissecting knife. When a slight wind stirred, the men noticed the strong smell of decaying flesh. The doctor removed the lungs, heart, kidneys, and part of the thigh bone. He cut out the tongue, and half of the brain, which had been removed, examined and returned to the skull in the previous autopsy. Each part was put into a large stone jar, and when the doctor had finished the jar was covered with parchment paper, tied with a string, and sealed with Dr Barron's seal.

In the morning, Inspector Baxendale took the large jar to Mr Davies at the Royal Institution Laboratory.

On Wednesday morning, the *Liverpool Daily Post* said, 'The Coroner, as if to make amends for the secrecy with which he carried out the preliminary inquest, was extremely courteous to the thirty or forty journalists who were drawn to the spot.' His courtesy was rewarded with sensational press coverage throughout England. *The Times* detailed the testimony of each witness under the headline, 'THE CHARGE OF POISONING AT AIGBURTH.' The *Liverpool Daily Post* and the *Courier* printed the transcript and consistently referred to 'The Aigburth mystery'. Almost no report failed to reprint Mrs Maybrick's letter to Alfred Brierley in its entirety. The public was now in full possession of the evidence of adultery, though it had no proved evidence of the cause of death.

Newsboys were hawking 'Flypapers again!' through the streets of Liverpool. The *Daily Post* reported on Thursday that the Maybrick affair formed the all-absorbing topic of conversation on the Exchange. Large headlines proclaimed 'THE FLY-PAPER THEORY : A REMINISCENCE' and invited readers to rehearse once more the details of flypaper poisoning by Mrs Flanagan and Mrs Higgins in 1884.

On the 30th May, Inspector Baxendale called once more at the Royal Institution Laboratory. This time he left one tin of Hamilton's carbolic disinfectant and one sheet of Moure's flypaper for Mr Davies to analyse. The analyst made out a receipt, but did not make note of where the two items had been found.

The *Liverpool Courier* kept the flypaper theory stirring on Friday ('The suggestion of the prosecution is that the flypapers were obtained in order that arsenic might be mixed with the food and medicines given to the deceased.') Other headlines proclaimed 'THE STRYCHNINE THEORY' and offered 'DETAILS OF THE LIFE INSURANCES,' stating that Mr Maybrick carried a £2,000 policy in favour of his wife. 'MRS MAYBRICK'S FINANCIAL DIFFICULTIES' headed still another story, this one detailing an active sporting life at Cheshire and Aintree and saying that 'it came to her husband's knowledge that, like many other ladies who take an interest in matters of sport, she risked a little on the races.' The story went on to say that Mrs Maybrick had had frequent transactions with private loan offices, that only a fortnight before his death her husband had repaid a loan amounting to £50. The paper added that Mrs Maybrick had

'advanced as security for these borrowings a deed showing she had extensive estates in the Southern States of America.'

Having avoided a public reading of their brother's will at the Coroner's
Inquest, Michael and Edwin Maybrick now privately broke the seal and
read the document. It was written in James's rather shaky hand on blue
paper. They learned its principal terms : that they were made trustees of
everything Maybrick possessed, that the furniture was to remain intact
and belong to the children but was to be used to furnish a home for the
widow and children, that all moneys were to be invested and the income
used for the children's educations, that the widow was to have the insurance policies of £500 with the Scottish Widows' Fund and £2,000 with
the Mutual Reserve Fund Life Association of New York, that the widow
was to live under the same roof with the children so long as she remained
his widow, and that she was to have the sole use of the interest from the
£2,500 in life insurance policies during her lifetime, the principal then
to revert to the children.

Saturday readers of the *Liverpool Daily Post* who were of a ghoulish
inclination had much to savour. 'THE MAYBRICK MYSTERY. The Exhumation. Description by an eyewitness,' said the headlines. The details which
followed were as ghastly as promised. Liverpool had Saturday evening
and all day Sunday to indulge its lurid taste.

It was a taste that fed upon itself. By Monday morning, the *Post* was
able to say, 'The mystery surrounding Mr Maybrick's death seems to have
taken a greater hold on the public mind.' Referring to one of many tales
being circulated, it remarked :

> The police have resorted to an extraordinary stratagem, in order to
> procure evidence of a peculiar character, which they require in the
> case. The story goes that at their instigation a lady was employed to
> write a letter to a person well known in Liverpool, purporting to come
> from Mrs Maybrick. It is alleged that the writing so closely resembled
> that of the prisoner as to have deceived the person to whom it was
> addressed, and to have brought from him a response. This remarkable
> proceeding, we are informed, took place immediately prior to Mr
> Maybrick's death.

The *Courier* also had stories whose origin it could not disclose :

ALLEGED REMARKABLE LETTER OF THE DECEASED

We have it upon the authority of a gentleman who affirms that he
saw the document that, prior to his visit to London in April last, the

late Mr James Maybrick wrote to his brother Michael, a letter which, in view of the present circumstances, is extraordinary. The deceased gentleman said that he could not understand exactly the nature of his illness, and he thought it would be desirable, in the event of his illness proving fatal, if his body was subject to medical examination.

On Monday, 3rd June, the previous remand of the prisoner was due to expire. Magistrate W. S. Barrett joined Clerk Swift in the long trip to Walton Jail, where the magistrate issued a further remand until Wednesday.

In his laboratory, Mr Davies broke the seal on the large stone jar containing parts of Mr Maybrick's disinterred body. He tested the kidneys, and found about 1/100th part of a grain of arsenic. It was not pure enough to weigh. He tested the liver – a test he found difficult because of the presence of a large quantity of bismuth, which prevented him from getting liver pure enough to weigh. He found two 1/100ths of a grain of sulphide of arsenic. The other parts yielded no trace of arsenic.

All through the day, the analyst kept samples of flypaper soaking.

By Tuesday, 6th June, the *Liverpool Daily Post* was able to add to its interpretation of the news. 'It is impossible just now to test the veracity of these flying rumours,' it said, 'and we only mention them to show the absorbing interest which the development of the drama is exciting.'

The development of the drama included a report that young James Maybrick had been born eight months after the marriage of his parents, as well as strong hints that the cause of Mrs Maybrick's lingering illness in jail was a pregnancy resulting from her London weekend with Alfred Brierley. And, to feed the absorbing interest of their readers, the papers stated that Mrs Maybrick's father had died suddenly and mysteriously in Mobile, Alabama, and that her mother's second husband had died suddenly and mysteriously at sea while on a mission to England for the Confederate government. The ship's captain, it was stated, had been suspicious and was about to return the body to the American shore when the widow insisted on burial at sea. As for the mother's marriage to the Baron von Roques, it had failed to last and she had had one or two lovers since then. The implication was clear : Mrs Maybrick was following in her mother's footsteps.

In Bold Street in Liverpool, a photographer's window displayed pictures of Mrs Maybrick. One enlargement showed the crowd at the Grand National, and Mrs Maybrick and Alfred Brierley could be clearly seen watching the race.

Photographs appeared in the newspapers, too. One picture of James Maybrick, published in the *Liverpool Echo*, caught the eye of Edwin Garnett Heaton, who had recently retired after thirty years as a registered chemist. He recognised Maybrick as a customer who had regularly called in his shop, near the Cotton Exchange, for his 'pick-me-up'. Heaton remembered that, during the last year he was in business, the gentleman's prescription had called for increasingly larger doses of liquor arsenicalis.

On Wednesday, 5th June, Florence Maybrick was well enough to be driven to Garston for the resumption of the Coroner's Inquest. The day was hot and clear. All England was enjoying a spell of particularly fine weather. A large crowd watched the prisoner descend from the cab. The Reading Room was filled, but those inside got no glimpse of the prisoner. She was taken to the library next door to the room, where she could be identified by witnesses for the prosecution.

Among the lawyers, officials, and witnesses who were arriving was Alfred Schweisso, who had been subpoenaed from his job as waiter and clerk at Flatman's Hotel in London. An inspector asked him, 'Will you be able to recognise Mrs Maybrick?'

Schweisso said he would not.

'Keep with me,' said the inspector, 'and I will take you so as you can see her, because you will be sworn, as to whether you can recognise her or not.'

Following the inspector, Schweisso passed twice through the library, where he saw a woman wearing the bonnet and veil of deep mourning.

In the Reading Room, the heat of the day already was combining with the humidity supplied by a packed gallery to make the atmosphere stuffy and uncomfortable.

Mr Pickford had now had time to study the case. As the room was called to order, he addressed the Coroner. 'I think that we should before going further in this case have some evidence as to the cause of death.'

'It is a pity, Mr Pickford,' said the Coroner, 'that this application was not made before.'

The barrister suggested that the results of the tests of the organs of the deceased be made known. Superintendent Bryning said the testimony of the doctors must come first.

Doctor Hopper told of Mrs Maybrick's concern about Maybrick's habit of dosing himself, and described how he effected a reconciliation after their quarrel.

Dr Richard Humphreys admitted that he himself had prescribed

Fowler's Solution, which contained arsenic, and stated that his impression that Maybrick was suffering from an irritant poison was strengthened after certain suggestions were made to him the day before Maybrick died.

Dr William Carter told of testing the meat juice and finding arsenic. He said the cause of death was an 'irritant poison . . . most probably arsenic,' and that he had formed this opinion before the death but after a suggestion was made to him.

During the luncheon recess, the inspector who had led Alfred Schweisso through the library said that he had seen him standing near Alfred Brierley all morning. 'I suppose you recognised him,' said the inspector.

Schweisso said that he had not.

As they went back into the Reading Room, the inspector told Schweisso to nod to him when he recognised Brierley, as he would be in court in two or three minutes. Schweisso watched, but recognised none of the gentlemen coming in. Finally a policeman pointed out Mr Brierley to him.

Arthur B. Flatman, proprietor of Flatman's Hotel, identified the letters and telegram he had received in March, then testified that someone purporting to be Mrs Thomas Maybrick stayed at his hotel from 21st to 24th March. He was asked no questions about the death or cause of death of James Maybrick.

Alfred Schweisso said that he remembered a lady whom he understood to be Mrs Maybrick coming to the hotel. Schweisso was taken into the library, and on returning said that the lady in that room was the one. He testified that a young gentleman called for her at dinner time, and that next morning she had been joined by another gentleman who lived with her as man and wife until Sunday afternoon.

'Who is the gentleman?' asked the Coroner. 'Have you seen him in the room?'

Schweisso pointed toward Alfred Brierley. 'To the best of my belief,' he said, 'he is that gentleman there.'

The spectators began hissing. The Coroner announced that if there was the slightest manifestation of feeling he would have the court cleared.

Next came Mrs Briggs. She described how, after Mrs Maybrick was in custody, she wrote to Brierley for help. The letter was read aloud by the Coroner.

When the Coroner adjourned the inquest until next morning, the spectators stampeded into the street, joining the huge crowd that hoped to glimpse Mrs Maybrick as she was escorted from the building. It took a large number of policemen to maintain order.

To avoid the long trip back to Walton Jail, the authorities sent Mrs Maybrick to the County Police Station in Lark Lane. There a plank board, with a blanket supplied by a considerate policeman, provided the bed in the cell. A nearby greengrocer named Mrs Pretty, to whom Mrs Maybrick had occasionally given orders for fruit, sent in a basket of food with a note of sympathy.

The authorities let it be known on Thursday morning that Mrs Maybrick would not be brought to the inquest, and the crowd in Wellington Road was smaller.

Edwin Maybrick was the first witness of the day. He told of Alice Yapp handing him the letter from Mrs Maybrick to Brierley, of directing the nurses to take full charge of his brother, of Alice Yapp finding the chocolate box with the packet labelled 'Arsenic', and of the search that led to the hatboxes.

Frederick Tozer, druggist employed by Clay and Abraham, said he had made up the prescriptions during Maybrick's illness, and that none contained arsenic.

Now came the key technical witness, Edward Davies of the Royal Institution Laboratory. Spectators and principals leaned forward in a renewed effort to overcome the room's poor acoustics. Davies estimated that the bottle of Valentine's meat juice passed on to him by Dr Carter contained half a grain of arsenic. The analyst had obtained crystals of arsenic from the handkerchief found round the bottle in Mrs Maybrick's dressing table. One bottle found in the chocolate box in Mrs Maybrick's trunk contained arsenic 'strong enough to poison two or three persons.' A bottle from the first hatbox contained a saturated solution of arsenic, with solid arsenic at the bottom, and another had several drops of arsenic in solution 'strong enough for several drops to prove fatal.'

'You are not talking about the chronic use of arsenic?' asked the Coroner.

'No,' said Davies. 'A single dose.'

The Coroner went on. 'To put it on the safe side, we will say there is a grain in the bottle. Would that quantity produce unpleasant sensations, without causing death?'

'I do not know,' said the analyst. 'I suppose it would depend upon a person's idiosyncrasies. I cannot take much of a dose myself.'

The Reading Room burst with laughter.

'I have had it ordered for me,' he continued, 'but it did not suit me.'

The spectators howled.

The Coroner rapped sharply for order. Davies told of arsenic in a third bottle found in the first hatbox, arsenic in the tumbler that held a handkerchief in the second hatbox, arsenic mixed with powdered charcoal in the packet marked 'Arsenic. Poison for cats', arsenic in a bottle found in the lavatory, arsenic in a medicine bottle found in Maybrick's office, arsenic in bits of dried food found on the jug carried to the office, and arsenic in Rice's patent glycerine. The flypapers yielded arsenic, he said, and when questioned by one of the jurymen he added that in twenty-four hours a solution sufficient to poison any ordinary person could be obtained by soaking flypaper in cold water. He went on to say that he had been unable to find any trace of arsenic in Maybrick's stomach or its contents, but had found unweighable traces in some of the intestines and kidney and 1/50th of a grain in part of the liver. In closing, under questioning by Mr Pickford, Davies said that he had found in the liver less than half the quantity of arsenic which he had found in previous fatal cases of arsenical poisoning.

Amid considerable buzzing throughout the Reading Room, Mr Davies was excused. The Coroner once more rapped for silence, and turned to a letter. Those who had been following matters closely nudged each other and hunched forward to listen carefully. A letter from Alfred Brierley to Mrs Maybrick, found in her dressing table, was about to be read. The Coroner cleared his throat.

Mr Pickford interrupted. 'I understand,' he said, 'a communication was made to you, Mr Coroner, by a gentleman originally sworn in as foreman of the jury, and I should like to know whether it is proposed to call him or not. I understand it was something so important that the gentleman thought he ought not to sit upon the jury.'

'I feel certain it is not relevant,' said the Coroner. 'I communicated it to Mr Steel, who was then acting for the relatives, and to Superintendent Bryning. And I said, if you think this statement is useful to you, and that it is evidence, and that the foreman ought to appear as a witness, then I will discharge him. They both thought that would be the better course, for me to discharge him, and I did so.'

'I rather gathered,' said Mr Pickford, 'it had been a statement favourable to my client Mrs Maybrick. Do you say it was a matter you would not allow to go before the jury?'

'I ought not to tell the jury,' said the Coroner. 'The gentleman called upon Mr Cleaver and gave him his statement, and therefore it rests with Mr Cleaver or Mr Bryning to call him.'

'That is not quite correct,' said Mr Pickford.

'It was a statement made by deceased,' said Coroner Brighouse, 'and not in the presence of a certain other person. Deceased was not at the time in fear of death, and I don't see how the statement could be evidence.'

Mr Pickford was surprised to learn that a statement of such material importance as to cause the discharge of the foreman could not be evidence because the deceased had not made it in the presence of a certain other person.

The Coroner began his summing-up by advising the jurymen to put aside the comments they had seen in the press, as well as anything they had heard, and find their verdict on the evidence alone. They must consider three questions: Did they believe that death resulted from the administration of an irritant poison? If so, by whom was the irritant poison administered? And if it was administered by Mrs Maybrick, was it administered by her with an intent to take away life?

The jury retired. They had been told nothing of Maybrick's statement to the jury foreman at the Wirral races, and nothing of the negative results of the doctors' tests of faeces and urine two days before their patient died.

While the jury was out, Mrs Maybrick was brought from the police lock-up in Lark Lane. The crowds in the street surged toward the cab and roared when she was escorted into the building.

The jurymen returned to the box within thirty-five minutes. The Coroner asked, 'Have you agreed upon your verdict, gentlemen?'

The foreman rose. 'We have.'

'Do you find that death resulted from an irritant poison?'

'Unanimously.'

'Do you say by whom that poison was administered?'

'By thirteen to one we decide that the poison was administered by Mrs Maybrick.'

'Do you find that the poison was administered with the intention of taking away life?'

'Twelve of us at least have come to that conclusion.'

'That amounts to a verdict of murder.' The Coroner turned to the guards at the door of the ante-room. 'Bring in Mrs Maybrick.'

The Reading Room was silent as she came through the door. All who could somehow see over or around those straining in front of them watched a small, erect young woman dressed fashionably in the black of deep mourning. She stepped forward with perfect composure. Behind her came a woman warder and two policemen.

Mrs Maybrick looked straight ahead, and her eyes fell on the jury box. Glancing quickly from one gentleman to another, she realised that nearly all of them had been guests in her home.

The Coroner spoke. 'Florence Elizabeth Maybrick, the jury have inquired into the circumstances attending the death of your husband, and they have come to the conclusion that he was wilfully murdered by you. It it my duty to commit you to the next assizes, to be holden at Liverpool, there to take your trial on that charge.'

Almost simultaneously with Mrs Maybrick's appearance, the weather broke. Great clouds that had been gathering in the humid air throughout the afternoon burst with thunder and lightning. The electrical display lasted several hours, and the temperature dropped nearly thirty degrees as the cooling rains came down.

The prisoner was hurried to the waiting cab and rushed through crowds that clamoured to glimpse her despite the downpour. Once more she was formally remanded, pending the next step in the chain of justice – the committal proceedings in the Magistrates' Court.

While she was being returned to the lock-up in Lark Lane, the formal inquisition was handed round among the coroner's jurymen for their signatures. It declared :

> That James Maybrick on the 11th of May, 1889, in the township of Garston, died from the effects of an irritant poison administered to him by Florence Elizabeth Maybrick – and so the jurors say – that the said Elizabeth Florence Maybrick did wilfully, feloniously, and of her malice aforethought kill and murder the said James Maybrick.

That the name of the accused was put backward the second time it was given, and that the Coroner now formally compounded the police superintendent's earlier error as to the township in which Maybrick had lived and died, seemed to offend the legal sensibilities of neither juryman, solicitor, nor barrister.

It was decided to keep Mrs Maybrick at the Lark Lane police station during the week. There she was treated kindly by the jailer's wife, and good food was sent in from a nearby hotel. Her mother was staying nearby, too, and could see her often. When the Baroness came to the jail, she found that Florence was able to move about freely, for her cell door was left wide open.

Mrs Maybrick's lawyers came often that week. The dimensions of the case against her were now clear. The effort in her defence would have to be considerable and it would be expensive. It might involve bringing witnesses from America to testify on James Maybrick's medicinal habits. The Cleaver brothers, under pressure from the Baroness von Roques and their own desire to have cash in hand against the expense of the defence, wrote to the Mutual Reserve Fund Life Association of New York, applying for a claim on the £2,000 policy carried by Maybrick with his wife as beneficiary.

Public interest and excitement were still running high a week later. The police decided to avoid the difficulty of handling an overwrought crowd on the morning of the hearing in the Magistrates' Court. They moved the prisoner from her Lark Lane cell to the Courthouse in Islington during the evening of Tuesday, 11th June.

A makeshift bedroom was arranged. While a policeman stood guard all night at the door, his daughter, acting as a female warder, stayed in the room with the prisoner. As Mrs Maybrick was going to bed, she knelt at the bedside. She felt a hand on her shoulder, and heard the soft voice of the young woman say, 'Let me hold your hand, Mrs Maybrick, and let me say my prayers with you.'

Wednesday, 12th June, was overcast and gloomy. The sun had not shone since Saturday. But Liverpudlians turned out in large numbers to see Mrs Maybrick brought to the courthouse, only to learn that she had been inside the building all night.

In the courtroom, five magistrates occupied the bench, with Sir William Forwood presiding. In a special gallery to their right sat a large number of well-dressed ladies, with most of the witnesses just below them. The police superintendent and inspectors joined Michael and Edwin Maybrick and a few of the remaining witnesses at the solicitors' table, which was crowded as well with the lawyers who had represented the family, the accused and Alfred Brierley at the inquest. The analyst, Edward Davies, finding no other accommodation, took the seat of the court crier, and began almost immediately to adjust his eyeglasses and tug at his beard as he concentrated nervously on the proceedings. Opposite the bench, on a raised platform, crowded the general public. A far larger number waited on the steps of the building and in the street.

At ten o'clock, Mrs Maybrick was escorted from the ante-room to the dock by a sergeant of police and a female warder. A comfortable armchair not usually found in the dock had been provided for the young widow. Again she was dressed in deep mourning and wore a heavy veil over her face.

Mrs Maybrick looked around the room. Neither in the special gallery of well-dressed ladies nor in the general crowd of spectators did she see a single face familiar to her from her own Liverpool circle. The Baroness von Roques, whose impressive figure had become recognisable to all, sat in the first row of spectators only a few feet away. Mrs Maybrick sat down facing the magistrates.

Now came Florence Maybrick's first opportunity to hear any detail of the evidence against her. Superintendent Bryning delivered a long charge. He detailed the circumstances of James Maybrick's illness and death, including suspicions and letters and post-mortem analysis. Following him came the witnesses, mostly well known to Mrs Maybrick, who gave evidence similar to that produced at the Coroner's Inquest. They included Dr Hopper, Mrs Briggs, Alfred Schweisso, Bessie Brierley, Alice Yapp, Mary Cadwallader, Elizabeth Humphreys, and Edwin Maybrick.

When the inquiry adjourned for the day, Mrs Maybrick had to pass the tier of well-dressed ladies. These spectators immediately began hissing her. One spat disgustedly in her direction. Sir William shouted to the policeman to close the door, and the demonstration was brought under control amid general confusion.

Mrs Maybrick slept again that night in the makeshift bedroom in the courthouse. She was returned to the dock promptly at ten in the morning. The courtroom was as crowded as on the day before. Many were now experienced enough to bring along their opera glasses.

The witnesses came again in the same order as at the inquest, and with the same evidence. Mr Pickford, however, in his cross-examinations now sought testimony helpful to his client. He asked Michael Maybrick if he could produce the letter he received from his sister-in-law in March.

'I did not keep the letter,' said Michael.

The barrister pressed him for details of the letter.

'I believe she spoke about her husband taking some particular medicine,' said the witness. 'I think it was a powder she spoke of, but I really don't remember. My recollection is very vague. Something was said about my brother being very irritable when spoken to about this medicine.'

The chemists who made up Maybrick's final prescriptions, and those who sold flypapers to Mrs Maybrick, were heard. The nurses appeared, and Mrs Hughes told of finding the letter from Alfred Brierley while searching for keys. Dr Humphreys admitted again that the idea of irritant poisons did not occur to him until the suggestion was made, and Dr Carter and Dr Barron repeated their inquest testimony.

The printed list of items tested by the analyst was again provided, and Mrs Maybrick pored over it as Mr Davies repeated his findings in testing some 250 bottles and other items. At last Mr Pickford rose and addressed the magistrates.

'I understand this concludes the evidence for the prosecution,' he said, 'and I should like to ask for the guidance of the bench. If they have formed a clear opinion that they ought not to dispose of this case, but send it before a jury, then I will not trouble them. I would not think it right to go fully into the defence here. If, on the other hand, they think it a case they should decide themselves, then that is another matter.'

The magistrates retired to chambers. When they returned, Sir William said, 'Our opinion is that this is a case which ought to be decided by a jury.'

'If that is clearly the opinion of the bench,' said Mr Pickford, 'I shall not occupy their time by going into the defence now, because I understand whatever defence may be put forward the bench may think it right for a jury to decide it.'

Sir William ordered Mrs Maybrick to stand up, and the formal charge was read to her. As the presiding magistrate finished, Mr Pickford turned to his client. 'Do not speak,' he said. 'I will reply for you.'

He turned to the bench and said, 'I reserve my defence.'

The magistrate cleared his throat and addressed the prisoner. 'Florence Elizabeth Maybrick, it is our duty to commit you to take your trial at the ensuing assizes for the wilful murder of the late James Maybrick.'

Florence Maybrick stood erect and proud. She had only a moment to look around and, through her heavy veil, catch her mother's confident eye before the sergeant and the warder began to escort her from the room.

The escort and the prisoner went directly to a cab at a side door, and departed for Walton Jail. The cab had scarcely begun to move, however, when the excited crowd, including those who had been waiting in front of the building and those who had just emerged from the courtroom, caught sight of it. The mob shouted, the driver whipped his horses, the cab sped recklessly through the charging mob. Some raced along with it for a few moments, hooting and shouting at the flypaper poisoner, before the galloping horses pulled away.

In the courtroom, the lawyers and officials picked up their papers. The medical witnesses departed, again without having mentioned that tests of the patient's faeces and urine two days before death had revealed no trace of arsenic.

Mrs Charles Samuelson, who at the coroner's inquest had testified that Mrs Maybrick said she hated her husband, had not appeared at the hearing at the Magistrates' Court.

PART TWO

The Trial

VI

*'The next case I will mention to you
is a case which has excited very great
attention in this country.'*

'The Maybrick Mystery' was now the most eagerly read headline in the newspapers of Liverpool, Manchester, London, and indeed all of England. It had replaced 'The Aigburth Poisoning Case' as the cue to the first topic of conversation in household, office, club, mill and pub. The testimony at the Coroner's Inquest and the Magistrates' Court had been published verbatim. Liverpudlians, including all who might be drawn to sit upon the jury, knew the details by heart. And all the details added up to one conclusion: the woman was, as Michael Maybrick said when Edwin showed him the letter, an adulteress.

It was a fact, an accusation, an insult to the prim middle class morality of Victorian womanhood. Murder was the accusation? Well, what could one expect from a woman – an American woman, at that – who rewrote the codes of conduct to fit her own torrid, sinful desires? What could one expect from a woman who betrayed not only husband and small children but the strict ethic of her class?

Letters poured in to editors. Parsons preached in church. Speakers harangued assemblies. Writers opined in magazine and newspaper. As the Coroner's Inquest had turned out to be an investigation not of the cause of death but of a woman's conduct, so the continuing rise of public outrage was a reaction not to the alleged criminal act of murder but to the proved immoral act of adultery.

Conjecture over the defence tactics to be used by Mrs Maybrick's lawyers filled column after column, day after day, in the newspapers. Each new day brought a new theory for the avid reader to think through, weigh, and test against his already extensive knowledge of the case.

One day in mid-June, William Pickford, who was working around the clock preparing Mrs Maybrick's defence, received a letter from a man named R. Thompson, who was aboard a ship recently arrived in Liverpool harbour. He said that he had information about Mr Maybrick.

Pickford sent for Thompson. To his office came a man who bore the constitution of more than forty years at sea and the authority of one who had held a master mariner's certificate for thirty-six years. Captain Thompson said that upon landing in Liverpool he had read the details of the death of his old friend Maybrick, and of the accusation against his wife. What he had to say might be helpful to her defence.

He had sailed between Liverpool and Norfolk for many years, he said, and through his friend Nicholas Bateson of Norfolk he had met Jim Maybrick and known him well in 1880. He had not forgotten a visit he made with Maybrick to a drugstore, and he remembered something the druggist said to him a few days later.

In Walton Jail, Florence Maybrick searched her memory for incidents when her husband had used his white powders. She continued to hope that her old prescription for a face wash including arsenic would be found, but her lawyers told her that Battlecrease House had been entirely emptied by the Maybrick brothers. Not even her strong box, which might contain the prescription, had been turned over to them.

The lawyers decided to concede the question of the compromising letter to Alfred Brierley. It was best for the defence to ignore the letter. The Baroness asked her daughter how she could have written such a letter.

'Mamma,' said Florence, 'he had been kind to me.'

Few were kind to Brierley. Reporters dogged him wherever he went. He refused to talk to them. He began to avoid his many close friends. He stayed in his apartment for days at a time and sent his valet to fetch newspapers and groceries. Among the valet's regular stops was the office of the Cleaver brothers, for Brierley had begun to contribute to Florence Maybrick's defence funds.

The question of funds was vital. The Baroness von Roques was determined that her daughter should have the finest legal minds in England on her side. She had insisted that the Cleaver brothers call in Mr Pickford, and if a barrister better than Pickford could be found, they would have him.

There was Holbrook land in America. It would not be the first time those million acres had stood the Baroness in good stead. She wrote to New York and Louisville to start the process of liquidation.

Throughout the month of June, the press continued to keep the Maybrick Mystery stirring. By 28th June the case had been so much tried in the Liverpool papers that Mrs Maybrick's lawyers were considering a motion to move the trial to a place where, they hoped, the details would be less well known to prospective jurors. Mrs Maybrick wrote that day to her mother :

> I sincerely hope the Cleavers will arrange for my 'trial' to take place in London. I shall receive an impartial verdict there, which I cannot expect from a jury in Liverpool whose minds have come to a 'moral conviction', *en attendant*, which must influence their decision to a certain extent. The tittle-tattle of servants, the public, friends, and enemies, and from a thousand by-currents, besides their personal feeling for Jim, must leave their traces and prejudice their minds, no matter what the defence is.

Her letter went on to speak again of the face wash prescription, saying, 'I had it at home, but, of course, it won't be found now.'

There was something else at home, and, on the day when Florence wrote to her mother, Edwin Maybrick went to get it. He unlocked the linen closet in Battlecrease House and took out Florence's dressing gown. Edwin handed the gown to Inspector Baxendale, pointing out a brown stain on a handkerchief in the pocket, and then handing him an apron which had been found with the dressing gown.

The inspector waited until Monday morning to take these new pieces of potential evidence to Mr Davies at the Royal Institution Laboratory. Davies found stains in the pocket of the dressing gown and below the waistband of the apron as well as on the handkerchief. He turned once more to his testing apparatus.

Now it was not only the news columns that caught the eye of the follower of the Maybrick Mystery. Advertising columns carried a special sale notice :

The Late Mr James Maybrick

By order of the trustees

> That valuable furniture, costly ornaments, Continental porcelain, silver plate, modern electro, oil paintings, proof etchings and engravings and other contents of the residence 'Battlecrease', Grassendale, removed to the Hanover Rooms, by Messrs Branch and Leete, on Monday and Tuesday, the 8th and 9th of July, at eleven of each day, in the Hanover Gallery and Sale Rooms.

Messrs Branch and Leete were auctioneers. It was to their Hanover

Street showroom that trustees Thomas and Michael Maybrick had sent the vanloads of furnishings from Battlecrease House.

The public neither knew, as did trustees Thomas and Michael, nor cared, as they did not, that James Maybrick's will specified that 'The furniture I desire to remain intact, and to be used in furnishing a home which can be shared by my widow and children, but the furniture is to be the children's.' The auctioneer's hammer rose and fell, and households all over Liverpool gained a picture here, a vase there, a sofa, a chair, or, in one case, a piano. Among the items for which bidding was intense was Florence Maybrick's writing pad and blotter. By nightfall on 9th July, nothing from Battlecrease House was left in the Hanover Gallery.

When a number of bills had been paid, Michael Maybrick passed on £300, representing one-half of the total sale, to the defence fund for his sister-in-law.

Mr Arnold Cleaver sailed for America. It was an expensive and time-consuming trip, but New York lawyers Roe and Macklin had cabled that they had found men in Norfolk who had valuable testimony to give.

There were other cables. On 11th July the Mutual Reserve Life Association of New York cabled its Liverpool representative that, in view of Mrs Maybrick's need of funds and in view of strong American sympathy for her plight, it had decided to waive the customary waiting period of three months for all claimants. The agent was told to advance $1000 to Mrs Maybrick.

When she learned of the payment, the Baroness von Roques insisted again that the finest lawyers in England take Mrs Maybrick's defence. Mr Pickford said there was only one man to ask. His name was Sir Charles Russell, and he was a Queen's Counsel, the highest rank to which an English lawyer might aspire. It indicated he had practised as a barrister for at least ten years and had been approved for advancement by the Lord Chancellor. A Queen's Counsel was known as a silk because he wore a silk gown in Court. A barrister, Mr Pickford added, wore an ordinary stuff gown. Sir Charles was an Irishman, he went on, who over thirty years had won many controversial cases. He had served in Parliament, and had been Attorney-General under Gladstone in 1886. But perhaps his most notable achievement had come this year, when he had appeared before the Parnell Commission of Parliament as leading counsel for the Irish hero, Charles Stewart Parnell, who with sixty-five Irish members of Parliament had been charged with sedition. In a stunning victory just a few weeks ago, Sir Charles had won their vindication.

The Baroness von Roques needed little encouragement to agree with

Mr Pickford's choice. Sir Charles Russell, she said? The man was, then, a knight.

Knight Commander of the Bath, said Mr Pickford. He added that, as he recalled, Sir Charles had declined a judgeship back in 1882.

The Baroness drew herself up proudly. Would Mr Pickford take the earliest opportunity to ask Sir Charles if he would take Florie's case?

When Mr Pickford began to tell him about the Maybrick case, Sir Charles had the air of a weary man. Yes, yes, he said impatiently, any man in England who could read or hear knew all about the Maybrick Mystery.

Pickford went straight to the point. Sir Charles would know Mrs Maybrick's great need for a vigorous defence, for, in a word, a champion whose reputation and rhetoric could be of greatest help. The evidence was much against her, but the defence was sound. Would Sir Charles lead for her? Pickford himself would continue as junior barrister, and they would be instructed by Messrs Richard and Arnold Cleaver, who had handled the case from the beginning.

Sir Charles looked at Pickford. He drew from his vest pocket a large snuff box and carefully sniffed a pinch of snuff in each nostril. He was exhausted, he said. He had faced 340 witnesses during the sixty-three violent and bitter sessions of the Parnell Commission.

Yes, said Pickford. He remembered the distinguished cross-examination of the forger, Pigott, which Sir Charles had made. And he knew that Sir Charles's final speech in defence of the Irish members had lasted for six days.

Sir Charles asked about Mrs Maybrick's funds. His usual brief fee was £500, with a daily fee of £100.

Pickford said frankly that Mrs Maybrick's resources were not that great. There were, however, properties in America which her mother, the Baroness von Roques –

A gesture with the snuff box interrupted the barrister. Very well. In view of the cause, said Sir Charles, he would forego his customary fee. Weary as he was, he must respond to Mrs Maybrick's need. He would take the case.

On Tuesday, 16th July, Arnold Cleaver landed in New York. He was met by Alfred Roe, and they went directly to the offices of Roe and Macklin at 156 Broadway to discuss the defence of Mrs Maybrick. Next day, Cleaver and a member of the New York firm took the train for Norfolk, Virginia.

In Liverpool, meantime, Cleaver's brother Richard again asked Edwin Maybrick where Mrs Maybrick's cash box was.

In Norfolk, Arnold Cleaver and his New York associate went to the St James Hotel. There they found a Negro waiter named Thomas Stansell, who had worked as valet to James Maybrick from 1878 to 1880. When they had finished questioning Stansell, Cleaver offered him the opportunity of a trip to England.

The prosecution of Mrs Maybrick was now well into preparation. As Counsel for the Crown, John Edmund Wentworth Addison would appear. Like Sir Charles Russell, he was an Irishman who had made a name for himself in the Northern Circuit of England. He had taken silk as Queen's Counsel nearly ten years earlier, and had been a Conservative Member of Parliament since 1885. Junior Counsel for the Crown would be William Robert McConnell, still another Irishman, whose father had been magistrate of County Down. Addison and McConnell would be joined by Thomas Swift, a bright young barrister whose father's firm of solicitors were conducting the prosecution on behalf of the Treasury.

It was on Swift's orders that Inspector Baxendale boarded the LMS for London on 22nd July. The inspector carried eleven jars from Mr Davies of the Royal Institution Laboratory. They contained parts of the viscera of James Maybrick. Inspector Baxendale took them up to Guy's Hospital, where Dr Thomas Stevenson, an eminent toxicologist, lectured on forensic medicine and chemistry. Dr Stevenson acted as analyst for the Home Office and for the Treasury in cases of poisoning. He would test the organs for arsenic.

The newspapers now reported that the Liverpool Assizes were called for 26th July. Following the Grand Jury's one-day hearing, the trial would probably begin on the last day of the month.

Mr Valentine Blake saw the announcement of these dates. He was busy and distraught trying to trace his son, who seemed to have been lost at sea. But he was nagged by the Maybrick Mystery. Now he wrote to Messrs Richard and Arnold Cleaver, who were always named in the papers as Mrs Maybrick's solicitors. He had met James Maybrick only last January, he wrote, when looking for help in placing a substitute for cotton on the market. His letter disclosed that he and Maybrick had talked at length about arsenic, which was used in processing his fabric, and in February he had given Maybrick 150 grains of arsenic, some white and some black, in three separate packets.

In conference with their client in Walton Jail, Mr Pickford and Mr Richard Cleaver explained why they had decided not to apply for transfer of the trial to London. In the first place, the expense would be considerable. And, they reasoned, it showed greater confidence to stand trial where the case was best known – in Liverpool. There was another factor, too. The judge who had been assigned to the Liverpool Assizes was known as a 'lawyer's judge' and a 'jurist's jurist'. He was Sir James Fitzjames Stephen, a man who had had a long and distinguished career and had written important books on criminal law. He was especially knowledgeable, said the solicitors, on the law of evidence.

On Friday morning, 26th July, Mr Justice Stephen opened the Liverpool Assizes. It was not necessary for Mrs Maybrick to attend. The judge represented the Crown, and the Grand Jury represented the people. It was their duty to decide whether the Crown could expose to the risk of a trial by jury any person whom the magistrates, who represented the Crown, had committed for trial. Their function, indeed, was to stand between the Crown and the accused person. The Grand Jury was a selected, rather than random, jury, purposely chosen from persons of sufficiently high rank to be free of local influence and equally free of constraint by the Crown.

The Grand Jury had before them a long calendar of cases. The twenty-one jurymen went through them patiently, until the judge said, 'The next case I will mention to you is a case which has excited very great attention in this country, and certainly if the prisoner is guilty of the crime alleged to her in the charge, it is the most cruel and horrible murder that could be committed.'

Case No 24, Florence Elizabeth Maybrick, had begun. Mr Pickford and the Cleaver brothers saw the judge pick up the folder containing the depositions of the witnesses for the prosecution. 'I refer to the case of Florence Elizabeth Maybrick, who is charged with the wilful murder of her husband, James Maybrick.' The judge set forth the facts, including Mrs Maybrick's 'adulterous intrigue with a man of the name of Brierley,' the violent quarrel after the Grand National, the soaking of flypapers, the illness of Mr Maybrick, the letter opened by the nurse and the expressions, such as 'He is sick unto death', found therein.

In referring to the letter, the judge said, 'She had been to London, and there met Mr Brierley, with whom she slept on two occasions during her absence from home. Of course, if that is proved, there can be no doubt as to what her relations to him were. But certainly if a woman does carry on an adulterous intrigue with another man, it may quite supply – I won't go further – a very strong motive why she should wish to get rid of her husband.'

A moment later, the judge, referring to the letter, said, 'This took place on Friday, and he died on Saturday afternoon.'

William Pickford and Richard Cleaver exchanged glances. How had the judge failed to grasp that the letter, the most circumstantial evidence in the case, had been opened on Wednesday, and that Maybrick had died on Saturday evening?

Mr Justice Stephen continued, mentioning the presence of arsenic in articles found in the house as well as in the body of the deceased, and pointing out that Mrs Maybrick had nursed her husband throughout most of his illness. He repeated that the jury had 'to consider not whether she is guilty or not guilty, but whether there is sufficient evidence to put her on trial for poisoning her husband with arsenic.' His final words to the jury were, 'If you think it desirable that the matter should have further investigation, you will find a true bill against her.'

A true bill was found. The grand jury agreed that, according to the indictment, Mrs Maybrick must be called upon to plead guilty or not guilty to the accusation that she had 'at Garston on the 11th of May, 1889, feloniously, wilfully, and of her malice aforethought, killed and murdered James Maybrick.'

Lawyers who were following the case noted that the specific charge of murder stood alone. In club and office it was remarked that the indictment might have included charges of the administration of arsenic and of attempting to administer arsenic with intent to murder, except that the evidence thus far revealed no specific dates or places or facts of such felonious acts.

The trial was set for 31st July.

The newspapers next day printed the full text of the judge's charge to the grand jury. Sir James thus reached all of England with his indictment of adulterous intrigue and with the erroneous impression that Mrs Maybrick had written to Brierley the very day before her husband died.

On Monday morning, 29th July, a number of gentlemen appeared before Mr T. E. Paget, District Registrar of Liverpool. They were there to probate the will of James Maybrick, and they included Thomas and Michael Maybrick, George R. Davidson and George Smith, each of whom had witnessed Maybrick's signature to the will, and a solicitor, Mr Steel of the Liverpool firm of Layton, Steel and Springman. No executor being named in the will, the brothers were sworn, and the administration of Maybrick's personal estate was then granted to them as universal legatees in trust under the terms of the will. The gross estate was recorded as £5,016, and the net estate as £3,770.

In Walton Jail that morning, Florence Maybrick received Sir Charles Russell. He had come to question his client. It was an unusual step, for the accused would not be permitted under the law and the precedents of court procedure at that time to testify or be cross-examined. But Sir Charles was perplexed by certain instructions in the brief, and was determined to hear her answers to certain questions.

At the Liverpool Assizes, meantime, the calendar call continued. In a forgery case, the lawyers asked to have the trial postponed until after the Maybrick case. Mr Justice Stephen reluctantly agreed, and the lawyer, Mr Cottingham, asked his lordship to tell the witnesses on what day to come. His lordship said he could not, and that Mr Cottingham should use his own discretion in telling them when to come. 'And you know,' he added, 'Sir Charles Russell may very likely wish to plead guilty.' The courtroom rang with laughter.

The judge's words were in print next day. 'THE JUDGE AND THE MAY-BRICK CASE. Extraordinary Judicial Joke,' said the headline in the *Liverpool Daily Post*. It gave prospective jurors something to think about.

In Walton Jail on the day before the trial, Mrs Maybrick's composure surprised those who saw her. Some who were in charge said she was without feeling.

She was visited that morning by Mr Cleaver. With the approval of the Baroness von Roques, he had drawn a mortgage for $5,000 on a twenty-one-year lease on a house at 17 East 14th Street in New York City. The lease had been obtained by the Baroness more than ten years earlier, and had been signed over to her daughter. The mortgage terms included interest at five per cent payable half yearly. Mrs Maybrick, relieved that a way had been found to add to her defence fund, signed the mortgage. It was made to 'Richard Stewart Cleaver of the city of Liverpool, gentleman.'

VII

Wednesday, 31st July, 1889

Soon after eight o'clock in the morning, a female warder escorted Mrs Maybrick from her cell to the rear of a black van, stepped into the van after her, and the door was shut upon them. In the confined space, Mrs Maybrick suddenly felt as if she had been buried. As the van started to move, she learned that a section in front contained a number of male prisoners who were also awaiting trial.

Already the crowd had gathered in the broad Lime Street plaza before St George's Hall in Liverpool. They thronged the wide steps below the lofty columns of the Grecian porticos and pushed and tussled for position. When the immense brass doors swung open at nine o'clock, many were disappointed to learn that most of the seats in the courtroom had been reserved for ticket holders. These favoured ones, arriving by carriage and dressed in the latest fashions, marched proudly past the disappointed majority and down the echoing halls past art gallery and music chamber to the vaulted courtroom all England wished to occupy. Many carried fans against the heat, opera glasses against distance from the dock and witness box, and picnic baskets against losing one's place during the luncheon recess.

As they drew near, Florence Maybrick could glimpse St George's Hall through the curtains of the van. The building's vast limestone solidity stirred memories. How many pleasant afternoons had she spent wandering through the galleries admiring the aquatints in their ornate gilt frames? How many evenings, with friends now so far away, had she enjoyed string quartet or chamber group in St George's recital rooms?

A turn brought the Lime Street Station in view. Here she had come and gone on the London train. She remembered how proudly she had followed James Maybrick through the teeming concourse when he escorted her to the train after they stepped ashore in Liverpool as an engaged couple. And – was it possible that Alfred Brierley had come down from London this morning? She felt her heart jump at the thought.

She looked at the warder opposite her. The woman's gaze was fixed on the wall above her prisoner's head. Again Florence Maybrick's eyes turned to the bit of view beyond. Now St John's Church loomed. She had steeled herself successfully through the trip from Walton Jail, but the thought of her children, of their pony cart rides, of their shrill voices shouting above the clamour of the street, seemed more than she could bear.

What did she hear? Above the creaking of the van and the clatter of the horses' hooves on the cobblestone, a great clamour arose. She leaned toward the window, craning her neck to look down into the street below the high wheels of the van.

They were surrounded by a mob. For a moment the van scarcely moved. Florence Maybrick looked at the warder. The woman had neither moved nor changed expression. She seemed not to hear the angry curses shouted in the name of 'Mrs Maybrick'. Outraged faces, hissing and spitting, strained at the van almost within arm's length of the window. Florence Maybrick sat upright again. She would keep her dignity no matter what happened. If a mob surrounded her, it was a mob to be ignored. Sitting on the edge of the van's hard bench, her back unsupported by the rough wall behind her, she stared firmly at the warder. As if reacting to her determination, the clatter of hooves sped up, the jostling vibration increased, and they hurried on. Within moments they stopped again, the compartment door swung open, and Mrs Maybrick was quickly escorted to a detention room in the basement.

In the courtroom, the spectators' attention was caught by some motion in the dock. Could the prisoner be mounting the steps from the basement, which rose only into the iron-railed dock? No. It was a court attendant, carrying a cane chair. A buzz of disapproval swept the room. Was it not customary for the prisoner to stand throughout the trial?

Just before ten o'clock, the Clerk of Arraigns appeared. His authoritative shuffling of papers gave the cue that the drama was to begin. Now Sir Charles Russell appeared, leading a bewigged and berobed procession. With him came Mr Pickford and Mr Richard Cleaver, then the Crown prosecutor, Mr John Addison, with his juniors, Mr William McConnell and Mr Thomas Swift. The lawyers for prosecution and defence settled at tables opposite each other.

A burst of trumpets was heard. The fanfare continued as four trumpeters, in the traditional garb of the High Sheriff's retinue, entered at the head of the solemn Assize procession. All in the courtroom rose. A liveried guard – the judge's javelin men, in cream and crimson – escorted his lordship. Sir James wore his full-bottom wig and his robe of scarlet velvet trimmed with ermine. With him came the High Sheriff, resplendent in the uniform of the deputy-lieutenant of the county, next the Earl of Sefton, and finally the High Sheriff's chaplain, in gown and hood.

The bailiff called the court to order, his high voice commanding all to 'tend the Queen's business'.

With so much attention called to the Assizes procession, few had noticed two figures climbing into the dock. They were the governor of Walton Jail, and its chief warder. The Clerk of Arraigns now commanded them, 'Put up Florence Elizabeth Maybrick.'

Below, Florence Maybrick had heard the blast of trumpets and the commands of bailiff and clerk. Now she stepped carefully up the narrow, winding stone stairway. She felt the presence of the two matrons close behind her, and as she rose into the dock she could hear the hush in the courtroom fall away into dead silence.

As she set foot on the floor of the dock, she felt giddy. Why was she so high in the air? The room seemed to fall away on all sides. She reached for the iron railing that stood almost to her chin. Now she looked down. There at a table sat Mr Pickford and Sir Charles. They seemed pre-occupied. Didn't they know she had been brought into the dock? A sense of boxes upon boxes drew her attention. Above the lawyers she saw a panelled box in which sat several men. One or two stared at her, but mostly they chose to gaze in other directions. Above them, under a canopy of scarlet and gold, rose the judge's bench.

Florence Maybrick studied the massive man who sat, even higher than the dock, on the bench. He seemed to be such a heavy old man. His long face sagged down from close-set eyes. The prominent nose, the protruding lower lip, the great jowls edged with untrimmed sideburns that hung down below his wig – all gave him a stern and frightening appearance.

She turned slowly. To her right was a long box with two rows of empty chairs. That must be the jury box. And over there to the left – that tall, narrow box – was that the witness box? It looked like a pulpit. Now, turning, she faced what she had already sensed in the hushed air of the room : the expectant crowd in the gallery. Here were no diverted gazes. All stared at her. Some, as she looked back at them, burned into her mind as familiar faces. Yes, there were ladies who had dealt cards to her across the whist table, ladies with whom she had served on charity committees. They stared, unblinking and disdainful.

One figure was more familiar than all the others. The Baroness von

Roques sat not far away. As their eyes met, Florence could feel her mother's confidence – always expressed in ramrod posture and determined jaw – stretching across the courtroom to her. It enabled her to relax her tight grip on the iron railing and stand proudly in the centre of the dock as she continued to scan the room.

Another gaze was familiar. Alfred Brierley sat far across the room. He gave no sign of recognition. Very well. The coldness of his gaze, combined with the judge's frown, the disdain of familiar faces in the gallery, and the determined confidence of the Baroness, gave Florence Maybrick a compulsion, despite the warm closeness of the air, to shudder as if from a chill. She controlled the impulse and turned again toward the bench. All would know, if they had not known it before, that she was a lady. She would maintain her composure.

The spectators saw in the dock a diminutive young woman dressed entirely in black. She wore a crepe jacket with short, open sleeves, white cuffs and black gloves. Her matching crepe bonnet gave streamers of black ribbon down her back. Through her thin black veil, her face was sharply white. Despite the hollow, sunken look around her eyes, her demeanour seemed unconcerned.

All rose again as the court chaplain led the opening prayer.

When his monotone had died away in the vaulted ceiling, and the rustling skirts of the ladies had settled again into their seats, the judge nodded to the Clerk of Arraigns. The clerk read the charge, indicting 'Florence Elizabeth Maybrick, aged twenty-six, for having, at Garston, on the 11th of May, feloniously, wilfully, and of her malice aforethought, killed and murdered one James Maybrick.'

The clerk paused and looked at Mrs Maybrick over the top of the paper in his hand. 'How plead you?'

She answered in a clear and steady voice. 'Not guilty.'

It took an hour to empanel the jury. All were Lancashiremen from the towns around Liverpool, but not one came from the city of Liverpool. The foreman and two others were plumbers, and two more were farmers. A woodturner, a provision dealer, a grocer, an ironmonger, a milliner, a painter and a baker made up the rest. One of them could neither read nor write so much as his own name. Some were very young. They averaged perhaps thirty-five years of age.

Florence Maybrick studied them as they took their places in the jury box. These, she knew, were her judges. Sir James, the hulking, square-jawed figure in wig and red velvet, was not her judge – so Mr Pickford had explained – so much as he was her counsel. He was there to see that this jury treated her as innocent until such time as her accusers might prove, beyond all reasonable doubt, that she was guilty. Looking at them, she felt for the first time since she was taken to Walton Jail that she was to be treated as an innocent person. The handsome figure of Sir Charles Russell, with his strong aquiline nose, his white wig and black silk gown, added to her feeling of confidence.

At last the jury was complete. Mr Addison rose to begin his opening speech for the prosecution. He was a burly, heavy-set man with a large round nose. His voice rang out in clear tones. Those who had attended the Coroner's Inquest settled back : There would be no trouble hearing what was said in this room.

The prosecutor began with a concession to the vast coverage which the case had received in the press.

'Each and every one of you,' he said to the jury, 'know that the charge against the prisoner is that she murdered her husband by administering to him doses of arsenic, and it would be idle in me to suppose that each and every one of you do not know some of the circumstances of the case, and that probably you have discussed the matter, but I know equally well that now – '

Mr Addison was interrupted by Sir Charles, who whispered that, excepting the scientific witnesses, all the witnesses should be requested to leave the Court. All withdrew except Mr Michael Maybrick, who was allowed to remain.

In the gallery, attentive barristers observed that the witnesses should have been excused before Mr Addison began. The oversight had given Sir Charles his first opportunity to show his concern for the fair treatment of his client.

The prosecutor reminded the jury that, as they were now 'sworn to decide the case according to law between the prisoner and the Crown, you will have no difficulty whatever in dismissing from your minds all that you have so heard and seen.'

If Sir Charles was tempted to interrupt to point out that no jury in England was ever sworn to decide a case according to law, but rather according to the evidence, he resisted the temptation. Now the prosecutor touched upon this point. 'It is upon the evidence, and upon the evidence alone, that the issue must depend.'

The prosecutor went into precise details of the case, beginning with 16th March, when Mrs Maybrick telegraphed to Flatman's Hotel in London for rooms. He recited the entire story of the rendezvous there, of the Grand National quarrel and the fight at Battlecrease House, of the onset of Maybrick's illness, of Mrs Maybrick's buying flypapers, of Maybrick's prescription that was afterward found to contain arsenic.

The gallery stirred at the first mention of the word that all had come to hear. Mr Addison, ignoring the reaction and yet appealing to it, explained that a single deadly dose, capable of killing a man, would be a dose of at least two grains or more. The symptoms, he said, are nausea, a sinking, purging, and vomiting without relief. Burning pains in throat and stomach, and external tenderness of the stomach, are felt, with cramps of the thighs and the stomach. A furred tongue, intense thirst, and tenesmus or bowel straining appear.

'The same symptoms are produced by what may be called smaller doses,' said the prosecutor. 'If you administer a dose of arsenic less than a fatal dose, twice a day, the same symptoms will be produced. But in a couple of days the patient will get better. But if before he gets better he goes on repeating the dose before there is a complete recovery, then in the course of time he will die. Another word on this subject. It is not a cumulative poison. It does not collect in the system in the same way, for instance, that lead does; on the contrary, it rapidly passes away, and it is the arsenic which passes away which kills, and not that which remains, and this makes it one of the most dangerous of poisons, inasmuch as in small doses it produces symptoms which may not be recognised as being peculiar to arsenic, and producing these effects death results.'

When the prosecutor read Mrs Maybrick's letter intercepted by Nurse Yapp, all quieted. Opera glasses rose to eyes that would themselves be pleased to read the letter if they could. At the words 'He is sick unto death' and again at the phrase 'my own darling' the room whispered its excitement, and as Mr Addison finished and said, 'That letter was given to Mr Edwin Maybrick at five-thirty,' the whispering rose like a flock of starlings set loose in the courtroom.

The gallery quieted again as the prosecutor described the symptoms and treatment during Maybrick's last days and Mrs Maybrick's furtive handling of the meat juice bottle. Mr Addison said, 'The accurate examination afterwards by Mr Davies showed that in that bottle there was half a grain of arsenic. If half a grain of arsenic was put into it, and no more, it showed that he was being poisoned by doses repeatedly administered. Half a grain of arsenic administered about twice a day would produce these illnesses of which you have heard.'

Immediately upon Maybrick's death, said the prosecutor, the housemaid and nurse were sent to see what they could find, and they discovered the packet of 'Arsenic. Poison for cats.' Mr Addison added a confused description of the finding of the hatboxes, with both Sir Charles and his own junior counsel, Mr McConnell, correcting him. Then he went on to describe the bottles which were found to contain arsenic, as well as the tumbler with the soaking piece of handkerchief. In the pocket of a dressing gown worn by Mrs Maybrick, he added, as well as in a handkerchief that was in the pocket, traces of arsenic were found.

Sir Charles leaned toward his junior counsel and whispered. A dressing gown, Mr Pickford? He could recall no previous mention of a dressing gown. Mr Pickford whispered that it was the first that he had heard of it, too.

Mr Addison went on to read the short note written to Alfred Brierley by Mrs Maybrick at the suggestion of Mrs Briggs. The sensation that ran through the gallery was more of silent pity than of scandalous titillation.

The prosecutor had reached almost the end of his presentation of the case. 'Gentlemen, there is no reason to doubt that James Maybrick died by arsenic, and arsenic given to him by repeated doses. Who did it? I am compelled to submit there is very cogent evidence to show it was his wife who administered it. Undoubtedly if she administered these repeated doses to him, then, gentlemen, she is guilty of the offence of wilful murder, and it will be your painful duty to say so.'

Mr Addison paused for the echo of his words to die, then nodded to his junior, Mr Swift, who said, 'Call Mr Clemmy.' The prosecutor sat down.

William Henry Clemmy was a surveyor from Bootle. He produced plans of Battlecrease House and explained the positions of rooms, hallways and stairs.

While the prosecutor mopped his brow and the back of his neck with his handkerchief – the exertion of his hour-long speech had combined with the heat of the last day of July and the confinement of shoulder-length wig, barrister's robe and traditional lace jabot and cuffs to leave him dripping with perspiration – Mr McConnell called Mr Michael Maybrick and examined him.

The testimony of the composer brother went as it had gone at the Coroner's Inquest and at the Magistrates' Court, from James's London visits to Dr Fuller through the witness's removal of the meat juice from the sickroom, and the discovery of the various bottles and packets after his brothers' death.

Sir Charles Russell rose with authority to cross-examine. His gaze was penetrating. He lost no time establishing that a bottle of brandy Michael suspected turned out to be harmless, that as a result of his directions nothing was administered to his brother from the meat juice Mrs Maybrick had handled, and that another bottle she handled contained no arsenic. He probed the witness's recollection of quinine pills, of several small phials, of solution of morphia, of the chocolate box, and of the packet of insect powder, asking in each case about Michael's awareness of the contents, and, specifically, of arsenic. In series, the answers were, 'I do not remember', 'I really do not know', 'I am not aware', 'I did not follow the evidence', 'I do not know', and again, 'I do not know.'

Now Sir Charles brought the witness round to the letter Mrs Maybrick had written asking him to investigate his brother's habit of taking a white powder. Michael said that he had destroyed the letter, and related James's sharp response, 'Whoever told you that, it is a damned lie,' when he brought up the subject.

Sir Charles was not reluctant to turn to 'this man Brierley'. 'As far as you are aware, your brother died in ignorance of the guilty meeting in London?'

'Yes, I am convinced of it.'

'The only complaint having to do with her was in reference to the quarrel about the Grand National?'

'Yes, I believe he knew nothing except what took place on the race-course.'

'You are aware there were complaints on both sides?'

'Yes.'

The last two questions and answers sank into the spectators. If there were complaints on both sides . . .

'Have you come across the cashbox from Mr Maybrick's wardrobe?'

'I have seen it, but it is not here.'

'Are you aware it has been asked for by the representatives of Mrs Maybrick?'

'No, I am not aware.'

Sir Charles had established the picture of a household in which the accused woman not only was up against suspicious friends and in-laws but couldn't even retrieve her cash box. This was a small point. Much larger was the question of complaints on both sides. It stood to reason that even an adulteress need not murder an adulterer in order to gain her freedom. Obviously, if another woman was involved, Mrs Maybrick could have obtained a legal separation or divorce.

Mr Addison was ready to examine the next witness, Dr Arthur Hopper. As family physician to the Maybricks the doctor looked the part. He was short of stature, fatherly and matter-of-fact. He gazed across the courtroom at Florence Maybrick as one might look at an old friend not seen in a long time.

Mr Addison's questioning brought out that Maybrick had complained to the doctor from time to time of dyspepsia and nervousness, and that he had once discussed arsenic. Maybrick had been taking quinine in America. 'As he said that quinine did not suit him,' the doctor testified, 'I suppose I suggested arsenic.'

In Sir Charles Russell's cross-examination, the doctor agreed that he would call Maybrick distinctly hypochondriacal, and said that 'when he came to consult me, I was disappointed to find that between the visits he had been trying some new remedy recommended by friends, and different from the medicines I had prescribed.'

This happened frequently, he said, and Maybrick had taken to doubling the dose. 'I said to him,' he added, 'it was a dangerous habit. Although he might escape scot free, he would some time do himself great injury.'

Now Sir Charles established that Maybrick had complained of numbness as early as 1882, and that Maybrick had given Dr Hopper a bundle of aphrodisiac prescriptions written by Dr Seguard of New York. The doctor agreed that arsenic was commonly used as a 'nerve tonic of the aphrodisiac character'.

The defence lawyer turned now to the time when Mrs Maybrick asked the doctor to remonstrate with her husband about taking a strong medicine, and Dr Hopper said he had looked in Maybrick's room for bottles, but not for a powder.

Sir Charles got the witness to make it clear that Mrs Maybrick's black eye was inflicted by her husband, and then he again turned to arsenic. Attentive listeners were beginning to see a pattern in the cross-examination : Sir Charles kept coming back to Maybrick's knowledge of arsenic and his habit of dosing himself.

Next Sir Charles questioned Dr Hopper as to his personal experience of men who used arsenic habitually. His experience, the doctor admitted, came only from books. Asked whether the sudden cessation of stimulants was injurious, he replied that it was 'risky rather than injurious'.

When Sir Charles had finished, Mr Justice Stephen intervened with a question of his own. 'Did you attend Mr Maybrick in his last illness?'

'Oh, no, my lord,' said the doctor.

The lawyers at the counsel tables looked at each other. Surely his lordship had not missed the fact that neither Mr Addison's opening speech nor the doctor's testimony had in any way connected him with Maybrick's last illness.

William McConnell took the next witness, Mrs Briggs. Mr McConnell's beaked nose, his downturned mouth and muttonchop sidewhiskers, and his gaunt figure seemed apt for one who had to question this clearly determined woman. Asked about any signs of disharmony in the marriage, she said that Mrs Maybrick 'only made a complaint about her husband after the Grand National'.

The judge interrupted. 'How long after?'

'The day after,' said Mrs Briggs.

Again the men at the counsel tables were puzzled. Mr Addison's opening remarks and Dr Hopper's testimony had clearly established the complaint on the day after the Grand National. Had his lordship not noted this important date?

On cross-examination, Sir Charles Russell pursued the question of Mrs Briggs's impression of Maybrick's condition on 8th May.

'The fact was, Mrs Briggs, when you saw this poor gentleman you came to the conclusion he was in a very bad way?'

'Yes.'

'Is it not a fact that he was in a very much more serious condition than you would have thought up to that time?'

'Yes.'

'You formed a very serious opinion of the man's condition? You thought him in peril?'

'Yes.'

'Serious peril?'

'Yes.'

Mrs Briggs now agreed that she knew that Maybrick used the writing table in which she found a bottle, that the hatboxes contained not women's hats but men's, that none of the furniture or boxes in which arsenic was found was in any way secured or locked, that a very large number of medicine bottles were found in the house, that she knew that Maybrick dosed himself, and that he used to recommend medicines to her.

Sir Charles turned to the moment when Mrs Maybrick lay ill in the spare bedroom. He asked Mrs Briggs to recollect telling her, when Nurse Wilson was present, that arsenic had been found in the bottle of meat juice she had handled.

'Do you recollect telling her that fact?'

'I think I mentioned it.'

The answer was not precise enough for Sir Charles. 'Do you recollect Mrs Maybrick beginning a sentence when a policeman came into the room and stopped her?'

Mrs Briggs hesitated. The courtroom hushed. Would Sir Charles be able to draw from this prim woman the admission that Mrs Maybrick had tried to explain the condition of the meat juice?

He pressed the point. 'Do you recollect the policeman coming into the room?'

'No.'

'You and the nurse were in the room, and your sister at the door. Was there any conversation which was interrupted?'

'Yes. My sister said to me, "You are not to say anything," and the policeman said, "You are not to speak." '

'It was upon the conversation in this room on Valentine's meat juice that the policeman said you must have no conversation?'

'Yes.'

Sir Charles had no more questions for the witness. He sat down pleased to have established that this busybody had bustled into Battlecrease House, given it as her opinion that Maybrick was in peril, and recommended summoning a nurse – all on the very day when Mrs Maybrick wrote that he was 'sick unto death'.

In addition, the cross-examination had revealed that this confidential friend of Mrs Maybrick had offered sarcastic advice when Mrs Maybrick was in dire need of friendship, and that Mrs Briggs was an evasive witness capable of saying first that she herself told Mrs Maybrick of the finding of arsenic in the meat juice, then that Nurse Wilson had told her, then that she did not recollect and finally that she did recollect the conversation and its interruption by her sister and the policeman.

It was Edwin Maybrick's turn to mount the narrow steps into the witness box. His testimony revealed that he had locked up Mrs Maybrick's dressing gown, apron and handkerchief until he turned them over to Inspector Baxendale after the Coroner's Inquiry and the committal proceedings at the Magistrates' Court.

The chief point which Sir Charles wanted to establish by cross-examination was summed up in his question, 'From the Wednesday morning until the death had you privately forbidden any intervention by Mrs Maybrick in the nursing or administration of medicine or food?'

The witness told of his instructions to Nurse Gore.

'Now, I want this quite definitely – your instructions were distinct, that neither as to medicine, nor as to food, was Mrs Maybrick to have anything to do with it?'

'I never mentioned her name in the matter, but I told the nurses I should hold them responsible for all foods and all medicines given to him, and that nobody was to attend to him at all except the nurses. But I did not mention any names.'

'Still, that would be the effect of the orders?'

'Yes, it would.'

Having made it clear that it would have been difficult for Mrs Maybrick to administer arsenic or anything else to her husband during his last four days, Sir Charles Russell calculated to raise sympathy for the mistress of Battlecrease House. 'Now,' he said, 'I should like to ask you if you have seen the cash-box which Mrs Maybrick said was hers?'

'Yes. It is at the house now. It is locked up in the linen closet.'

'Is there any objection to its being produced?'

'None, so far as I know.'

The chemist Thomas Symington Wokes, examined by Mr Swift, stated that Mrs Maybrick had bought flypapers from him on 24th April, and that he was not aware of cosmetic use made from flypapers. Sir Charles established that Wokes knew Mrs Maybrick by name and openly sent the flypapers to the house.

The chemist Christopher Hanson testified that he sold flypapers to Mrs Maybrick on 29th April. Sir Charles brought out that Hanson's shop was only a ten-minute walk from Battlecrease House, that the flypapers lay in a conspicuous position when Mrs Maybrick was ordering a cosmetic lotion, and that arsenic was an ingredient in many cosmetic preparations.

'It softens the skin?' he asked.

'I don't know what it is for,' said the chemist.

'You know, I presume, it is a depilatory?'

The judge looked across at the jury of plumbers and farmers and such. 'That is,' said his lordship, 'it takes off hairs.'

When his lordship adjourned the trial until next morning, weary spectators hurried home to tell those less fortunate all about it, and to read in the papers the testimony they had heard during the day. Others went only a short distance across Lime Street to the Grapes Hotel and the Lime Street Hotel, where the public rooms were crowded with those from inside the courtroom who were eager to give their reports and those from outside who were eager to listen. At the North Western Hotel, where Sir Charles Russell was staying, the crowds were equally large and excited.

In the compartmented prison van, Mrs Maybrick was again isolated – a feeling she had had all day. She had spent the long hours almost in the centre of the room. Behind her had rustled and coughed and whispered and fanned an eager crowd, while before her the judge and jurymen, counsel, court attendants and witnesses had questioned and answered and shuffled their papers and mopped their brows. But throughout, as the accused person on trial under English law, she had been an exhibit rather than a participant. She had paper and pencil with which to write notes to her lawyers when she wished. But she was permitted neither to speak nor to be spoken to.

As the van moved off, Florence Maybrick knew the crowd was different. It did not hiss, as it had in the morning. It was a subdued crowd, if not a respectful one. What Mrs Maybrick sensed, through the narrow openings in the curtains of her moving cell, was not sympathy. But it was not antipathy, either.

The jurymen were taken to a nearby hotel. They had been warned by the judge that they would not be able to go home. They might send and receive letters and telegrams, but were not to be subjected to outside influence.

Later, in the billiard room of another hotel, the Imperial, the bailiff of the court, who was in charge of the jury, was seen. Then a number of the men playing billiards were recognised as jurors. Still another group was seen talking casually with passersby. The jurymen seemed to come and go as they pleased.

The public devoured the testimony, which was printed verbatim in, it seemed, every paper in the land. In New York, the *World* devoted a column and a half of its front page to the first day of the trial. Its cabled story observed:

> Matters bear an exceedingly ominous aspect for the prisoner, and her friends have been able to derive but little comfort from the manner in which the trial has progressed until now. The counsel for the prosecution, in opening the case, indicated that they were in a position to prove not only all the charges on which the indictment for murder is based, but a good deal more besides.

The paper also reported that great surprise was expressed in Liverpool at James Maybrick's will, which had just been probated.

> He left in all about $50,000 personally, most of it in trust to his brothers for his two children. He left his widow less than $800 a year, the income being principally made up of the interest on a sum derived from insurance policies on his life.

VIII

*'I put it to you again for the last
time. Did you not open the letter
deliberately, because you suspected your mistress?'*

Thursday, 1st August, 1889

As Florence Maybrick arrived in the detention cell in the basement of
St George's Hall, she was met by Richard Cleaver. He had drawn up a
deed which assigned to him the £2,000 insurance policy with the Mutual
Reserve Fund Life Association. The deed stated that the costs of Mrs
Maybrick's defence had already amounted to £500, and might amount
to £1,000.

The crowds at St George's Hall were larger than on the day before. A
stranger who did not know what was going on, if such a person could
have been found in England, might have thought a festival was being
held. Vendors hawked sweetmeats and ices, and the Keeper of the Hall
with all his men tried to handle the vast number who demanded what
few tickets were left after leading citizens, visiting barristers and solicitors
had been granted their reservations.

The festive atmosphere seeped into the courtroom. The trumpeters of
the Assizes procession, who on the day before had blared their customary
fanfare at the entrance of the judge, now sounded forth with a well-
known Roman Catholic hymn. It brought indignant comment from
outraged Protestants, who forgot or did not know that Messrs Addison
and McConnell, Counsel for the Crown, and Sir Charles Russell, counsel
for the prisoner, were staunch members of the Roman Church.

In the dock, Florence Maybrick found that her straight cane chair had
been replaced by a more comfortable armchair appropriated from the
grand jury room.

The first witness of the day was Dr Charles Fuller, Michael Maybrick's
London physician. He told the prosecutor that Maybrick had never

suggested to him that he had been taking arsenic during any part of his life. Sir Charles Russell's cross-examination brought the observation that the doctor thought Maybrick was a nervous man who exaggerated his symptoms. The skilful questioning of the defence lawyer brought out the various symptoms of habitual arsenic eating, the admission that it is impossible to say that any one symptom is distinctly from an over-use of arsenic and from nothing else, and the further admission that the effect of doses varies according to the individual and that much depression occurs on the withdrawal of the drug from those who take it in very large doses.

Mr Addison decided to re-examine his witness. The doctor now said he really had no experience of the arsenic habit. Asked what people generally take arsenic for, he said, 'Generally for skin eruptions.'

Christopher Robinson and Frederick Early Tozer came next. As assistant chemists employed by Clay and Abraham of Liverpool, each swore there was no arsenic in the prescriptions for Mr Maybrick.

The courtroom buzzed when Nurse Alice Yapp climbed into the witness box. Everybody knew this was the woman who opened the letter. Mr Addison led her through the quarrel after the Grand National, the discovery of flypapers soaking, the mistress's pouring something from one bottle to another, her comment to her husband that he always wanted his hands rubbed and it did him no good. At last the prosecutor came to the letter. All eyes strained to see the small, dull-looking piece of paper as it was placed in evidence. Finally, the nurse told of finding the chocolate box with its packet of 'Arsenic. Poison for cats'.

The witness was subdued throughout. Her brashness had been left in the third-floor nursery at Battlecrease House. The prosecutor had to caution her sharply. 'Do try and keep up your voice. You give us a great deal of trouble.'

The approach of Sir Charles Russell, whose snapping snuffbox and sweeping robe spoke almost as eloquently as his precise questioning, did not increase Nurse Yapp's self-confidence.

He said, 'About this question of flypapers. Have you ever acted as lady's maid?' The question rang with implications about the nurse's position in the domestic hierarchy of Battlecrease House and her knowledge of her mistress's habits.

'No, sir. Only as nurse.' The answer reflected Yapp's acceptance of the position to which it had pleased the Lord to call her.

Questioning her closely about the flypapers, Sir Charles made it clear they had been in sight from the time when Bessie Brierley saw them in the morning. 'And you,' he said, 'out of curiosity, went into the room after the dinner was over?'

'It was about two hours after when I went into the room.'

'You had no business in the room?'

'No.'

'Where were they?'

'On the washstand.'

'In the principal bedroom?'

'Yes, sir.'

'And in a position in which you could see the washstand on entering the door of the bedroom?'

'Yes, sir.'

'These were reported to you by Bessie Brierley as having been there early in the morning, and you have no reason to suppose that they did not continue there the whole of the day till you saw them?'

'No, sir.'

Having made it clear to the jury that the witness was a busybody and that whoever was soaking flypapers made no attempt to hide them, Sir Charles went on to produce from the witness testimony that Mrs Maybrick had chosen the most public place in Battlecrease House in which to pour medicine from one bottle to another. 'Is that the landing which all in the house who desire to go up and down stairs must pass?'

'Yes.'

'Now,' said Sir Charles, his glance sweeping round the courtroom as if he was at last getting down to brass tacks, 'with regard to this letter.' The desired effect was produced: all rustling in the room ceased, and most of the large paper fans hovered in mid-air. He handed the letter to the witness. 'You had heard the name of your mistress coupled with the name of Brierley before you got the letter?'

'Never.'

'Why did you open the letter?'

'Because Mrs Maybrick wished that it should go by that post.'

Sir Charles stared at the evasive nurse. 'Why did you open that letter?'

She did not reply.

The judge decided to lend a hand. 'Did anything happen to the letter?'

'Yes,' said Nurse Yapp, 'it fell in the dirt, my lord.'

Sir Charles put his question once more. 'Why did you open that letter?'

The nurse found the impudence she had lost when she took the stand. 'I have answered you, sir.'

The judge spoke again. 'She said because it fell into the dirt.'

Sir Charles turned to the bench, his patience almost out of control, and spoke slowly and carefully. 'I think, with great deference to your lordship, she did not say so. Your lordship is referring to something before.'

Mr Justice Stephen was stubborn. 'She has just said so now.'

Sir Charles looked at his lordship. He was now more than a little impatient with this interruption to the very kind of work – the difficult art of penetrating cross-examination – which had numbered him amongst the greatest advocates in England. He could not understand this blundering interference by any judge, but especially one of his lordship's reputation. 'Well,' he went on, 'I did not catch it, anyhow. I want to have it out again.'

He turned back to the witness. 'Why did you open that letter?'

'I opened the letter to put it in a clean envelope.'

'Why didn't you put it in a clean envelope without opening it?'

There was no reply.

'Was it a wet day?'

Again no reply.

'Aye or no?'

The nurse looked down at Sir Charles and said nothing.

'Was it a wet or a dry day?'

The nurse looked around the courtroom. She said nothing.

Sir Charles tried another tack. 'Had the day before been a dry day?'

'It was showery.'

'Will you swear that on Wednesday it was showery?'

'I cannot say positively.'

'Was the child able to walk?'

'Yes, sir.'

'What do you say you did with the letter?'

'I gave it to Mr Edwin Maybrick.'

'No, no,' said Sir Charles. 'I mean when you got it from Mrs Maybrick?'

'I gave it to the child to post.'

'Did you ever do that before?'

'Always, and Mrs Maybrick always gave letters to the baby to carry to the post.'

'Did this incident ever happen, or anything like it, before?'

'No, sir.'

Sir Charles reached up to the witness box. 'Let me see the letter. Where did the child drop it?'

'Right by the post office, in crossing the road.'

'Which side?'

'Near the post office.'

'Then you had securely passed the road and were stepping on to the curbstone?'

'Yes.'

'Then you picked it up?'

'Yes.'

Sir Charles looked at the envelope in his hand. 'And you saw this mark upon it, did you?'

'Yes.'

He handed it to her. 'Just take it in your hand. Is the direction clear enough?'

'It was very much dirtier at the time.'

'You didn't rub the mud off. What did you do?'

'I went into the post office and asked for a clean envelope to re-address it.'

Sir Charles let the full power of his scorn come down upon the witness. 'Did it never occur to you that you could get a clean envelope, and put it unopened into that?'

'Oh, I never thought of that.'

'Then, between the picking of it up and going into the shop you formed the design of opening it, and did, in fact, open it as you were going in?'

'Yes.'

'If, as you suggest, this fell in the mud, there is no running of the ink.'

'No, sir.'

'Can you suggest how there can be any damp or wet in connection with it without causing some running of the ink?'

'I cannot.'

Sir Charles fixed his most devastating accusation. 'On your oath, girl, did you not manufacture that stain as an excuse for opening your mistress's letter?'

'I did not.'

'Have you any explanation to offer about the running of the ink?'

'I have not.'

'I put it to you again for the last time. Did you not open the letter deliberately, because you suspected your mistress?'

'No, sir, I did not.'

Sir Charles sat down abruptly, ending his cross-examination.

Elizabeth Brierley, the second domestic servant to give evidence, said that she saw Michael Maybrick take something off the washstand on the Thursday evening before the master died. Sir Charles Russell then brought out that Mrs Maybrick was in the room when the witness noticed the flypapers, and that when the inner room, in which the hats were kept, was used as a bedroom it was occupied by Mr Maybrick, and only Mr Maybrick's hats were kept there.

When Mary Cadwallader followed Bessie Brierley, Sir Charles observed that a stable witness had taken the stand. With firm, emphatic questions – 'Some medicine had come from London by post?' 'You yourself had taken it in?' 'Your master told you this?' – he made it clear that the master had told Cadwallader he had taken an overdose of medicine from London.

As the court adjourned for luncheon, Florence Maybrick was certain she had not seen Alfred Brierley. She went to her detention cell with Mary Cadwallader's confident testimony on her mind, feeling for the first time that a friendly witness had taken the stand.

During the recess, Edwin Maybrick approached the crown prosecutor. From his pocket he took a pillbox. He seemed uncertain what to do with it.

After lunch, Mr Swift, the assistant crown prosecutor, interrogated the cook, Elizabeth Humphreys. Mounting the stand with complete self-assurance, the cook beamed a smile at her former mistress. Mr Swift produced the cook's story of Mrs Maybrick saying that if the master had taken 'that much more' (the cook pointed to her finger) of his medicine he would have been a dead man.

'Do you suppose that she meant the London medicine?'

'I thought she meant the London medicine. She said that "horrid" medicine.'

'I don't want to know what she meant,' said Mr Swift, contradicting his previous question, 'but what she said.'

'She said that "horrid" medicine.'

The cook was questioned about her offer to make lemonade for the master. She said that Mrs Maybrick took it and said he was to have it only as a gargle.

Once more Mr Swift's examination technique ran afoul of Sir Charles. 'Do you remember asking her something about pulling through?' he said.

Sir Charles interrupted. 'I must ask you not to ask leading questions.'

'Don't speak to me, if you please, Sir Charles,' said Mr Swift huffily. 'Speak to the court.' The gallery burst into laughter. It quieted only when the judge's narrow eyes and heavy jowls looked their sternest.

In cross-examination, Sir Charles took full advantage of the witness's sympathy for the accused. She agreed that she thought her mistress was doing her best under the circumstances and that Mrs Maybrick was very much grieved over the situation. He cleared up the point that Humphreys had not known that liquids were forbidden to the patient, except as a gargle, until after she had made the lemonade, so that Mrs Maybrick had simply been following the doctor's orders.

Mr McConnell rose to question Dr Richard Humphreys. The doctor looked the general practitioner: smallish, homespun, comfortable. The junior prosecutor asked him about a visit to Battlecrease House two years earlier, when the children had whooping cough, and he recalled Mrs Maybrick's asking him about her husband's taking a white powder. 'I said that if he took a large enough dose he would die,' he said, and added, 'I said to Mrs Maybrick, not meaningfully, however, "Well, if he should ever die suddenly call me, and I can say you have had some conversation with me about it." '

The courtroom buzzed at the implication that Mrs Maybrick might have been planning an explanation for her husband's death two years before the fact.

The doctor went on to testify in great detail, through more than two hours of examination, on Maybrick's symptoms and treatment during his final illness.

When he came to the patient's condition on the Thursday before he died, the doctor said that it was not as favourable as before.

'What were the unfavourable symptoms?' asked Mr McConnell.

'They were diarrhoea and straining. I saw the faeces that afternoon.'

'Did they present any characteristic that led you to make more than a casual observation?'

'They themselves did not. But I had a conversation with Mr Michael Maybrick which led me to believe that something more might be seen.'

'Was any further examination made?'

'Yes.'

'What examination did you make?'

'I boiled them in copper with a little acid.'

'What were you testing for then?'

'I was testing for some metal, probably antimony, arsenic, or mercury.'

'How much did you subject to the test?'

'About a tablespoonful.'

'With what result?'

'Nothing conclusive.'

'Be a little more explicit, doctor?'

'I go no deposit on the copper.'

'Had your patient had bismuth in his medicine before?'

'He had.'

'Was there any deposit of bismuth on the copper?'

'There was no deposit of any metal.'

'The result was negative?'

'Yes.'

'Did you examine the urine at all?'

'I did the same afternoon, but the result was negative.'

As the doctor's testimony about testing the faeces and urine proceeded, Sir Charles and Mr Pickford compared notes. They recalled no testimony on this point during either the Coroner's Inquest or the Magistrates' Court hearing. Mr McConnell had blundered into entirely new evidence: Two days before death, tests for arsenic had turned out negative. It was a development greatly in favour of the defence.

Among the spectators, the point was not missed. Had not Mr Addison said yesterday morning that arsenic did not collect in the system but rapidly passed away, and that it was the arsenic which passed away which killed and not that which remained? Here was Maybrick's doctor testifying that no arsenic had been passed by his system two or three days before death.

Turning to the post mortem examination, Mr McConnell asked if his witness might refer to notes made by the doctors during the autopsy. The judge permitted the notes to be handed to him and he described the examination. It was not a description for the ladies present, least of all Florence Maybrick, but, while the matron beside her offered smelling salts, she managed to turn the bottle away. In the gallery more than one such bottle was sniffed.

The doctor made it clear that all the organs of the deceased seemed healthy except those in the digestive tract, from the tongue through the bowels.

Mr McConnell now came to the key question: 'From what you saw during his life and from the post-mortem examination, what do you say was the cause of death?'

'Arsenic,' said the doctor. 'Arsenical poisoning.'

'Were you present when the matters contained in these four jars were taken?'

'I was.' The doctor paused. He seemed to have an afterthought. 'Just now you asked me what I thought was the cause of death. I said arsenical poisoning. I said that knowing that an examination has been made of the contents of the stomach. But, asking me what conclusion I came to after the post mortem, recollecting the symptoms that he died of, I could only say that it was due to some irritant poison, most probably arsenic. But I should not like to swear that it was.'

Sir Charles Russell had kept one eye on his large pocket watch, which lay on its back, its hinged gold front open, on counsel's table before him. He had been concerned at the prospect of beginning his cross-examination just before an adjournment. Usually a defence lawyer could make little headway with an important witness during the closing few minutes of the day. Now, however, the kindly doctor had volunteered to qualify his own testimony as to the cause of death. And there – Mr McConnell had turned and sat down.

Sir Charles rose, picking up his watch and snapping it shut just before he dropped it by its chain into his deep waistcoat pocket.

'When you gave the answer in the first instance,' he began, 'you were taking into account not merely the symptoms before death, but the statements of the results indicated to you by others?'

'I was when he asked me the question.'

'Excluding these results, were you when examined before, and are you now, able to say more than that the symptoms during life, and the post mortem appearances after death, are consistent with death from some irritant poison?'

Mr Justice Stephen interrupted. The word 'consistent,' he said, was so very misleading. He asked the witness if the symptoms pointed to death by poison.

'I mean to imply that they point to death by irritant poison,' said the doctor.

Sir Charles continued his cross-examination. 'Did you not go on to explain that, when you used the word irritant poison, you meant anything, as, for instance, impure food, would cause these symptoms?'

'I mean,' said the doctor, 'that I did not know what the post mortem appearance of an irritant would have been. An irritant food, causing certain symptoms during life, would probably produce a similar appearance after death.'

'You have never assisted at a post mortem examination of any person supposed to have died from arsenical poison?'

'No.'

'Up to the time that the communication was made to you which suggested that there might be some foundation for supposing foul play, did it in any way occur to you that there were symptoms present during life of arsenical poisoning?'

'No.'

'When was it that the idea was first suggested to you?'

'I think on Thursday, or on the Wednesday night.'

'From a communication made to you by Mr Michael Maybrick?'

'Yes, that there was something unsatisfactory.'

The court adjourned.

The spectators burst into Lime Street. Each was eager to be first to tell a mob of rapt listeners that Sir Charles had just proved that Maybrick's doctor would never have thought of poisoning if Michael Maybrick had not suggested it.

Sir Charles could hardly have planned a better moment for adjournment. When he stepped forth from St George's Hall and crossed Lime Street to his hotel, he was loudly cheered all the way. He went to bed that night the hero of the city.

Through the evening, rumour and conjecture wrestled with each other in every Liverpool household and public room. Early editions of newspapers, having gone to press before Sir Charles's cross-examination began, disagreed with late editions. Everywhere, new theories were expounded and old theories were revised.

The correspondent of the New York *World* had an advantage over the English newsmen and those from New York's morning papers. His paper would not be on the streets of New York until noon the next day, when it would be five o'clock in the afternoon in England. He could afford to take his time before filing his dispatch. He sauntered from the Grapes Hotel to the North Western, then back to the Imperial, listening everywhere. He read the reports in all the papers he could get hold of, missing none sold in Liverpool that night. When at last he made his way to the telegraph office to write his cable dispatch, he was able to assemble all the reactions he had gathered into a story that caused his editors in New York to compose the headline, 'HER ACQUITTAL PROBABLE.'

His story began, 'Sir Charles Russell put in some sledge-hammer work in the way of cross examination today, which caused a great rebound of popular opinion in Mrs Maybrick's favor, and makes a disagreement of the jury, if not an absolute acquittal, look quite probable.' A number of items of information came not from the courtroom but from the populace.

Mrs Briggs, the all-round friend of the family, will also come in for more close questioning by Sir Charles Russell. Whether rightly or wrongly the friends of the accused regard Mrs Briggs's conduct previous to Mr Maybrick's death with some degree of suspicion. Reference may be made to the fact that before he met the American girl, Mr Maybrick intended to marry the sister of Mrs Briggs, a Miss Janion, and that her family were much displeased when Mr Maybrick married Miss Chanler [sic] instead.

A brand-new theory was this : 'It is rumored also that Sir Charles Russell will score a strong point on the will which Mr Maybrick made before his death. It is alleged that Sir Charles is going to show that he had discovered his wife's relations with Brierly [sic] and that he was determined to kill himself.'

The most degrading rumour was stated as fact : 'It is beginning to leak out that no baby will be born, her hopes in that direction having been destroyed by the illness from which she suffered during her incarceration in Walton Prison.'

Still another rumour was authoritatively scotched :

The *World* correspondent is also assured today by one in a position to know that Brierly [sic] never had a thought of turning State's evidence against the accused, but that he had, in fact, given his check for over $1,000 towards her defense fund.

And there was another good word for Sir Charles :

The *World* correspondent was told today that Sir Charles Russell has gone into the case largely on the grounds of public interest and in sympathy for the woman, and that he really is taking a much lower fee than he has been represented as receiving.

IX

*'I found two one-hundredths of a grain
of arsenic in the whole handkerchief.'*

Friday, 2nd August, 1889

The admission of the more privileged public and the pageantry of the solemn Assizes procession were now routine. The crowd returned ready for an immediate continuation of the exciting cross examination of the homespun doctor. Sir Charles Russell started his questioning as if only a five-minute recess had intervened : the Wirral races, the weather, twitchings of the arm, strong tea, nervous symptoms, headache, palpitation, stiffness of the lower limbs, the sciatic nerve, nux vomica, chronic derangement of the stomach, pain in the thighs, the morphia suppository, the Turkish bath, hawking versus vomiting – Sir Charles peppered the doctor with short, specific questions which omitted no detail of James Maybrick's symptoms and reactions.

Sir Charles proved himself so well versed in medical matters that he sometimes overlooked the jury's considerably lesser knowledge. 'With a view to stopping the retching,' he said to the doctor, 'you prescribed ipecacuanha wine. That would be upon the homeopathic principle?'

'It was upon the knowledge that small doses would stop vomiting.'

'If taken in large doses it would be a thing to cause vomiting?'

'Yes.'

'Then you applied it on the principle *similia similibus*?'

'Upon that knowledge.'

Sir Charles did not stop to translate from the Latin for the uneducated jury, nor to elicit an explanation of the homeopathic principle, which meant trying to cure the patient by administering minute doses of remedies which would produce in a healthy person the same symptoms as the patient's.

Presently Sir Charles turned to the subject of the slops. 'You took on the Thursday some faeces, and you applied what is known as Reinsch's test?'

'Yes.'

Alert barristers leaned forward. Here was Sir Charles at his best. The witness had inadvertently introduced the matter of testing the faeces only yesterday, though it had never come up in the Coroner's Inquest or the hearing at the Magistrates' Court. But yesterday Dr Humphreys had not even identified the test by name. Clearly, Sir Charles had done his homework last night.

'You applied that test both to the urine and the faeces – that is to say, you added hydrochloric acid in each case, and then introduced a piece of copper foil?'

'Yes.'

'And you found no deposit?'

'No. I got no deposit.'

'That would be a negative test?'

'No, not of necessity.'

'Why?'

'Because the quantity that I used was so small, and the time I boiled it such a short period, that there might not have been time for any deposit of any kind to take place. Further, I am not skilled in the details of testing.'

'That is candid, doctor,' said Sir Charles. 'Then you mean to convey that, although you tried this experiment, you were not able to conduct it successfully?'

'I cannot say. I do not pretend to have any skill in these matters.'

'It is not a difficult test?'

'No.'

'And if there is arsenic, it is supposed to make a deposit upon the copper?'

'Yes, if it is boiled long enough, and if there is some quantity there.'

'I must ask you, how long did you boil it?'

'About two minutes.'

'What quantity did you take?'

'Perhaps an ounce.'

'Do you suggest that for an experiment properly conducted that was sufficient?'

'It was sufficient if there had been an appreciable quantity of arsenic in it.'

'Did you at that time think your experiment was properly conducted or not?'

'I was satisfied there was nothing on the copper. I had no books at the time to refer to. It was only from recollection I worked.'

'So far as the urine is concerned, you followed the right course?'

'Yes, so far as the deposit upon it is concerned. I do not know whether the copper was absolutely pure, but I have a very strong impression that it was pure.'

Sir Charles paused. Here might be an admission that would counteract the admission that the test might not have been properly conducted. 'But see, Dr Humphreys,' he said, 'in proportion as there is any doubt about the purity of the instruments you were using, would there not be a greater certainty of getting a deposit?'

The doctor seemed confused. 'I should like you to say that again.'

At this point, Sir Charles could afford patience. He spoke slowly. 'You say you are not sure that the instruments were perfectly pure?'

'I was told they were pure, but I am not sure.'

'But if they were not pure, would you not get a greater deposit?'

'If they were not pure, it depends on what the impurity was.'

'Well, what impurity do you suggest may have existed?'

'In the copper, arsenic.'

'Then, if there were impurities in the form of arsenic in the copper, would it not make it the more certain that you would get a deposit on the copper?'

'If there was that impurity.'

'Did you find any?'

'I found none.'

Sih Charles was now ready to put his climactic question to the agreeable doctor. 'I think you said that the idea of arsenic did not occur to your mind until it was suggested to you? Had it not been for the suggestion of arsenic, were you prepared to give a certificate of death if he had died on Wednesday?'

'Yes.'

'And in your judgment what was the cause of death?'

'Gastritis or gastro-enteritis.'

Mr Justice Stephen leaned forward, anxious to double-check this important testimony. 'Then if nothing about poisoning had been suggested to you,' he said, 'you would have certified that he had died of gastritis or gastro-enteritis?'

'Yes, my lord.'

Sir Charles now asked the witness to mention any post mortem symptom which was distinctive of arsenic poisoning and which was not

also distinctive of gastritis or gatsro-enteritis. The doctor said he could not
give any.

'That is because you believe there is none?'

'I should not like to swear to distinguish between them.'

Sir Charles drove the point home. 'No distinctive symptom apparent
to a post mortem examination distinguishes arsenic poisoning which does
not distinguish gastritis or gastro-enteritis?'

'I can't swear to distinguish between them.'

Mr Addison rose quickly to re-examine. 'Does an irritant poison produce irritability of the stomach?'

'Yes.'

'And can you distinguish it from irritability caused by dyspepsia?'

'No. I could not.'

'You didn't suspect irritant poison at that time?'

'No, I did not.'

'You did not suspect arsenic given on purpose?'

'No.'

Dr William Carter was a local celebrity, and he knew it. 'I am a physician
of considerable experience in Liverpool,' he said in his opening testimony.
'On Tuesday, 7th May, I was called in in consequence of my general
position in the town.' The humility of the family doctor was not to be
found in this witness. He testified at length on the drugs and other treatment administered to James Maybrick.

'From the post mortem examination,' he said, 'I came to the conclusion that there had been an irritant of some kind, and now, since I
have heard the evidence given by Mr Davies, I have no doubt whatever
that arsenical poisoning was the cause of death. I judge that the fatal
dose had been given on Friday, the 3rd, but a dose might have been
given after that.'

Mr Addison questioned the doctor on the symptoms of arsenical
poisoning, and at last asked, 'Now, taking the whole history of the case,
your conclusion is – '

The doctor interrupted. 'I can have no doubt about it.'

The prosecutor was taken aback by the impetuosity of his witness.
'Excuse me. You can't have any doubt about what, doctor?'

'That it was arsenical poisoning.' The doctor spoke so authoritatively
that the courtroom buzzed. Mr Addison sat down.

Sir Charles Russell reminded the doctor that at the Coroner's Inquest
he said he formed no opinion that Maybrick was suffering from poison
until the suggestion was made to him. He had also said that something

eaten after the Wirral races must have set up gastritis. Sir Charles asked if the doctor would expect the symptoms from impure food and arsenic to be the same, and the doctor said, 'Except generally the last symptom of all, which is less common – death.'

'I should not have called that a symptom, doctor,' said Sir Charles. The courtroom burst with laughter.

The tension broken, Sir Charles pinned down the witness. 'Have you yourself ever assisted at the post mortem examination of a person as to whom it was alleged death had been caused by arsenic?'

'Not by arsenic.'

'Have you ever before attended a patient as to whom it was alleged that death had resulted from arsenic?'

'Not death.'

Again displaying a detailed knowledge of medicines, symptoms and treatment, the defence lawyer led the doctor into stating his view that Maybrick's was a case of acute, rather than chronic, poisoning, and that a large and fatal dose must have been taken on Friday, 3rd May.

Dr Alexander Barron, who had attended the post mortem on behalf of Mrs Maybrick, was the first witness after lunch. Mr Swift examined him, and was confounded to find that the doctor would testify only that 'some irritant poison', but not necessarily arsenic, had probably caused Maybrick's death.

Sir Charles Russell's examination drew Dr Barron's testimony that, though he had been present at about five hundred post mortem examinations, he could not differentiate between the symptoms of food poisoning and those of arsenical poisoning.

As Edward Davies was called to the witness box, the clerk handed out copies of the printed list of items found in Battlecrease House. Mrs Maybrick was given one. She immediately began to mark it with her pencil.

The bottle of Valentine's meat juice was introduced as an exhibit. The analyst said that he had found arsenic in it, and that he believed it had been put in in solution, because it contained no solid arsenic.

There was much squirming for better view and much lifting of opera glasses when the chemist came to the bottle, containing arsenic in a black powder, which was wrapped in a handkerchief.

The identification of bottles became so confused that the judge ordered Inspector Baxendale into the witness box to stand beside the witness. Then Mr Davies, with the inspector's help, identified the hatbox bottle with its twelve to fifteen grains of solid arsenic in powdered charcoal, another containing a saturated solution of arsenic with solid arsenic at the bottom, a bottle from Humphrey Jones, chemist in Llangollen, with ten to twelve grains of solid arsenic, the tumbler from the hatbox, with thirty to forty grains, and the packet of 'Arsenic. Poison for cats' from the chocolate box, which contained sixty-five grains of arsenic in charcoal powder. Mr Davies then described his tests of the utensils from Maybrick's office, in which he found distinct crystals of arsenic.

Next, the chemist turned to a large tin box. From it he lifted a dressing gown. Though wrinkled and soiled, it was clearly of fashionable cut. The chemist said it was Mrs Maybrick's and that he had received it from Inspector Baxendale on 1st July.

The courtroom buzzed. No dressing gown had been produced at the Coroner's Inquest or at the Magistrates' Court hearing. All eyes turned to the defence table. Sir Charles and Mr Pickford were clearly surprised to see the gown.

The chemist said that he had found traces of arsenic in the pocket of the gown. As to the handkerchief in the pocket, he said, 'I steeped the handkerchief in dilute acid. I found two one-hundredths of a grain of arsenic in the whole handkerchief.' Producing an apron and testifying that it had accompanied the gown, he added that he had found a trace of arsenic in the apron as well.

Observant spectators noted that Mrs Maybrick followed the chemist's testimony with more intense interest than she had showed for any other witness. They could see that she made many notes along the margin of the printed list.

Mr Richard Cleaver handed a note up to Mrs Maybrick. She wrote an answer and spoke to the matron beside her, who handed her an envelope. She sealed her answer in the envelope and passed it down to Mr Cleaver.

For the first time since the description of the post mortem examination, Mrs Maybrick seemed to be in a state of extreme nervous excitement. One matron gave her a glass of water. Another hurried down the stair from the dock, returned with a chair, and sat down close to Mrs Maybrick's armchair. Throughout the afternoon, the prisoner seemed on the verge of swooning.

The judge asked for Frederick Tozer to be recalled. 'Is this the boy, Mr Davies, who gave you the samples from which the prescriptions were made up?'

'This is the gentleman,' said Mr Davies, 'who made up the prescriptions.'

Sir Charles Russell now asked the chemist, 'Does arsenic easily reveal itself?'

'Yes.'

'Have you got the tube showing the crystals you obtained from the liver?'

The witness produced a test tube. Sir Charles said it required a strong magnifying glass to see the film upon the tube. He added that he should like his lordship to see it.

'Oh,' said Mr Davies, 'you can see it distinctly on a black background.'

The judge looked at the tube through an ordinary magnifying glass, then through an extremely powerful one. He said he could not find the film, and asked Sir Charles to show it to him.

Sir Charles did not forget which side of the case he represented. 'You must look for it yourself, my lord.'

Mr Davies offered to help the judge.

'Please, Mr Davies,' said Sir Charles, 'don't volunteer. Remember, you are a witness.'

Mr Justice Stephen tried once more to see the film on the tube. He requisitioned the court chaplain's slate-coloured hat, using its dark background to look for the speck of arsenic.

The courtroom was silent a long moment while the judge examined the tube. At last he passed it to the nearest juryman, along with his two magnifying glasses. He explained that one was much more powerful than the other, and that the more powerful one had to be held so near to the eye, on the one hand, and so close to the object, on the other, that it was almost impossible to manage. Handing tube and glasses from one to another, and holding them this way and that against each other's black coats, the jurymen tried to see the crystals of arsenic.

In cross-examination, Sir Charles said, 'Now, having found arsenic in the liver, and traces in the intestines and kidneys, I want to enumerate in what parts of the body you found no traces.' And he produced a negative reply concerning arsenic in the stomach, the spleen, the bile, some fluid which escaped from the body, the heart and lungs, the bedding, and the clothing.

Sir Charles would let no detail escape. Referring to the arsenic found in the liver, he said, 'You got two one-hundredths of a grain of sulphide of arsenic?'

'Yes.'

'Have you got it with you?'

'No. I converted it into arsenious acid.'

'Well, have you that?'

'I converted that into arsenite of silver.'

'Have you that with you?'

'No. I have not brought it.'

Florence Elizabeth Chandler Maybrick in 1904, after her release from prison. This wistful photograph was published as frontispiece in *Mrs Maybrick's Own Story: My Lost Fifteen Years*, a book Mrs Maybrick had been forbidden to write.

James Maybrick. This photograph of his father was kept by James Chandler Maybrick Fuller throughout his boyhood and young manhood. He took it with him to Canada, settling in Rossland, British Columbia. There young Jim Fuller accidentally drank poison and died within minutes.

Mrs Maybrick. The photograph was taken some time before her arrest and trial. The picture may be the one that was displayed in the shop of a Liverpool photographer during her trial.

Sir James Fitzjames Stephen (Mr Justice Stephen). His two-day charge to the jury may have caused the conviction of Mrs Maybrick more for adultery than for murder.

Sir Charles Russell, who led eloquently for the defence of Mrs Maybrick. He broke
precedent by visiting her in jail before her trial and in prison afterwards. During the
years of her imprisonment, he pleaded often for her release and for changes in the
law of appeal.

Mr John Addison, QC, MP, who led for the prosecution of Mrs Maybrick.

St George's Hall, Liverpool. On these steps and in these streets thousands hissed Mrs Maybrick when she was brought to trial. Within days, the same crowds cheered her and her counsel Sir Charles Russell, and hissed Mr Justice Stephen, then demonstrated again and again to demand her release.

Wednesday

Dearest
Your letter under cover
to John C— came to hand, just
after I had written to you on
Monday. I did not expect to
hear from you so soon & had delayed
in giving him the necessary
instructions. Since my return
I have been nursing day &
night — he is sick unto death.
The doctors held a consultation
yesterday & now all depends
upon how long his strength
will hold out. Both my
brothers-in-law are here & all
are terribly anxious. I cannot
answer your letter fully to day
my darling, but relieve your
mind of all fear of discovery
he has been delirious since
Sunday, & I know now that
he is perfectly ignorant of everything even
as to the name of the Street & that he has not been making

The letter to Brierley. Dropped in the mud by little Gladys Maybrick, read by Nurse Alice Yapp, it was the key piece of circumstantial evidence against Mrs Maybrick.

The Baroness von Roques. Southern American and twice widowed, she was separated from her third husband. She had been a powerful influence on her daughter, Mrs Maybrick; for fifteen years she fought unsuccessfully for Mrs Maybrick's release from prison.

The face-wash prescription. Found by the Baroness von Roques in her daughter's Bible long after her conviction, it provided substantiation of Mrs Maybrick's trial statement – too late.

James Chandler Maybrick Fuller. A photograph published in Rossland, British Columbia, newspapers after his tragic death.

Gladys Maybrick Fuller. The last picture of her daughter that Mrs Maybrick received
in prison before her son forbade communication with her. Mrs Maybrick kept this
photo with her for more than 45 years, until her death.

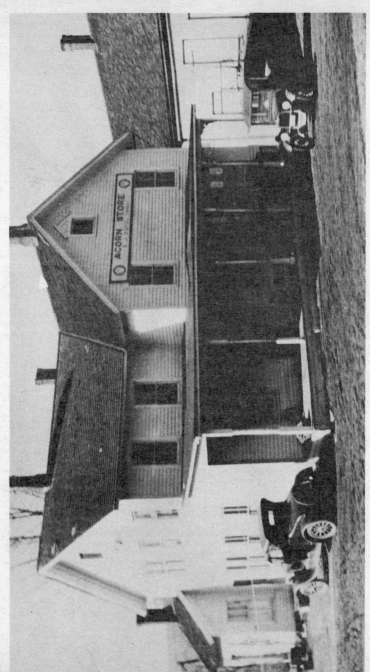

Rob Boyd's Acorn Store, South Kent, Connecticut, in the winter of 1928–1929. Here Mrs Chandler bought provisions for herself and her growing number of cats, and received her mail, during the last fifteen years of her life. The store was a long walk (a mile and a half) from her cottage.

Mrs Chandler at age 77 in September, 1939. An avid reader, she received the *New York Times* daily through the mail, her subscription maintained by a friend from twenty years earlier. Probably the copy of *Life* magazine was given to her by South Kent School Nurse Amy Lyon.

Mrs Chandler's cottage near Gaylordsville, Connecticut, in 1922. She captioned this snapshot, 'The Cat.'

Mrs Chandler's cottage, a few days after her death in October, 1941.

'You can bring it tomorrow, I suppose?'

'Yes, but it has turned black now.'

'Never mind. Bring it.'

Now Sir Charles asked about the small bottle which contained a weak solution of arsenic in a light liquid with some scent, as if it was scented water. He tried to get the witness to agree that it might have been used for toilet purposes, and that the handkerchief found round the bottle in the chocolate box might have contained a rouge stain. In each case, Davies only generally agreed.

Sir Charles went on. 'The next thing I wish to call your attention to is part of the contents of the wooden box that was under the hatbox – the black powder. Did you come to the conclusion that that was carbonised arsenic?'

'It was a mixture of powdered charcoal and arsenic.'

'Is it not the fact that arsenic is sold mixed with soot or carbon?'

'It ought to be mixed with soot or indigo. But this is not in exact compliance with the Act. It is neither soot nor indigo.'

Having established that the powdered charcoal and arsenic was not prepared according to regulations for public sale, Sir Charles now made a passing reference to Mrs Maybrick's dressing gown. 'A handkerchief soaked and put into the pocket of a dressing gown would leave traces of arsenic in the pockets?'

'It would leave a great deal more. I believe what was found in the pocket did come from the handkerchief.'

The gallery now expected some reference to Mrs Maybrick's using arsenic as a cosmetic. But Sir Charles asked no more questions about the dressing gown. Instead, he returned to the analysis of Maybricks' liver, the only organ in which arsenic was found in a weighable amount. 'You have told us what would be the entire quantity of the entire liver from the fractional portion you dealt with?'

'What I found would amount to an eighth of a grain.'

'But you did not find one-eighth of a grain. You found two one-hundredths of a grain of sulphide of arsenic in the six ounces?'

'Yes.'

'And assuming that the arsenic was distributed equally over the entire liver, it would amount to one-eighth of a grain?'

'Yes. It was one-half of what I found in the case of Margaret Jennings, and that was half of the smallest amount I have ever known.'

'Who was Margaret Jennings?'

'One of the women poisoned by Mrs Flanagan.'

'And you found double the amount in her liver?'

'The quantity I found was four one-hundredths of a grain, but in that case there was no bismuth to make the analysis more difficult. I got the whole quantity in the other case, and in this case I believe I only got about half.'

'Have you ever until this moment said you did not get more than half?'

'Yes, at the Coroner's Court. I said I believed I did not get more than half.'

Sir Charles turned to the counsel table and picked up a sheaf of papers. 'Is not this what you said, "I believe that to be the minimum quantity, because the process of separation necessarily involves some loss"?'

'I do not know the exact words, but I said words to that effect.'

As Mr Davies stepped down from the stand, the gallery buzzed. One-half of one-half meant that the analyst had found only one quarter of the smallest amount of arsenic he had ever known in a fatal case. The evidence scored well for the defence.

In the courtroom, it was now nearly six o'clock. Upon adjournment, it seemed likely that the prosecution's case would be completed next day. As the spectators crowded out of the courtroom, Mrs Maybrick was led down the stairway. For the first time since the trial began, she leaned heavily on the arm of one of her matrons.

In the evening the Cleaver brothers found their office in a state of pandemonium. Clerks and secretaries did not know what to do. Letters and telegrams had been arriving all day from all over England, offering encouragement to Mrs Maybrick and advice to her solicitors. They were piled up everywhere, and the post office kept delivering more. To read them all was impossible. To answer them was out of the question.

Mr Richard Cleaver asked the morning papers to announce his thanks to all who had written and sent telegrams. He went to bed tired but buoyant with the hope expressed by the countless messages.

X

*'I share the anxious duty of defending,
upon the most serious charge that can be preferred,
this friendless lady in the dock.'*

Saturday, 3rd August, 1889

When Sir Charles Russell stepped forth from the North Western Hotel on Saturday morning, he was roundly cheered by a large crowd. The number of men in the throng seemed to have increased, perhaps because it was a Saturday morning. The lawyer found an even larger mass awaiting him at St George's Hall, and again they let him know that he had their enthusiastic approval.

Others who came to St George's were not in such good favour. The witnesses who had testified for the prosecution, all of whom were easily recognised by those who had occupied gallery seats, found themselves booed and hooted at. Nurse Yapp was called a variety of opprobious names. Alfred Brierley was generally hissed as he hurried up the steps.

The procession trumpeters outdid their earlier triumphs by playing a lively Welsh air, *'Jennie Jones'*. It was remarkably inappropriate. The gallery, crowded with more men than women for the first time since the trial began, wondered audibly who was responsible for the trumpeters' selection.

The spectators were treated to more entertainment when the judge spoke. 'I have received a letter from Messrs Clay and Abraham, chemists, in reference to a witness who appeared yesterday. It seems I spoke of a witness named Tozer as a boy.'

The knowing nudged each other. They remembered the judge saying, 'Is this the boy, Mr Davies, who gave you the samples of the various ingredients from which the samples were made up?' And they remembered Mr Davies's emphatic reply, 'This is the gentleman who made up the prescriptions.'

The judge went on: 'He is very much more than a boy, being over thirty years of age, and has, moreover, had much experience in his business in both London and Paris, and holds a certificate of the Pharmaceutical Society, empowering him to carry on business on his own account. Of all that I was unaware. I heartily apologise to him, as I don't wish to hurt any young man's feelings.'

All eyes found Mr Tozer, a slight and boyish-looking gentleman who added to his youthful appearance by turning bright red and trying to hold back a sheepish grin.

Now Sir Charles Russell asked Nurse Gore for precise detail on the bottle of meat juice, making sure it had been opened by no one before her, and establishing that after Mrs Maybrick handled it none was given to the patient.

Mr Justice Stephen cleared his throat and interrupted, addressing the witness. 'I understand you to say that you had put out some stock in water, tasted it yourself, and then you gave him some?'

'Yes.'

Sir Charles was dismayed at the judge's confusion. 'That was before this incident, my lord,' he said, 'and before Mrs Maybrick took it in.'

'Yes,' said Nurse Gore.

Sir Charles took a deep breath. 'Let us go back on that.' He questioned the nurse about how she prepared the diluted meat juice from the new bottle and fed the patient before Mrs Maybrick took the bottle to the dressing room. Then, referring to Nurse Gore's warning to Nurse Callery not to give Mr Maybrick anything from that bottle, he said, 'I think it is quite clear that the person to whom the communication you referred to was made was Nurse Callery?'

'Yes.'

The judge now revealed that he was confused as to whether Mrs Maybrick was carried into the spare bedroom before her husband died, or afterward.

Mr Addison re-examined the nurse. 'You said something about your suspicions. What was it that excited your suspicion?'

Sir Charles pushed his chair back from the counsel table and rose as he spoke. 'I really must object to that question. She has told us what she saw.'

Mr Addison shrugged. 'My friend has cross-examined about the suspicions.' He turned back to his witness. 'The bottle of meat juice was taken away out of the room and brought back. Now, what made you suspicious?'

Sir Charles was insistent. 'Well, really, Mr Addison, I can't allow that.'

'I'm very sorry,' said the prosecutor, 'but she has told us what she saw.'

The judge at last took a hand in the debate. 'Her manner excited suspicion in taking away the Valentine's meat juice. What was it in her manner?'

'She did not take it openly,' said Nurse Gore.

'How did she take it?' asked the judge.

'She took it in her left hand, and covered it with her right hand.'

'Yes,' said Mr Addison, 'and then?'

'She brought it back with her right hand on my other side.'

The judge spoke again. 'Was it in such a position when she brought it back that you could see it openly?'

'I could see her put it on the table, but she had it in her hand by her side.'

When the name of Alfred Schweisso rang out in the courtroom, a rapt silence fell over all. Mr McConnell examined, and the waiter identified Mrs Maybrick as the lady who had come to Flatman's Hotel on Thursday, 21st March, to occupy the house's finest bedroom and adjoining sitting room. 'Was there any gentleman called to see the lady, in the afternoon of that day?' asked Mr McConnell.

'Yes, sir.'

'What time?' asked the judge, his pencil poised over his notepaper.

'About half-past six.'

The assistant prosecutor learned that Schweisso did not see Mrs Maybrick again until Friday morning, when he took breakfast to the sitting room. There he saw a gentleman in the room with Mrs Maybrick. It was not the gentleman who had called the previous evening.

'At what time would that be?' asked the judge.

'About half-past nine.'

The witness was asked to identify the gentleman. His eyes swept the gallery, finding Alfred Brierley in a seat high up near the back. That, he said, was the gentleman, and he pointed to him.

Schweisso now testified, amid breath-holding silence, that Brierley had occupied the same bedroom, in which there was only one bed, as Mrs Maybrick. They occupied it, he said, until Sunday afternoon. When they left, he added, Mrs Maybrick paid the bill.

'No cross-examination,' said Sir Charles Russell.

The silence broke into a wave of sensational whispering. The defence would take no issue with the waiter's testimony. The adulterous weekend in London was, then, frankly admitted. Curious opera glasses swept from the handsome bearded face at the back of the gallery to the pale round

veiled face in the dock, and back again. The two who were on exhibit
stared into space, seeming oblivious to the titillation brought to the crowd
by the testimony of Alfred Schweisso.

Dr Thomas Stevenson climbed into the witness box. He was identified as
a London toxicologist who had known a great many cases of poisoning
by arsenic, both purposeful and accidental. He told of the eleven vessels
delivered to him by Inspector Baxendale on 30th July, and said that he
found 'about one one-hundredth of a grain' of arsenic in the intestines.
When he mentioned the amount of bismuth he encountered in his tests,
his lordship interrupted.

'Just repeat the quantity of that last, will you?' said the judge.

'That is bismuth, my lord,' said Mr Addison.

'Yes, I know,' said the judge.

Dr Stevenson's testimony went on to state that he had found about a
third of a grain of arsenic and a grain of bismuth for the whole liver.

His lordship spoke again. 'Just tell me how much?'

'One grain,' said the witness.

'What does that result in in your mind?' asked Mr Addison.

'That the body at the time of death probably contained a fatal dose of
arsenic. I have found a little more or a little less than the quantity I did
find here in undoubtedly fatal cases of arsenical poisoning.'

'Have you formed an opinion upon the evidence given?'

'I have.'

'What do you say, doctor?'

'I have no doubt that this man died from the effects of arsenic.'

The words came so rapidly and so dogmatically that they caused an
immediate sensation in the courtroom. The judge glowered for silence.

The witness had been asked for an opinion on a case which he knew
only from listening to trial testimony. Mr Addison continued to take the
witness through the details of the fatal illness, asking him time after time
to draw inferences and express opinions about the symptoms until finally
Sir Charles was driven to object.

The judge ruled, 'I must agree with Sir Charles. There is strong
mystery about all the circumstances, but I think you are going too
minutely into some matters.'

Mr Addison went on. 'Now, the question has been raised whether
gastro-enteritis presents any post mortem appearances?'

'This was a death from gastro-enteritis,' said the doctor. 'It is a special
disease set up by arsenic. I have no knowledge that gastro-enteritis occurs
independent of the introduction of some irritant.'

Once more the prosecutor put the question. 'Taking all the symptoms and appearances before death and after, what do you say was the cause of death?'

'No doubt it was due to arsenical poisoning.'

Sir Charles Russell had sat patiently through nearly an hour of Dr Stevenson's authoritative testimony. Now he rose to question the grounds for that authority. The doctor could not say exactly when he last saw a whole post mortem in a case of arsenical poisoning. He could not name a post mortem more recently than 'some years ago' in which he himself took part. Recalling a case of suicide some years earlier, he said the dose taken was unknown and the amounts of arsenic found in the post mortem had not been analysed.

After nearly ten minutes of searching for positive answers, Sir Charles said, 'I want to know, can you give any case, the circumstances of which you have in your mind, in which you assisted at the post mortem examination?'

'I do not know of any case where I assisted at the post mortem, knew the circumstances, and made the analysis. It is rare with any one.'

'Then you cannot give me a case where death followed the administration of arsenic, where you assisted in the post mortem, and followed this with analysis?'

'Not where any definite known quantity was given.'

'After hearing the history of the case and the result of the post mortem examination, would you withhold any opinion until you had heard the analysis?'

'I should have had a pronounced opinion that the deceased had died from an irritant poison, but I should have been cautious in saying that it was arsenic until it was proved to me in the analysis.'

'Will you indicate any one symptom which is distinctly an arsenical poisoning symptom, and which is not to be found in cases of gastro-enteritis caused by other means than arsenic?'

'There is no distinctive diagnostic symptom of arsenical poisoning. The diagnostic thing is finding the arsenic.'

Sir Charles paused to wipe his brow and take snuff, letting the last words ring in the vaulted ceiling of the courtroom and in the minds of the jurors. Clearly, one might call it arsenical poisoning when one had found arsenic.

Now Sir Charles asked what was the actual weighable quantity of arsenic obtained from the liver. The doctor said the total was seventy-six thousandths of a grain. From the intestines he added fifteen thousandths of a grain, for a total of ninety-one thousandths. Mr Justice Stephen was busy writing down the figures.

Two grains, the defence lawyer reminded the witness, was considered a fatal dose? The analysis had found something less than one twentieth of a fatal dose?

The doctor agreed. He added that no arsenic was found in the contents of the stomach, nor in the bile, the fluid from the mouth of the deceased, the spleen, the heart or the lungs.

Doctor Stevenson stepped down. Mr Addison rose to announce that the evidence for the prosecution was closed.

Mr Justice Stephen adjourned the court and, with what appetites they could muster, the principals, the court attendants and those in the gallery who had not brought picnic baskets went out to lunch.

'Gentlemen of the jury, with Mr Pickford I share the very anxious duty of defending, upon the most serious charge that can be preferred, this friendless lady in the dock. And as I shall have an opportunity at the close of the entire evidence to address you again, I propose at this stage to say but few words.'

So began Sir Charles Russell's opening speech for the defence of Florence Maybrick. It was a speech for which the gallery had long waited and to which still more followers of the trial tried to gain admission. Word had gone round at lunch time that the prosecution had closed, and those unwise enough to have left gallery seats in search of food hurried back, some in time to regain their places and some to find them already occupied. Attendants who had previously been unyielding in their interpretation of the rules took into consideration the fact that it was Saturday afternoon and that Sir Charles was opening for the defence. They permitted standing in the aisles and sitting upon the steps and crowding in the doorways so that as many of the crowd as possible could hear one of England's greatest advocates.

'Gentlemen,' he continued, 'the question that will be put to you by my lord will be whether Florence Maybrick is guilty or not guilty of the charge here preferred against her, that charge being the deliberate and cruel murder of her husband. Two questions must enter into your consideration – was it a death by arsenical poisoning? If it were, was that poison administered by his wife? Whatever cloud of doubt and mystery may surround the case, nothing short of the deliberate opinion that you can arrive at one conclusion, and one conclusion only, will justify you in pronouncing the verdict which must snap the thread of this poor woman's life.'

Sir Charles looked at the Maybrick brothers. 'It is an extraordinary fact that, although from Wednesday, the eighth of May, this lady was deposed from the position of mistress in her own house, no adequate search or inquiry was made. For it does not seem that there was any one manly enough, friendly enough, honest enough, to go to her and make to her a statement of the charge against her, in order to see whether she had any explanation to offer. The only approach was when she was formally charged by the policeman, which would afford no opportunity except for a mere denial or admission.

'Gentlemen, the further question comes : Granted that arsenic was in Mr Maybrick's body, was it that which caused his death?' Sir Charles promised to produce well qualified opinion that it was not.

Sir Charles now turned to the next question. 'If you should come to the conclusion that this was death due to arsenical poison, does this prove to you that the lady in the dock was the administrator of the poison? The only evidence showing the acquisition by the prisoner of any substance containing poison is the evidence of the chemists Wokes and Hanson as to selling her flypapers. That arsenic was in the house is undeniable, that arsenic was in the house in such quantities as to indicate that at some time there was a considerably large quantity is undeniable. How comes it, then, that, after all the publicity that this case has had, there is no attempt to prove any suggestion that at any time, at any place, from any person, under any circumstances, Florence Maybrick purchased substances which were poisonous, except in this instance of flypapers?'

Sir Charles seemed to have finished outlining the case for the defence. He paused to gather his thoughts. 'I presume my lord will follow the course which he has followed on similar occasions, namely, treating the statement of the prisoner as evidence for the defence, and will allow her to make a statement.'

Sir Charles was asking for something that was not permitted in English courts of law : for the accused person, in effect, to give informal testimony. Mr Justice Stephen understood, for he had long advocated change of the laws which denied this right to the accused. He said he would allow the prisoner to make a statement, but that she could not be sworn, nor could she be questioned about it.

Sir Charles suggested that she address the court from notes.

Mr Justice Stephen said that all judges refused this, but that several practised what he now proposed – that she be allowed to say whatever she pleased. But he could not go so far as to permit her to write it down.

'I think it would meet your lordship's views,' said Sir Charles, 'that no one should communicate with her between this and Monday morning.'

The judge agreed. 'Then let it be regarded as an order to the persons who are in charge of her. If she likes to make notes, by all means let her do so.'

Sir Charles now underlined the judge's dissatisfaction with the law's refusal to allow a defendant to give evidence. 'In the interests of justice, in the interests of innocence if there is innocence, in the interests of penal justice if there be guilt, the prisoner should have the opportunity of making a statement under such solemn sanction as evidence is ordinarily given – ay, and I will go further, and of having that statement tested in open court by cross-examination. It is an extraordinary statement, which will need every scrutiny and examination by you, in relation to which you will have to ask yourselves the question, If it be not a true statement, how comes it that the woman, who might make other excuses and explanations, comes to make that?'

Then Sir Charles said that only one concluding observation remained. 'I refer to that dark cloud that passed over her life, and rests upon her character as a woman and a wife. But I would entreat you not to allow any repugnance resting in your minds against a sin so abhorrent as that to lead you to the conclusion, unless the evidence drives you irresistibly there, that, because a wife has forgotten her duty and faithfulness to her husband, she is to be regarded as one who deliberately and wickedly will seek to destroy his life.'

Sir Charles turned and moved slowly to the defence table. The effort of expressing his deep concern for his client, coming in the afternoon of the fourth long hot day of the trial, had obviously drained him. He sat down wearily, wiping his brow and his chin, then slowly and deliberately taking snuff.

Mr Pickford stood and asked the clerk to call Mr Nicholas Bateson as the first defence witness. Bateson was a Liverpudlian who was in the cotton business in America. From 1877 to 1881, he said, he had shared bachelor quarters in Norfolk with James Maybrick. He remembered that in 1877 Mr Maybrick had malarial fever, and that on prescription from Dr Ward of Norfolk he had taken arsenic and strychnine for about three months. 'He constantly rubbed the back of his hands in the morning,' said Bateson, 'and complained of numbness in his hands and limbs.'

Mr Addison cross-examined, and learned that quinine had first been prescribed for Maybrick but that it had no effect on his malaria and so arsenic was given.

Mr Pickford re-examined. Referring to the arsenic, he said, 'What you mean is this, that it cured him of malaria, but the symptoms of rubbing of the hands and numbness were left?'

'These symptoms increased.'

Sir Charles Russell rose to question the next witness. The gallery now saw a sight common to the waterfront but not the courtroom : the solid figure, the rolling gait, the weathered hands and face of a man who had spent forty years at sea. He climbed nimbly into the witness box. He was Captain Robert Thompson, the master mariner who had landed in Liverpool a few weeks ago, read of the Maybrick mystery, and made himself known to Mr Pickford.

Under questioning, Captain Thompson explained how he had met Mr Maybrick in 1880 when he transported two hunting dogs from Liverpool to Norfolk for Mr Bateson. One day when he and Maybrick were on the way to have a drink together, Maybrick stopped in a Main Street druggist's and said, 'I want my *desideratum.*' Without question, the druggist's assistant handed Maybrick two powders.

'Did you hear the assistant say anything?' asked Sir Charles.

'My lord,' interrupted Mr Addison, 'I object to what a druggist's assistant said being received – an unknown assistant in an unknown shop in Virginia, years ago.'

'It will be followed up by other evidence,' said Sir Charles.

'I think it safer,' said the judge, 'to take the evidence offered.'

Sir Charles put the question again. 'What did he say to him?'

' "It's all right, Colonel Maybrick." One of the packets was a white paper and the other a yellow paper. He put his finger on the yellow paper, and said, "Now, Mr Maybrick, be careful." That is all I heard him say.'

The captain now told of returning alone to the druggist's a few days later. He said that the assistant recognised him and made a statement to him. Soon afterward, Maybrick visited the captain in his cabin aboard ship.

'Now,' said Sir Charles, 'did you say anything to Mr Maybrick as to what was told you by the assistant in the druggist's shop?'

'We were on familiar terms, and I took the liberty of speaking to him about taking this arsenic.'

Mr Justice Stephen interposed. 'What did you tell him?'

'I said, "I believe, Mr Maybrick, you are in the habit of taking a dangerous and noxious drug." He said, "What is that?" I said, "Arsenic." And he said, "Who the devil told you?" I said, "I asked the druggist's assistant, and he told me you are in the habit of taking it." And he said, "Damn his impudence." '

One of the jurymen spoke up. 'Did you know this shop before?'

'I had been there once before.'

Sir Charles resumed his examination. 'Did you have any further conversation with him on the arsenic?'

'No, he was very touchy on the subject, so I dropped it. He neither admitted nor denied taking it.'

Sir Charles sat down. Mr Addison declined to cross-examine.

Now came Thomas Stansell, the waiter found at St James's Hotel in Norfolk by Mr Cleaver. He testified that he had been engaged as a servant to Mr James Maybrick and Mr Bateson when they lived together in York Street, Norfolk, from 1878 to 1880. Two weeks after he was first in their service, he said, Mr Maybrick gave him fifty cents and told him to stop at the druggist's and get him some arsenic.

'And did you go to the druggist's?' asked Sir Charles.

'Yes, sir.'

'Were you asked who it was for?'

'Yes.'

'Did you state?'

'Yes. I said, for Mr Maybrick.'

'Did you get it?'

'Yes.'

'What did you get?' asked Sir Charles, opening his snuffbox and taking a pinch of snuff.

'A very small package. Not as long as the box you have in your hand.'

Stansell now described how Mr Maybrick told him to make beef tea. Maybrick put a bit of the arsenic into the tea and stirred it. Sometimes, added the witness, he was told to get the arsenic in a bottle and sometimes in paper.

Additional testimony described Maybrick's habit of rubbing his hands and limbs after taking arsenic, and told of his many medicines.

Mr Addison chose to cross-examine this witness. His questions served only to add detail to what the servant had already told. 'Did you take a prescription to the chemist, or had he a prescription already?' asked the prosecutor.

'I did not take one. He told me to go to the druggist, and he gave me half a dollar.'

'What did he tell you to get?'

'To get arsenic.'

'Did he tell you how much?'

'No.'

'Did the chemist know?'

'He seemed to know very well.'

'Without any trouble?'

'Yes.'

'Did he seem to be well after taking his beef tea?'

'No, sir. He didn't seem to be very well, sir.'

When Mr Addison had finished, Sir Charles put one more question. It showed his eye for detail. 'When you asked for half a dollar's worth of arsenic, did you get any change?'

'No.'

Edwin Garnett Heaton was the next witness. For thirty-seven years, he said, he had been a registered chemist in Liverpool. He had retired a year ago. When he saw Maybrick's picture in the papers at the time of the coroner's inquest, he recognised him as a customer who had come in regularly for ten years to get his 'pick-me-up', a tonic indulged in by many members of the Exchange. He recollected Maybrick first giving him a prescription which changed the tonic by adding liquor arsenicalis.

'After the first few times,' he said, 'I used to give it to him at once. I used to receive the order merely by a motion or sign by him.'

Mr Heaton now testified that over a period of time the amount of liquor arsenicalis increased by about seventy-five per cent, from four drops to seven, and that Maybrick stopped in for it as often as two to five times a day.

'He gave you a reason why he wished it?'

'Yes.'

'Do you know that liquor arsenicalis has aphrodisiacal qualities?'

The chemist hesitated.

'Do you know that word?'

'I do not.'

Mr Justice Stephen leaned toward the witness. 'Did it excite passion?'

'Yes, sir, it had that effect.'

Sir Charles went on. The jury learned that when Maybrick was going away from home the chemist often made up eight or sixteen doses.

Cross-examining, Mr Addison set out to show there was no proof of Maybrick having been Heaton's customer, as his name was not in the chemist's books. Heaton insisted that he had recognised Maybrick when he saw his likeness in the *Liverpool Echo*. The druggist made it clear that many gentlemen from the Exchange had regularly taken liquor arsenicalis in their pick-me-ups, that seven drops would be seven-hundredths of a grain, and that he saw it do nobody, including Maybrick, any harm. When Sir Charles re-examined, Mr Heaton agreed that only a fraction of his many customers had liquor arsenicalis in their pick-me-ups, that whether it was harmful would depend upon the frequency of the taking, and that seven drops five times a day would equal one-third of a grain of white arsenic daily.

When the chemist stepped down, neither prosecution nor defence had noticed that proof that Maybrick had been his customer was present in the courtroom. It was held in the hands of the accused, among others. For in the printed list of items received by Edward Davies was one, bottle Number 10 among those found locked up in Mr Maybrick's private desk in his office, labelled 'Spirits of salvolatile. Edwin G. Easton, Exchange Street East, Liverpool. Contents: light-coloured liquid.' The Edwin G. Easton of the list and the Edwin G. Heaton now returning to the witness room were one and the same. Careless handwriting by a policeman compiling the list had changed the spelling of the chemist's name.

Dr J. Drysdale next told of Maybrick's several visits to him since the previous November, of his continuous headaches and frequent numbness of hand and leg, of his hypochondriacal self-dosing with nitro-hydro-chloric acid, strychnine, hydrate of potash and other drugs, and of his nervous dyspepsia.

William J. Thomson identified himself as a copper smelter at St Helens, and said that he knew the late Mr Maybrick and had seen him at the Wirral races. He quoted Maybrick as saying, when Thomson remarked that he seemed unable to control his horse, that he had taken a double dose of medicine that morning and felt unwell.

Wholesale druggist John Thompson told of employing a Maybrick cousin, and of Maybrick asking him to take the man back after he had been discharged. The cousin, he said, had access to all the drugs. Maybrick used to visit him in the warehouse, where he would have had not the slightest difficulty if he wanted to get drugs.

Saturday afternoon was drawing in upon the courtroom. Barrister, juryman and spectator alike were hot and tired from four days of testimony, much of it repetitious and almost all of it precise as to medical detail. No one would have asked for another expert witness at this point – no one, that is, except Sir Charles Russell. Having borne almost the entire weight of cross-examination and now of examination of the thirty-seven witnesses called thus far, and determined not to let the jury spend Sunday thinking about the case without having heard medical testimony for the defence, Sir Charles called Charles Meymott Tidy.

Dr Tidy was one of the highest authorities on medical and chemical jurisprudence in Great Britain. He was an Examiner of Forensic Medicine at the London Hospital and, like Dr Stevenson, was employed as an analyst by the Home Office. Since 1862, he testified, he had assisted at nearly a thousand post mortems, including some forty cases of arsenical poisoning.

Sir Charles asked if it were true that some symptoms might be missing in cases of arsenical poisoning.

'I fancy this is due,' said the doctor, 'to the fact that there is an infinitely greater number of cases of arsenical poisoning than of any other, and the result is that the anomalies become more apparent in the case of arsenical poisoning.'

The doctor said he had followed every detail in the case and read all the depositions. Asked about the account of the vomiting, he said that it was not the kind of vomiting that takes place in a typical case of arsenical poisoning. He would have expected diarrhoea long before it was reported – within two hours after the dose. He was aware, in addition, that there was no mention of pain in the stomach until the eve of the death of the patient. 'As a matter of fact,' said Sir Charles, 'exceptional cases where pain in the stomach and abdomen are wanting are excessively rare, far more than vomiting and purging?'

'I venture to call that a toxicological curiosity,' said the doctor.

Two or three members of the gallery tittered, and the strain of the day's listening was broken. General laughter followed. Sir Charles seemed displeased. He went on: 'You have never known a case in which there was absence of this distinctive symptom?'

'No. No case has ever come before me.'

'Taking the whole of the symptoms which have been before the post mortem and analysis, could any one, in your judgment, safely suggest to us arsenical poisoning?'

The doctor was careful. 'I can only speak for myself in the case.'

'And you say undoubtedly that these are not the symptoms of arsenical poisoning, nor do they point to such?'

'Certainly not.'

Sir Charles now turned to the post mortem appearances. To describe the internal redness which would be found over the entire stomach, the doctor introduced a drawing he had made from a cast of a stomach. The drawing was handed up to the bench, and the doctor pointed out small blots of redness called petechiae, which were found in no case of irritant poison except arsenic.

The witness now testified that, from the description he had heard and from the post mortem notes he had seen, there was no suggestion of such an appearance in Maybrick's case. The appearances of the stomach were, he said, perfectly consistent with death from gastro-enteritis.

'And not caused by arsenical poisoning at all?'

'Yes.'

Sir Charles questioned his witness carefully about the finding of traces of arsenic in the kidneys and of a certain weighable quantity in the liver and intestines.

Dr Tidy seemed quite sure of his ground. 'To take a certain quantity of the intestines and to find a certain quantity of arsenic, and then multiply by the weight of the entire intestines, is certainly not an assumption which is accurate. I happen to know that arsenic is not equally distributed over the intestines.'

'Therefore, to work out the calculation of the presence of those three-tenths of a grain of arsenic in the liver is wrong?'

'Yes.'

'The result of your view is that some of the symptoms found here are consistent – I think I may use the word here – with arsenical poisoning, but not distinctive of it?'

'That is so. Tenesmus and such are consistent.'

'But as regards the symptoms?'

'There is the absence of three or four of the leading symptoms. And if I had been called upon, I should have said it was undoubtedly not arsenical poisoning.'

'Is that view strengthened by the post mortem?'

'Very much strengthened. The post mortem has very much strengthened my view.'

'What conclusion have you come to as to the cause of death?'

'That it is due to gastro-enteritis of some kind or another, but that the symptoms of the post mortem distinctly point away from arsenic.'

Sir Charles sat down.

Mr Addison's cross-examination began with definitions. 'He died from an irritant poison?'

'Yes, an irritant. It becomes a question as to what precise meaning you attach to the word "poison".'

'We won't be very particular,' said the prosecutor, 'but what meaning do you attach to it?'

'It is a body which, introduced into the system, is capable of destroying life, either by chemical action on certain tissues of the body, or by a physiological action on the tissues of the living system.' The doctor added that pins or powdered glass kill but are not poison.

The doctor could not be budged from his firm refusal to use the word 'poison'. 'He died from gastro-enteritis,' said Mr Addison, 'caused by an irritant?'

'Yes.'

'It was some strong irritant, probably poison?'

'Some substance which to him acted as an irritant.'

'Which was poisonous enough to kill him?'

'Which to him acted as an irritant.'

'Can you suggest to us what it was?'

'No, I cannot.'

'What would you attribute intense thirst with a sense of hair tickling all the time to?'

'Something disagreeable in the stomach.'

'Is it due to poison of some kind?'

'Oh, dear, no.'

'An intense dry and glazed throat occur in arsenical poisoning. Do they occur in anything else?'

'Oh, dear, yes. With any irritant.'

'That is to say, any irritant poison on the stomach would produce them?'

'Any irritant *substance*.' The doctor gently emphasised the last word.

'You say it was not a typical case of arsenical poisoning?'

'I say that it is not only not typical, but absolutely points away from arsenic as the cause of death.'

Sir Charles Russell rose to ask a few more questions of his witness. He wanted to clinch just two points. 'As regards the question of dryness and thirst in the throat and gullet,' he said, 'do you find that also in many other illnesses?'

'Yes.'

'In no sense is it distinctive of arsenical poisoning?'

'Not at all.'

'Do you remember Dr Humphreys's evidence, where he said that he put the faeces and the urine in hydrochloric acid cold, and kept them there until it boiled, and then inserted a copper foil?'

'Yes.'

'Could you say if there had been any arsenic there that he would have found a deposit?'

'He would probably have got it instantaneously, if there had been an appreciable quantity.'

Sir Charles excused his witness. He looked at his watch, glanced toward the prisoner in the dock, and turned to the bench. 'In reference to an application that I made, I understood his lordship to say that the prisoner was to have no communication with any one outside between now and Monday.'

'I think that is understood,' said Mr Justice Stephen.

Although it was now six o'clock on Saturday evening, the spectators seemed less anxious than on previous days to crush each other in emptying the gallery. Many lingered to gaze at the prisoner as she was escorted down the stairway from the dock, and, as her silent and sombre image lingered there, some stared long after she had gone. A certain wistfulness hung about them.

In a pub near the Lime Street Station that evening, Alfred Schweisso ordered refreshment while waiting for his London train. He was recognised by an Irishman who, on behalf of Sir Charles Russell and Mrs Maybrick, knocked out three of his teeth.

XI

*'Because she sinned once is she, therefore,
to be misjudged always?'*

Monday, 5th August, 1889

It happened to be a general holiday throughout England. Mill, office and bank were closed, but St George's Hall in Liverpool was open. The crowds in Lime Street were the largest yet. Many had come from Manchester and Birmingham, some from London. In their Sunday papers they had read accounts now favourable to Mrs Maybrick. She was innocent, the correspondents of newspapers all over England had written after hearing the first defence witnesses on Saturday, and would be found so.

Liverpudlians, on the other hand, were still reading of her guilt. The local journalists, deeply entrenched in their longstanding knowledge-ability about the Maybrick Mystery, saw no reason to change their opinions.

Inside St George's Hall, Mr Richard Cleaver hurried to the witness room and looked for the housemaid, Bessie Brierley. Had it not been among her duties at Battlecrease House, he asked, to brush the clothes? It had. Well then, he asked, could she say whether Mr Maybrick's clothes were wet on the day of the Wirral races?

The housemaid tossed her head. She had given evidence on one side, she said, and she was not going to give any on the other.

Mrs Maybrick arrived in the black van from Walton Jail. She had been permitted no visitors all day Sunday. She seemed more pale than on Saturday, but her step was firm, her manner composed. She carried a roll of blue foolscap.

Sir Charles Russell continued the case for the defence by calling Dr Rawdon Macnamara, professor of Materia Medica at the Royal College of Surgeons of Ireland, and author of a standard work on the action of medicine. The doctor said that he had administered arsenic in many cases, frequently to the point of saturation. 'Hawking,' he said, indicated inflammation of the stomach rather than arsenical poisoning, while the sensation of a hair in the throat was unknown in the case of arsenic. And he had never known of pain in the thighs in cases of saturation or over-saturation with arsenic.

'Now,' Sir Charles concluded, 'bringing your best judgment to bear upon the matter, in your opinion was this a death from arsenical poisoning?'

'Certainly not,' said Dr Macnamara.

Mr Addison's first question confirmed the opinion. 'As you have listened to the case,' said the prosecutor, 'will you tell me what he died of?'

'To the best of my judgment and belief, he died of gastro-enteritis, not connected with arsenical poisoning.' The doctor added that he believed there could be outside circumstances which would result in gastro-enteritis.

'But do outside circumstances mean, taking something that produces it?'

'Oh, dear, no,' said the doctor. 'The case of a person troubled with a weak stomach – suppose dyspepsia – exposed to wet for some time, and not taking proper care against getting wet; the result is, that the blood is driven to the internal organs – amongst others, the stomach – and there produces congestion. And if, by any accident, such a patient committed any error of diet, the result would be gastro-enteritis – a gastritis that would extend down to the bowels, constituting the congestion of the stomach and of the bowels. A wetting, coupled with neglect of precautions and a weak stomach and circulation, may produce these consequences.'

'Do you mean that by getting wet this illness of gastro-enteritis – this acute inflammation, may be produced in the stomach and bowels?'

The Irish doctor looked steadily at the prosecutor. 'That, I think, is the evidence I have given.'

'In saying that gastro-enteritis would be produced by a man with a weak stomach getting wet, do you understand that to be the opinion of Dr Tidy as well?'

'I do not. Dr Tidy can speak for himself.'

'Do you agree or disagree with him?'

The doctor was not to be put into such a corner. 'Will you kindly tell me what Dr Tidy said?'

'Did you hear him?'

'I have heard so much that it would be very hard to tax my memory.'

'Dr Tidy said gastro-enteritis was produced by the introduction of some foreign substance into the stomach, producing the effect of an irritant.'

'I bow to Dr Tidy as a toxicologist, but not as a general practitioner.'

The judge leaned toward the witness. 'Please answer the question. Do you agree with him or not?'

'I do not,' said the doctor without hesitation.

Sir Charles re-examined. 'Assume a case where there was a chronic weakness of the stomach, in the case of a man who had been taking various drugs, and who in that condition gets a wetting, such as that described, is a man in that condition the more liable from a slight cause to have set up in his system this gastro-enteritis?'

'Yes. The weakest spot invariably suffers.'

'For instance, when you speak of cold or wet driving the blood to the parts and congesting, would it drive it to the weakest part?'

'Yes, to the lungs if they were, and the stomach if it was.'

Following the doctor came a Liverpool professor, Frank Thomas Paul, who taught Medical Jurisprudence at University College and was Examiner in Forensic Medicine and Toxicology at Victoria University. After establishing his witness's authority, Sir Charles asked, 'In your judgment, do you say this is a case of arsenical poisoning?'

'I think it is a case of gastro-enteritis. The post mortem appearances do not show that it was set up by arsenic.'

'If, in the case of a man who had been complaining for a considerable number of years of what you would call chronic dyspepsia, who had been drugging himself, or had been drugged, following the occurrences we heard of on the day of Wirral races – take the case of such a man, would a slighter cause be sufficient in such a man to set up gastro-enteritis than in a man perfectly well?'

'Certainly. Such a case in such a man would be more likely to be fatal.'

Mr Addison rose to cross-examine, and immediately got into a discussion with Sir Charles and the judge over whether the day of the Wirral races was wet.

The cross-examination proceeded. 'Have you any doubt that inflammation of the stomach was there?'

'Surely he would have complained of it.'

'Have you any doubt as to the condition of the stomach?'

'I don't think the condition of the stomach was at all unusual.'

'Do you mean that he did not die from it?'

'I presume that he died from exhaustion, produced by gastro-enteritis. I do not call this a severe case.'

'Don't you call a case which kills a man an indication of severe inflammation?'

'Some people are more easily killed than others. He merely had to get into a condition of exhaustion. I don't think there was pain in this case.'

Mr Pickford now called Mr Hugh Lloyd Jones, a chemist and druggist, who testified that ladies came to buy flypapers when no flies were about. He said that he knew there was an impression in the trade that arsenic was used as a cosmetic.

The chemist was followed by a hairdresser. Backed by thirty years' experience in Dale Street, James Bioletti testified that arsenic was used in toilet preparations and that there was an impression among ladies that it was good for the complexion. When cross-examined, he added that it was principally used as a depilatory.

'What is the label?' asked Mr Addison, referring to the mixture of arsenic and slaked lime which Mr Bioletti had just described.

'Depilatory.'

'Do you put nothing else on it?'

'Directions.'

'And nothing to show there is arsenic in it?'

'No, sir.'

'Do you mean that you sell the stuff without any other label? What weight is there in one of the packets?'

'It is generally in a two-ounce bottle.'

'What weight? You as a chemist and druggist ought to know the weights.'

'He is a hairdresser,' called Sir Charles Russell, without rising from his seat.

When Mr Bioletti had stepped down, the prosecutor spoke briefly to his lordship, then handed something to Sir Charles Russell. The barrister examined the object for several moments, then addressed the bench.

'I should like to call some one to speak to a box I have here, labelled, "Taylor Brothers, pharmaceutical chemists, Norfolk, Virginia." The description of the contents says, "Iron, quinine, and arsenic, one capsule every three or four hours, to be taken after food." At the bottom of it is the name, "Mr Maybrick".'

The prosecutor spoke. 'I shall call Mr Edwin Maybrick at once to speak to it.'

'I do not wish to make any complaint about this not being produced by any one,' said Sir Charles.

'It is in the printed list,' said Mr Addison.

'It is not,' said Sir Charles.

'Mr Edwin Maybrick will tell us all about it,' said Mr Addison.

'I will quite accept his statement,' said Sir Charles.

Edwin Maybrick testified that he had found the pillbox in the drawer of the washstand of his brother's bedroom, and that James was last in Norfolk in 1884.

Sir Charles cross-examined him briefly. 'Do you know how this escaped being recorded amongst the things found?'

'I found it at the time the furniture was being removed from the house.'

'When did you find it?'

'A week or two after he died – before the furniture was removed.'

'Did you know that Mr Cleaver was acting for this lady?'

'I did.'

'Did you communicate it to him?'

'No.'

Mr Addison now asked, 'What did you do with it?'

'I kept it.'

'When did you first give it?' asked Mr Addison.

'On the first of August.'

Now Sir Charles Russell called Sir James Poole, a prominent Liverpool merchant and former mayor of the city. In the spring of this year, said Sir James, he saw Mr Maybrick in the Palatine Club with one or two friends. The conversation turned on the use of poisonous drugs and medicines, saying that it was becoming a common custom. Maybrick had an impetuous way, said Sir James, 'and he blurted out, "I take poisonous medicines." I said, "How horrid. Don't you know, my dear friend, that the more you take of these things the more you require, and you will go on till they carry you off." I think he shrugged his shoulders, and I went on.'

Mr Addison saw no need to cross-examine the former mayor.

Sir Charles Russell turned to the bench. 'That is the evidence I place before you, my lord. I don't know what the desire of the lady may be now as to making any statement.'

Sir Charles went to the dock. Mrs Maybrick rose and stood close to him, whispering. Then he stepped back toward the bench. 'My lord,' he said, 'I wish to tell you what has taken place. I asked if it was her wish to make any statement, and she said, "Yes". I asked her if it was written, and she said, "No".'

The hush in the courtroom was punctuated briefly by the rustling of skirts as the gallery squirmed for better views of the dock. They saw Mrs Maybrick, her small figure demure as ever in black dress, cap and veil, wipe her eyes with her handkerchief. Then she moved to the side of the dock nearest the bench. She paused, looking at the judge, before she grasped the railing of the dock.

'My lord, I wish to make a statement, as well as I can, to you.'

Her low voice was scarcely audible on the far side of the room. Her audience hunched forward, straining to hear.

'A few facts in connection with the dreadfully crushing charge that has been made against me – namely, the wilful and deliberate poisoning of my husband, the father of my dear children.'

She paused, overcome by a flood of tears. As she wiped her eyes, more than one handkerchief in the courtroom was also put to use.

'I wish principally to refer to the use of the flypapers and to the bottle of meat essence. The flypapers were bought with the intention of using as a cosmetic. Before my marriage, and since, I have been in the habit of using a face-wash prescribed for me by Dr Greggs, of Brooklyn. It consisted of arsenic, tincture of benzoin, elderflower water, and some other ingredients. This prescription I mislaid last April, and, as I was suffering from slight eruption of the face, I thought I should like to try to make a substitute. I was anxious to get rid of this eruption before I went to a ball on the thirtieth of that month. When I had been in Germany many of my young friends there I had seen using a solution derived from flypapers, elder water, lavender water, and other things mixed, and then applied to the face with a handkerchief. I used the flypapers in the same manner. But to avoid the evaporation of the scent it was necessary to exclude the air as much as possible, and for that purpose I put a plate over the flypapers, and put a folded towel over that, and another towel over that.

'My lord, I now wish to refer to the bottle of meat essence. On Thursday night, the 9th of May, after Nurse Gore had given my husband beef tea, I went and sat beside him. He implored me to give him his powder, which he had referred to early in the evening, and which I had declined to give him. I was terribly anxious, miserably unhappy, and his evident distress utterly unnerved me. He had told me that the powder would not harm him, and that I could put it in his food. I then consented.

'My lord, I had not one true or honest friend in that house. I was deposed from my position as mistress, and from attending upon my husband. Notwithstanding the evidence of the nurses and servants, I may say that he wished to have me with him. Whenever I went out of the room he asked for me, and, for four days before he died, I was not allowed to give him a piece of ice without its being taken out of my hand.'

Mrs Maybrick paused. Her tears flowed freely for a moment or two, and she yielded to violent sobbing. Seeing her so shaken, a number of women in the courtroom let go their own emotions. Sobbing could be heard, with muffled gasps, in many directions. Finally the defendant regained her composure enough to go on.

'When I found the powder, I took it into the inner room, with the beef juice, and in pushing through the door I upset the bottle, and, in order to make up the quantity of fluid spilled, I added a considerable quantity of water. On returning, I found my husband asleep, and I placed the bottle on the table. When he awoke he had a choking sensation in his throat, and vomited. After that he appeared a little better, and as he did not ask for the powder again, and as I was not anxious to give it to him, I removed the bottle from the small table, where it would attract his attention, to the top of the washstand, where he could not see it. There I left it, my lord, until, I believe, Mr Michael Maybrick took possession of it.

'Until the Tuesday after my husband's death, and until a few minutes before Mr Bryning made this terrible charge against me, no one in that house had informed me that a death certificate had been refused, and that a post mortem examination had taken place, or that there was any reason to suppose that my husband had died from other than natural causes. It was only when Mrs Briggs alluded to arsenic in the meat juice that I was made aware of the nature of the powder my husband had asked me to give him. I then attempted to make an explanation to Mrs Briggs, when a policeman interrupted the conversation, and put a stop to it.'

The voice was lower now. There was no other sound in the courtroom. Breathing itself seemed to have stopped. 'In conclusion, I have only to add that, for the love of our children, a perfect reconciliation had taken place between us, and that on the day before his death I had made a full and free confession to him, and received his entire forgiveness for the fearful wrong I had done him.'

The silence continued for a moment as Mrs Maybrick's hands slipped slowly from the rail and she sank back toward her armchair. The matrons helped her into a chair and offered smelling salts. Then the gallery breathed as one, settling back into chairs, wiping eyes and noses, coughing and clearing throats as the sensation of the prisoner's last words swept over it.

Sir Charles Russell quickly took the floor. 'My lord,' he said, 'I now desire to call two persons to whom that statement was made before the inquest.'

'I wish to say it is very painful to me to have to refuse,' said the judge, 'but I think I cannot allow it. I cannot go beyond what the law allows.'

Sir Charles yielded. 'I do not for one moment make any complaint.'

In the gallery, more than one lawyer was surprised that Sir Charles did not press his point. He had clearly said, on Saturday, that when Mrs Maybrick made her statement he would offer in evidence the fact that she made it earlier, before the inquest. The judge had not indicated then that he would not permit testimony to be given on her earlier statement. And just what did the law allow? In truth, the law did not 'allow' such a statement as the prisoner had just made.

There were other questions, too, that more than one who had followed inquest, Magistrates' Court hearing and trial wondered about. Why had neither the Defence nor the Prosecution called certain people whose names had crept into the testimony, or who had appeared at the earlier hearings? Where was Mrs Samuelson, who testified at the inquest that Mrs Maybrick had said she hated her husband? Who was the man who took Mrs Maybrick to dinner on the Thursday night before Alfred Brierley joined her at Flatman's in London? Why had he never been called? James Grant, the Battlecrease House gardener, and his wife, Alice, who had been a maid in the house before her marriage – each had been mentioned in the testimony of the other servants, but neither had been called. What of Thomas Maybrick, who as trustee of his brother's will sold the furnishings that the will ordered left to the children and used by them and their mother? And George Davidson, who had been described as Maybrick's most intimate friend, who witnessed his will and held him as he died – why had no one asked him under oath about Maybrick's habits? Why had Mr Pickford and Sir Charles Russell overlooked some of these important witnesses and the possibility of valuable testimony from them? Might not the Prosecution have made deadly use of the mysterious dinner companion in London?

And now here was Sir Charles taking snuff again and already launching into his final speech for the defence.

'My lord,' he said, 'gentlemen of the jury, I will not at the outset make any allusion to the grave and remarkable statement which has been made by the woman in the dock. Hereafter I will allude to it.'

The defence lawyer went into the history of 'the unhappy man whose death we are inquiring into,' his hypochondriacal nature and familiarity with the properties and uses of poisonous drugs and medicines. He spoke of Mrs Maybrick's communications to the doctors and to her brother-in-law about the powders her husband was taking, and of Maybrick's visits over a considerable period to the shop of Mr Heaton. 'These are habits of which men are not proud,' he said, 'They would not care about publishing them in all their fullness to the world.'

Of the Brierley affair, Sir Charles said, 'I have not uttered one word of cross examination as to that story of what took place in London. This lady fell. She forgot her self-respect. She forgot her duty to her husband. The sole suggested motive in this case is that she desired to conceal from her husband the grave error which she had committed and was tempted by wicked, deliberate, foul, criminal means to end his life. If there were not this act of infidelity on her part, there would be no motive assigned in this case. Ah, gentlemen, for faults of this nature the judgments of the world are indeed unequal. In a man such faults are too often regarded with toleration, and they bring him often but few penal consequences. But in the case of a wife, in the case of a woman, it is with her sex the unforgivable sin. Those who should well consider throw stones at her from unworthy hands. Now, is it true, I ask you, because she has committed – admits she has committed so grave a fault as this – because she sinned once is she, therefore, to be misjudged always?'

Sir Charles now asked if it seemed likely that a person who sought flypapers in order to kill her husband would go where her name and address were well known. And since Mr Addison dated the beginning of the design to poison Mr Maybrick from the flypaper purchase, and the beginning of the attempt to execute the design from the Wirral races, what about the fact that Mrs Maybrick told Yapp her master was ill because he had taken a double dose that day, and that Maybrick told friends at the track that he had taken a double dose? What about Mrs Maybrick's administration of the mustard emetic next morning, and her call for the doctor twice that day?

Now Sir Charles reviewed the testimony that revealed how the suspicion of Mrs Maybrick began. All Mrs Maybrick's acts were, he said, at once suspected. The interception of the letter, he said, was 'so important that if it had not taken place you never would have heard of this charge. You may recollect my cross-examination of Nurse Yapp. That cross-examination was in order that you might see how rapidly and how strongly suspicion had been generated in the minds of the servants in that house.'

Knowing that her brothers-in-law were dissatisfied with her, and with her husband so ill, said Sir Charles, 'is it conceivable that she would not have made any effort to remove from that house proofs of her guilt? There is not one of these things that could not have been removed, destroyed, hidden, the contents vanished, leaving no trace behind by which her crime could be found out.'

After describing the prisoner's arrest, Sir Charles reached a stopping point. The court rose for luncheon.

It was, all agreed, a remarkable address. It had been made entirely from memory, without recourse to notes or papers. With steady force Sir Charles had reminded the jury of point after point of testimony in favour of his hapless client.

After lunch, he took up again the question, 'Are you satisfied beyond a reasonable doubt that this was a case of poisoning by arsenic at all?' He reminded the jury that the notion of arsenical poisoning did not occur to Drs Carter and Humphreys until it was suggested to them, that Dr Stevenson had said he would have abstained from expressing a pronounced judgment until he knew the results of the analysis, that the symptoms were the same as in gastritis or gastro-enteritis.

Sir Charles pointed out that he was not called upon to advance any theory as to what the cause of death was if it was not arsenical poisoning. 'I am sure my lord will tell you that the prisoner is entitled to stand upon a defence, and to say, "You have not proved the case which you allege".'

Now he came to his second question. Did the facts and the evidence bring satisfactory proof that Florence Maybrick administered the arsenic, if arsenic were indeed the cause of death? He asked why she would have resorted to the clumsy contrivance of steeping flypapers, considering the amount of arsenic found in the house. As for the gown and the handkerchief, Mr Davies had said that if Mrs Maybrick had been dipping the handkerchief and rubbing her face for cosmetic purposes the dampness of the handkerchief would account for the arsenic in the pocket.

When he took up the question of the bottle of meat juice, Sir Charles reminded the jury of Mrs Maybrick's remarkable statement. 'I have to ask you how comes it that this woman was persistent in making this statement, that Nurse Gore's account of the incident was a substantially true account?' The bottle could have nothing to do with the death, he added, because Maybrick had none of it after it 'was tampered with'.

'The statement the prisoner has made,' he went on 'is certainly a remarkable one. It is made by a woman who is upon trial for her life. I leave it to speak with such effect on your ears and hearts as the circumstances under which it was delivered, and the way in which it was delivered, and the tone in which it was delivered, will suggest to you what ought to be its legitimate result.'

The American evidence, said Sir Charles, had only one purpose : To show the knowledge which James Maybrick had years ago of the properties of arsenic. And, referring to Captain Thompson's evidence, he added, 'one of you gentlemen put a question, and it would certainly seem odd in this country that upon slight acquaintance an assistant should venture to speak of the habits of one of his customers. But in a community where Englishmen were not so numerous, and where an Englishman entered a shop for something which might be thought dangerous to his health or life, would it be an unnatural thing that some observations of that kind should be made?' Did any one think the servant, Stansell, would have made up the story he had told? Did any one believe that, when the chemist, Heaton, closed up his shop, the deceased suddenly gave up the habit of taking his pick-me-ups? Did not the pillbox introduced this morning help make it clear that the habits of this man were surrounded by certain curious phenomena?

Sir Charles now faced the jury directly. 'Gentlemen, the officer of this court informed you that the prisoner at the bar had put herself upon her country, which country you are. You are in number large enough to prevent the individual prejudices of one from affecting all, but in number small enough to preserve to each of you the sense of individual responsibility. The verdict is to be the verdict of each one of you, and the verdict of all of you. I am not making any appeal for mercy. You are administering a law which is merciful. You are administering a law which forbids you to pronounce a verdict of guilty unless all other reasonable hypotheses of innocence can be excluded. And now I end as I began, by asking each of you, in the perplexities, in the mystery which surrounds this case, can any one of you, with satisfied judgment and with safe conscience, say this woman is guilty? If your duty compels you to do it, you will do it, you must do it. But you cannot, you will not, you must not unless the whole burthen and facts and weight of the case fairly and fully considered with honest and impartial minds, drive you, drive you irresistibly, to that conclusion.'

Had the gallery dared to applaud, Sir Charles would have received an ovation. His gravity, his logic, his honesty – all profoundly impressed his audience of lawyers, privileged ladies, journalists, and citizens local and visiting. Those who had followed the career of Sir Charles Russell over the years were already whispering that it was one of the most powerful appeals he had ever made. What the jury of tradesmen, farmers and plumbers was thinking, no one knew.

A powerful speech for the defence it was indeed. Yet there were those – both thinking laymen and experienced lawyers – who could not reconcile the thoroughness of Sir Charles's defence with one glaring omission that he had made. Why had he not produced as a witness for the defence the mistress of James Maybrick, the mother of his five illegitimate children? How had Sir Charles been unable to bring himself to call upon this decisive proof that Florence Elizabeth Maybrick had the means to obtain a divorce from her husband if she wanted to be rid of him? The question had no answer – except the obvious answer that Sir Charles had conducted his case in the way he best saw fit, and that such evidence might be treated by the Court and the jury as an unfair attack upon the memory of the dead man.

Beginning his summary of the evidence for the prosecution, Mr Addison said that Maybrick appeared to be a strong, healthy man. He was a 'hyp' only in matters connected with his health. The prosecutor said that absolute reliance must be placed in Mr Bateson, but he implied some doubt about the testimony of the sea captain and 'the black servant' or 'the black man', as he subsequently called him. He noted Dr Humphreys's testimony that Maybrick prided himself on his knowledge of medicine, and Dr Drysdale's that Maybrick never mentioned arsenic to him. As to Mrs Maybrick's wonder about the white powder, 'Now, gentlemen,' he said, 'I ask you whether you believe him when he said it was a damned lie, or whether, recalling what she was doing between the 14th and 21st March, you believe her. Unfortunately this woman, at that very time, had so interwoven her adultery with her conduct that it was impossible to treat it as an ordinary case of adultery, and not treat it as having any actual connection with the alleged crime.'

From the published report of Mrs Maybrick's statement, Mr Addison read an extract relating to the cosmetics. He said that any woman who wanted arsenic for a cosmetic would have asked for papers for that lawful purpose.

Next Mr Addison reminded the jury that the defence did not attempt to explain the arsenic in the prescription from Clay and Abraham's. As for that found in the implements in Maybrick's office, he said, 'Where was the arsenic found? It was not found in the basin, it was not found in the pan. It was found in the jug.'

Sir Charles Russell rose quickly. 'That is not so. Dr Davies washed out the pan, basin, and jug, and boiled the contents of all in hydrochloric acid.'

'If I am wrong I hope I will be set right,' said Mr Addison. 'My impression was that it was taken from the jug, but it might be that he mixed all the washings together.' He went on to describe Professor Paul's experiments with the glaze of the pan, and Mr Davies's inference that arsenic was in the food.

'If Mr Davies is here,' said Sir Charles, 'he will say I was correct.'

'Where is Mr Davies?' said the judge.

Mr Davies stood up. He said the washings of the pan, the basin, and the jug were all put together and tested, but the acid for the test was not added in the pan or the jug or the basin.

Mr Addison reinterpreted. 'As my friend has said, after the washing of the jug there was something left which was mixed with the water in the pan, and these two together yielded arsenic. I will now pass on to the cause of illness.' He reviewed the testimony of Doctors Humphreys and Carter that no single symptom by itself could arise from arsenic and nothing else. He found it strange that Maybrick himself had never suggested that his symptoms might be due to arsenic.

The supposed solicitude for her husband that had been attributed to the defendant, Mr Addison continued, was so inconsistent with the feelings she had put on record that 'they drive you to the conclusion that a dreadful tragedy was going on.' He questioned why she had written, 'He is sick unto death.' 'Is that the natural expression of a woman who has tender solicitations for her husband? No, but it is the natural expression to write to her paramour, "The doctors held a consultation yesterday, and all now depends upon how long his strength will hold out." Gentlemen, you know nobody had said that. Whether she be guilty or innocent, I protest against the notion of any solicitude for a husband in a woman who wrote that letter. I can only say she was consummately cunning.'

As he took up the matter of the bottle of meat juice, Mr Addison said, 'She said that she put the white powder into it because she was asked to do so, as he said it would do him no harm. I cannot help recalling to you in this connection the story which she told at another time about the white powders to others, and was it possible that she could innocently have done this, thinking it would not do him any harm? If she had done it innocently, why did she not tell the nurse? It was not a time when she could put a white powder in his food innocently or unsuspiciously. She had said he was dying.'

Mr Addison went on to her statement that she had made a full confession to her husband. 'If it is true,' he said, 'it accounts for what he said in the presence of Nurse Wilson, "Oh, Bunny, Bunny, how could you do it? I didn't think you would treat me so." Can you believe the woman who, believing that he was dying on the Wednesday and that all the struggle was hopeless, can you believe that she, surrounded by suspicion, on the Friday night told him of her mistake?

'Now, there is another matter that my friend has not in the least attempted to explain. In her room there was a box, and in that box were found three bottles of arsenic, and no flypaper, and on the top was a bottle of Valentine's meat essence, without any poison in it. What do you infer from that? Who put it there?'

Among the spectators, more than one legal mind wondered where the prosecutor got the testimony that the box was in 'her room'. The dressing room, it had been clearly stated, was used by Mr Maybrick, and the hat-boxes contained his hats.

It remained only for the prosecutor to summarise the duties of the jury. 'If you find that our proofs have failed and the case is not made out, it is the carrying out of the law in you to say, "The prisoner is not guilty". Your duty is to act in accordance with the evidence. You have to disregard all those feelings of sympathy which the age and the sex and the position of this unhappy woman would naturally create in your bosoms, and deal out to her the same justice as you would deal out to a poor and ill-favoured person who might be found guilty of this terrible crime. If she be guilty, then, gentlemen, we have, indeed, in this investigation, proved a murder founded upon profligacy and adultery, and carried out with a hypocrisy and a cunning which have been rarely equalled in the annals of crime.'

It was late in the day when Mr Addison finished, too late for the judge to begin his summing up of the case. As the court rose, there were questions in the gallery. Mr Addison had made many small errors in his summing up. He had oversimplified, for this ordinary jury, the detailed medical evidence on gastro-enteritis and inflammation. He had confused London medicine and Clay and Abraham's medicine. He had ignored or discredited the evidence of several witnesses on Maybrick's reckless use of medicines. The honesty and simple logic of Sir Charles Russell's summation for the defence had been lacking in Mr Addison's address to the jury, and, whatever the jury's reaction, many of the spectators resented it.

When it was early evening in Liverpool, it was mid-afternoon in New York. The telegraph editor of the *World* received a cable from his Liverpool man transmitting in full Mrs Maybrick's statement to the court.

The editor had read only half way through it when he summoned a reporter. He dispatched him on the double to locate somewhere in Brooklyn a Dr Greggs who might have prescribed a face wash containing arsenic for a Miss Chandler.

That night, all England slept with the Maybrick case on its mind. Succeeding editions of the evening papers had reported the progress of the closing speeches for defence and prosecution as quickly as they were made. The brilliance of Sir Charles Russell was given much credit, and the small-mindedness of Mr Addison was much blamed, for a surge of optimism that swept the land. Sense and sentiment together now sided with poor Mrs Maybrick. It could be clearly seen that she had been unfairly treated and ought never to have been brought to trial.

In Brooklyn, the reporter from the *World* found Dr Greggs at 143 Lefferts Place and asked if he had any recollection of Mrs Maybrick.

'Yes,' said the doctor. 'I knew her as Florence Chandler. That was about ten years ago. She lived with her mother, the Baroness von Roques, and her brother, Holbrook St John Chandler, at Willow Street, near Pineapple. Miss Florence called upon me to attend her brother, Holbrook, who was suffering from lung troubles and afterwards died of consumption in Paris. All I know about Mrs Maybrick is that she called upon me to prescribe something for her complexion, which I did.'

'Was there arsenic in the preparation?' asked the reporter.

'Yes. That's about the only thing you can prescribe for the complexion.'

'Do you call it a cosmetic?'

'Well,' said the doctor, 'you can't call it anything else. A cosmetic means a wash for the face.'

'Do you remember what were the ingredients of the prescription you gave?'

'No, I do not.'

'From what you know of Mrs Maybrick, do you think she would be guilty of the crime alleged against her?'

'From what I did know of her she would be the last one in the world that I should think would be guilty of any such crime,' said the doctor.

XII

*'The mere fact of a man swearing this, that,
and the other, does not by any means give a reason
for unqualified belief in what he says.'*

Tuesday, 6th August, 1889

Once more the crowds gathered early before St George's Hall. On this day, they knew, Mr Justice Stephen would sum up the evidence for and against Florence Maybrick's plea of not guilty, and the trial would move into the secrecy of the jury room. What the jury would decide was almost a foregone conclusion : Now even the Liverpool newspapers, commenting on the brilliant work of Sir Charles Russell, had begun to anticipate the vindication of the widow of the arsenic-eater.

Sir James Fitzjames Stephen, judge of the Queen's Bench Division of the High Court of Justice, shared quarters with another judge of the same division when he came to Liverpool for the Assizes. As he set off toward St George's Hall this morning, he carried with him the advice of his brother judge that he keep his summing-up to one day and not let it extend overnight.

With one exception, the principals in the courtroom were the same as on previous days. The exception was Sir Charles Russell, who had gone that morning to the Nisi Prius Court to take part in a railway case that he had taken. He left Mr Pickford in charge of Mrs Maybrick's interests.

His lordship took his seat just after ten o'clock and, without even glancing at the dock to be sure the prisoner was present, began his summing-up.

'Gentlemen of the jury,' he began, 'I feel myself bound, in consideration of its importance, to go through the whole of the evidence which has been given.'

The many lawyers in the gallery shifted uneasily in their seats. If his lordship followed his intention to the letter, the case would never reach the jury today.

There was, in the judge's opening words, a tendency to ramble. It alarmed those who knew the distinguished mind of the jurist. They were further surprised when, after mentioning Mrs Maybrick's trip to London on 21st March, he said, 'The next date after that took place is the Grand National something. I don't know whether it is a race, or a steeplechase, or what it is – but it is something which is called the Grand National, as if everybody knew what the substantive was – but the Grand National took place on the 29th March.'

Here was more than a surprise. Here was a prominent Englishman, the most important person in the courtroom, who did not know or could not remember what the Grand National was. An undercurrent of whispering flowed through the gallery.

'Somewhere about this,' his lordship was continuing, 'about the 12th to 19th March, took place the purchase of flypapers, and shortly after that occurred – I think there were two purchases of flypapers – a matter occurred in the middle of April.'

Mr Pickford was on his feet trying to get his lordship's attention. 'Will your lordship forgive me. In regard to the flypapers, Wokes fixed the date as the 24th, and the second chemist the 29th April, not March.'

'I said April,' said the judge. 'There is no use disputing whether I used one word or another.' The judge turned to the testimony of the witnesses. Of Dr Hopper, the judge said, 'Though the doctor had arranged for the husband to pay her debts, you must consider whether that is a reconciliation. After a desperate quarrel there simply comes the family doctor, who intervenes. To say that is a reconciliation does not accord with my knowledge of human nature.' He went on to Mrs Maybrick's telling the doctor about her husband's white powders. 'She mentioned it once to the brother, and also mentioned it once to the doctor. This is a very important matter.'

Though the bench was littered with his notes and with newspaper clippings, the judge continued to confuse dates. 'He and his wife and Captain Irving dined together on Wednesday, the 5th,' he said, meaning Wednesday, 1st May, and a few minutes later he shocked all who understood court procedure and the judge's need for impartiality by saying, 'Friday was the day on which began the symptoms of what may be called the fatal dose.'

In the gallery, barrister looked at barrister with raised eyebrows. Did his lordship realise what he was saying? And now Mr Justice Stephen was weaving homespun philosophy into his address. 'Amongst other remarkable points in this case is the very, very remarkable one that at literally every stage of the case, almost every incident of it takes place under the eye of one at least, often of several separate medical men, and that all these medical men not only prescribed for, but examined and re-examined the patient. The consequence is that you have such minuted medical testimony as to what took place which has been rarely equalled in trials of this nature. He had an hour's consultation with Dr Fuller. An hour is a longish time to be in consultation with a doctor. Such doctors as I have seen would think an hour's consultation a great deal too long, and it certainly would be very unpleasant for the other party.'

'We come now,' he went on, 'to the evidence of the servants. I don't think there is any great difference between them as to the story they tell.' He detailed Nurse Yapp's testimony for some minutes, and then said, 'Well, then, the medicines were kept on the landing. On Tuesday, the 7th May, she saw Mrs Maybrick pour the contents of one medicine bottle into another. I do not know what to make of that at all. She was at that time managing in her own house, nursing her own husband, and I cannot see the act in itself can be called a suspicious one.'

As to the letter entrusted Nurse Yapp for mailing, his lordship said that 'the letter itself is of the greatest importance, and is one of the critical points of the case.' His comment upon it showed more confusion. As he said, 'Sir Charles Russell asked her several times whether she did not drop the letter in the mud in order to make an excuse to open it afterwards,' more than one spectator recalled the frustrating moments when Sir Charles had asked her several times whether she dropped the letter in the mud at all, and his lordship's confusion at the time of that exchange. Now he went on to dates. 'Then she is cross-examined, and she says there was no quarrel before the 3rd April.' Careful listeners knew the judge must mean 29th March. 'The husband and wife seemed to have lived on perfectly good terms until the 21st April.' Surely he must mean 21st March. The confusion of specific dates was inexcusable.

When he turned to the medical evidence, the judge read first the testimony of Dr Humphreys. He referred to Dr Stevenson as not recognising in it 'the particular kind of sickness which would be produced by arsenic,' and the knowing agreed quietly that his lordship must have meant Dr Tidy, not Dr Stevenson.

Sir James Stephen was ready to interrupt his charge for the luncheon recess. Mr Addison rose and asked, 'Would your lordship allow me to qualify a statement I made yesterday? My lord, I said in regard to the handkerchief found in the bottle saturated with arsenic, that it had been used – might have been used – on the deceased man's mouth, for the purpose of allaying thirst. Although that was prescribed, there seems to have been no evidence of it having been done, and I want to guard myself in that way for fear I should be unintentionally unfair.'

'I do not think the evidence justifies that assumption,' said the judge.

'I do not think so, my lord,' said Mr Addison.

After lunch his lordship reviewed the testimony of Dr Humphreys. He picked up a large book which seemed to contain newspaper clippings. 'In cross-examination he gave general answers, which I have not taken down so fully as I could wish. I will read them to you from one of the newspaper reports, which certainly agrees with my recollection of the examination.' The medical symptoms were described at length, and then the judge rambled into a long discourse on the cause of death.

'The evidence of a certain number of medical men,' said his lordship, 'is, "I think he died of arsenic poisoning," or "I don't think he died of arsenic poisoning, but of gastro-enteritis, caused by the administration, or, at any rate, caused by something capable of causing gastro-enteritis, but not necessarily arsenic," and in some instances "probably not arsenic." These parts may be passed over as more fit for medical jurisprudence than for a jury engaged upon the administration of criminal law. It is the tendency of cases of this kind to run into scholastic discussion.'

Scholastic discussion or not, thought some of the judge's listeners, it was a case of medical jurisprudence that confronted this ordinary jury. His lordship had, for the moment, put his finger precisely on the point.

'I think I shall be of more use to you,' he went on, 'by telling you what are the different views for which these gentlemen contend. You know perfectly well that there is such a thing in scientific and legal questions, and questions of forensic medicine more particularly – there is such a thing as subtle partisanship, which very much diminishes the value of the evidence given under such circumstances. Any person who has been in the habit of attending committees of the Houses of Parliament and hearing the evidence which is given there by different engineers, or of persons connected with the mechanical arts, must have learnt that the mere fact of a man swearing this, that, and the other, does not by any means give a reason for unqualified belief in what he says. You have to take off a good deal of discount from the testimony of skilled witnesses on the ground of their becoming, probably insensibly to themselves, advocates rather than witnesses.'

Among the spectators, elbows nudged ribs. How many of the twelve men in the jurybox – the twelve farmers, plumbers, and shopkeepers –

had been in the habit of attending committees of the Houses of Parliament, they wondered? First his lordship had gratuitously declared a large part of the testimony heard in this trial to be more fit for medical jurisprudence than for a jury administering criminal law, and now he wished to discount the testimony of skilled witnesses. This increasingly perplexing recapitulation was surprising for a jurist of Sir James's eminence.

Now he returned to the essential questions. 'It is a necessary step – it is essential to this charge – that the man died of poison, and the poison suggested is arsenic. Now, then, let us see what the doctors say. I think slight traces of arsenic were found in the intestines. There was none in the heart, none in the blood, nor in other parts of the body, where, in the case of death by arsenic, you would suppose arsenic to be found. But there certainly was arsenic found.'

The question of terrible interest was, said the judge, who put it there? Three answers were suggested: Mr Maybrick put it there himself, or it was improperly taken as medicine, or it was put there by crime.

His lordship dealt at length with each of the three possibilities. He reviewed the testimony of Mr Bateson, of the servant, Stansell and of Captain Thompson (whom he called 'the foolish ship captain'). As for the testimony of the chemist Heaton, Sir James said, 'You ought not to allow yourself to consider this absolutely proved. The man was only identified by a photograph.' He said that in the Divorce Court, where identification was constantly practised, the evidence of a photograph was not admitted.

His lordship turned now to the lack of conclusive testimony as to how long arsenic may remain in the body. 'A celebrated physician said that a physician spent his time putting drugs of which he knows little into a body of which he knows less. This is one of those pointed sayings, but there is truth at the bottom of it. It cuts against the prosecution, and it cuts against the defence, and it lowers the degree of assurance with which we receive medical evidence.'

Having discounted the medical witnesses, Sir James looked up at the courtroom clock high on the wall. 'It is now a quarter past four, and I have been addressing you now for six hours and a quarter, and I am afraid I shall not be able to go on much beyond five. I will go on with you for three-quarters of an hour. I hope tomorrow I shall have said all I have to say.'

The judge now reviewed the medical testimony at great length, and at last concluded: 'I think it all comes to the general argument advanced by all the doctors called for the prisoner on this occasion – the suggestion of gastro-enteritis unattended by any poisoning – a state of things which may arise from dyspepsia. But the doctors for the Crown say that they do not believe that gastro-enteritis was idiopathic, which means that it in a sort of way arises of itself. Dr Tidy expresses his opinion that this was not a case of arsenical poisoning at all. It was a case of gastro-enteritis, produced by so small a cause as a wetting. I may just remark that Dr Macnamara is almost the only witness called to prove that symptoms of this sort have been produced by so common a cause, and have also produced symptoms of irritant poisoning, and which have led a variety of other medical men to the opinion that this was actually a case of arsenical poisoning. But I have taken an analysis of it, and I thought there was time to read it before the Court rises, but I regret to say that I will have to leave that over till tomorrow. I feel that our duty is to consider it fully, and I am sorry to say that I must require your attendance tomorrow at the usual hour of ten o'clock.'

His lordship rose wearily and gathered his notes, clippings and scrap-books. The gallery pushed into the street to tell the waiting crowd there would be no verdict that day. Florence Maybrick, exhausted by the strain of concentrating for seven hours upon the judge's address, made her way slowly to the basement.

In Lime Street and in public rooms, barrister and solicitor compared notes. His lordship's rambling discourse, his confusion about dates and events that had been established repeatedly in the testimony, his erratic digressions and gratuitous observations on medicine, his characterisation of a defence witness as 'foolish' and his careless use of such terms as 'the fatal dose' – all were surprising and alarming. The clear mind that had, over the years, established his lordship as an authority on the rules of evidence seemed somehow clouded and cluttered.

Yet the absolute fairness for which he was so well known seemed to have begun to show itself toward the end of his address. After many hours, he had at last wallowed his way to the point that the testimony of eminent witnesses held that this was not a case of arsenical poisoning at all and that the symptoms most characteristic of arsenical poisoning were absent. All who were now convinced of Mrs Maybrick's innocence agreed that it was the best point at which to leave the jury overnight.

There were those who also agreed that the judge's address to the jury gave clear evidence that he had not fully recovered from a severe stroke suffered in 1885. After long recuperation, his lordship had regained all his physical powers and, one had been assured, his mental ability. Of the latter there now began to be doubt.

The evening newspapers promised the acquittal of Florence Maybrick. His lordship's summing up gave strong hints that she was not guilty. Certainly he found reasonable doubt. Before another sunset, the woman would go free.

XIII

*'It is easy enough to conceive how a horrible
woman, in so terrible a position, might be
assailed by some terrible temptation.'*

Wednesday, 7th August, 1889

Early in the morning, the judge who shared quarters with Sir James Fitzjames Stephen was awakened. He found Sir James pacing up and down in his dressing gown. 'That woman is guilty,' he was muttering. 'That woman is guilty.'

By ten o'clock, Lime Street traffic was at a standstill. Five thousand people stood outside St George's Hall. Each seemed confident of an acquittal.

The usual number of members of the bar and other prominent citizens held tickets for the gallery. Shortly before ten o'clock, the Clerk of Arraigns was shocked to learn that a delegation of well-dressed ladies had brought bouquets of flowers and planned to escort Mrs Maybrick from the dock upon her acquittal. He warned them of the penalties of contempt of court.

The defendant came into court pale and haggard. She climbed the stair leaning heavily on a matron's arm. She was seen to tremble as she reached the front of the dock. She clutched the rail for a moment, swayed as if she was about to faint, and sank into her chair.

Sir Charles Russell was present. His grave appearance set the tone of the courtroom. The gallery was quiet and tense even before the court was called to order – so much so that despite the solidity of the building those in the courtroom could distinctly hear the murmur of the crowd outside.

When his lordship resumed his address to the jury by saying that Dr Stevenson found one fifty-three-thousandths of a grain of arsenic in the intestines of the deceased, it was the beginning of greater confusion than his lordship had shown the day before. The correct figure was fifteen thousandths. He said that Dr Stevenson said the body contained a nearly fatal dose of arsenic, that Dr Tidy had no doubt the deceased died from the effects of arsenic, that Dr Stevenson said the symptoms were very anomalous, and that he theorised that there may have been several doses of poison. 'But,' he added, 'I do not know that there was any effort made to point out the precise times at which doses may have been administered.'

In the gallery, fellow members of the bar shook their heads. Sir James should have known very well that no such effort had been made. It was, indeed, one of the peculiarities of the case that the indictment contained no counts on the precise time of administration or attempts to administer poison.

Now, having touched on fractional parts of a grain of arsenic, the judge was philosophising again. 'I cannot convey anything to enable you to attach meaning to figures representing such very small quantities. The globules of blood in a man's body are so small that there are more than a billion, but really that conveys no idea whatever to our minds.'

He turned now to Dr Tidy's testimony that the symptoms were not symptoms of arsenical poisoning. 'I should feel inclined to say that a great deal of controversy of that sort depends upon the result. Still, the poison was present, and to my mind that means a great deal to consider. Dr Tidy says, "I cannot suggest what caused this death. I cannot suggest what substance it was which acted on him as an irritant. The sickness was not like that of arsenic." That is the whole of Dr Tidy's evidence, and I have given you the whole of Dr Stevenson's testimony also. So that you have the matter fairly before you as far as I know how to put it.'

The judge now reviewed testimony given by Professor Paul on the testing of the glaze of the pan. As he went on to the professor's testimony on the size of a grain of arsenic, his listeners realised that he had somehow reverted to Dr Tidy's testimony on the symptoms of gastro-enteritis. 'You are getting there,' he said, 'into that portion of the medical questions which I have warned you against at every step. You cannot decide upon medical refinements.'

Sir James now came to the question of motive. 'In this case,' he said, 'I am bound reluctantly to say that there is strong evidence of the prisoner having been actuated by a motive at once strong and disgraceful. In fact, we have it now stated by Mrs Maybrick herself, that she did, about the latter part of March last, carry on an adulterous intercourse with this man Brierley. What certainly is the most remarkable feature in the case is that Brierley is not the first person who appeared at the hotel in London. Some person, not being Brierley, met her at that hotel earlier in the evening, that he went out with her to various places. So that she had left her husband, coming to London, meeting a man who is not known, and with him passing a very large portion of this day apparently. Whoever this man is, she is seen at breakfast with another man, who may have been Mr Brierley, but he has not been positively identified.'

His lordship picked up some papers and remarked upon the extraordinary fact that certain letters had not been destroyed by Mrs Maybrick. Some concerned the mass of falsehoods which she had told her London relatives about her trip. 'It is not my business to speak as a moralist,' said the judge, 'but there is one horrible and lamentable result of a connection of that sort which renders it the strongest possible inducement, for entering upon a system of the most disgraceful intrigue, and telling a great number of lies.' He referred to Miss Baillie's letter of 13th April.

'Well, there is another letter on the 7th of May,' he continued, 'and that letter is signed "Your sincere friend, John." Who John is we don't know, but I don't think it matters in this case to ascertain who he was. The letter was found by Nurse Yapp, when Mr Maybrick was very ill. It says. "You certainly did make a mess of it when you were last in London, and really it was quite unnecessary and still worse to tell so many fibs. I told my aunts the truth, as it seemed to be the best thing for me to do. I said we went to the Grand Hotel, and went to the Gaiety, and went home in a cab." '

His lordship looked down at the jury. 'This certainly seems to imply that this John must have been the man who took her out when she came to London.'

A murmur fluttered over the courtroom. His lordship had read from a letter which had never been put into evidence. He had said it was found by Nurse Yapp when Mr Maybrick was ill, whereas it surely must have been one of those found by Mrs Briggs or Mrs Hughes after his death. As for not knowing or needing to know who John was – why should this link in the evidence be left missing?

His lordship was busy with another letter – one signed 'A.B.' 'Can you tell me, Mr Addison, about this letter? It commences, "My dear Florie." '

'Yes, my lord,' said Mr Addison.

'Do you know Mr Brierley's handwriting?'

'The handwriting is not proved. That is my recollection.'

'Well,' said his lordship, 'is there any witness in court who is acquainted with Brierley's handwriting? Is Brierley here?'

'Yes,' said Mr Addison, 'he was subpoenaed by the prosecution.'

'It is a very painful thing to call him,' said the judge, studying the letter. He thought a moment, then picked up another letter. It seemed to be the one from John which he had read a moment ago. 'However,' he mused, 'this letter is not brought for the purpose of evidence, but it was found in her possession.'

Even those across the room who had opera glasses in hand were confused. Was his lordship holding the letter he had just read, or another?

'The writer further stated,' said the judge, 'that there would be some difficulty about Mrs Maybrick's reception at their house again. He further said, "I forgot to say, also, that my aunts discovered that you did not stay at the Grand . . ." '

His lordship paused. Apparently he was reading additional parts of the letter from John. He resumed. ' "And now, I am not going to be led into telling any more lies. I am tired of all this scheming, which seems to be endangering your reputation at a most critical time. I shall be glad to have a long letter from you in reply to this, but I will have no abuse." ' Sir James glanced on through the letter and mentioned that the writer spoke of a previous communication as a 'staggerer'.

Again he put down the letter and looked at the jury. 'These two letters certainly do show in the most unmistakable terms what was the position of this woman as regards wicked falsehoods.'

In the gallery, neighbours looked at each other. Then there were two letters, after all.

'Here are different persons connected with her,' he went on, 'charging her with living in a maze of falsehoods.'

And now he had picked up the key letter – Mrs Maybrick's intercepted letter of 8th May to Alfred Brierley. He read it to the jury, sentence by sentence, commenting on each thought. He ended with the strong inference in the letter that she wished its recipient to believe that her husband was very ill and likely to die. 'It may be,' he said, 'a thought which gives a dreadful satisfaction if the woman really hopes and wishes that her husband should die. And if she tells a man with whom she has lately committed adultery, then is it not a very cogent reason for thinking that she wished she might be free to live with the man to whom she made the greatest sacrifice that a woman can possibly make? Gentlemen, I point out to you a motive which I feel to be my duty not to overlook. It is a sad and terrible case.'

Now the judge turned to Dr Hopper's reconciliation. 'Do you think if such a reconciliation had been sincere,' he asked, 'after that would she have made an assignation with the lover of whom he had apparently been jealous when he saw her with him after going up to London and living with him in adultery for two days?'

Mr Addison interrupted. 'May I point out, my lord, in favour of the prisoner, that the Grand National was on the 29th of March, and the reconciliation took place on the 30th – the week after she was in London.'

'You are quite right,' Sir James agreed. 'I have made a mistake, and I am sorry I have done so in a case of this importance. That which is called the reconciliation took place on the 30th March, the Grand National having taken place on the 28th or 29th.' He added that he thought, however, that his remarks were not deprived of all their weight, and said, 'I ask you if the reconciliation could be really sincere when it took place on the 30th April and this letter was written on the 8th May.'

This time, no one attempted to correct the date to 30th March.

Sir James now set forth the principles upon which he had permitted the defendant to make her statement. After several minutes of reasoning, he proposed to read a newspaper account of her statement, 'because it is within the competency of gentlemen connected with newspapers to take down a short statement of that kind in almost absolute accuracy. I feel, therefore, that in reading what I am about to read to you I am appealing to my own recollection of what Mrs Maybrick said.'

Then he took up the question of using flypapers for cosmetic purposes, remarking that if Mrs Maybrick knew of this habit, why were witnesses not brought from Germany? 'She is a person,' he said, 'who obviously has the means of procuring excellent legal advice, and of providing evidence which costs considerable sums of money. Why is there no evidence?'

His lordship added that, although they had heard what Mr Maybrick did many years ago in America, 'it is very singular there is no evidence brought forward to substantiate this part of the case about Dr Gregg, of Brooklyn.' He asked why her mother had not been called to testify to this arsenical face-wash habit of her daughter's. 'This is very curious,' he finished. 'I might say a much stronger word.'

Now Sir James took up Mrs Maybrick's remarks about the meat juice. He wondered that she would yield to her husband's plea for the powder when she had long ago consulted Dr Humphreys about it. He wondered at her behaviour on finding him asleep after she had put the powder into the bottle. 'Here is a man craving for this powder, and the woman goes to get it, and when she gets it she does not give it to him – a very strange result. If that story is true, it is a matter for you to decide, but you must take account of the imputations of falsehood made against her in those letters.' It seemed surprising also that Sir Charles had taken so little notice of the meat juice, and that Mr Pickford had reserved Mrs Maybrick's defence when she was charged. His lordship said he could not help thinking it would have been better for her to say then what she had to say about the flypapers and the meat juice.

He turned now to Nurse Gore's testimony about the meat juice incident, and read verbatim the account of her evidence published in the *Liverpool Daily Post*. When he came to Mrs Maybrick's suggestion that Nurse Gore fetch ice for Mr Maybrick, his lordship remarked that it 'certainly did suggest to my mind that Mrs Maybrick made an excuse, and tried, by sending Nurse Gore out of the room, to get an opportunity of putting arsenic into her husband's meat juice.'

Sir James observed that it was time for lunch, and said that he expected to finish soon afterward.

When they returned, Mr Pickford spoke to the judge. 'My lord, before the jury comes in, I should like to say something in reference to a remark of your lordship about the prisoner reserving her defence when before the magistrates. Whether it was wrong, my lord, it was entirely my act, and – '

'Oh, pray, Mr Pickford,' said his lordship, 'dismiss from your mind the notion that I in the smallest possible way censure what was done, or that I assume there was any kind of division between you and Sir Charles Russell.'

Mr Justice Stephen continued his summing up. He reviewed the analyses performed by Mr Davies and Dr Stevenson, and said that in one bottle 'a portion of the fluid was found to contain ninety-four per cent of arsenic.' No one corrected the judge, though the figure should have been two and ninety-four one hundredths, or slightly less than three per cent.

'Now, gentlemen,' he added, 'you cannot by any means exclude from the case the circumstances that a large quantity of different matters, all of them more or less infected with arsenic, were found in the room, and in the house and in the places where Mrs Maybrick continually was. I should say that a person is somewhat unfortunately situated who, being supposed to have been guilty of poisoning her husband, with a large quantity of arsenic such as I have described to you, distributed about with a variety of articles immediately under her command, at the time when it was suggested that she did not commit so horrible a crime.'

Around the courtroom, heads shook and faces grimaced. Could any one, neighbours quietly asked each other, make sense out of his lordship's last remarks? Solicitors and barristers, in particular, shook their heads in wonderment.

'Gentlemen,' he continued, 'I could say a good many other things about the awful nature of the charge, but I do not think it necessary. For a person to go on deliberately administering poison to a poor, helpless, sick man upon whom she has already inflicted a dreadful injury – an injury fatal to married life – the person who could do such a thing as that must indeed be destitute of the least trace of human feeling. You must remember the intrigue which she carried on with this man Brierley, and the incredible thought that a woman should be plotting the death of her husband in order that she might be left at liberty to follow her own degrading vices. You ought not to convict a woman of such a crime as this unless you are sure in your own mind that she really committed it. It is easy enough to conceive how a horrible woman, in so terrible a position, might be assailed by some terrible temptation.'

Again his lordship reminded the jury that they must consider the testimony of eminent medical men that Maybrick died or did not die of arsenical poisoning. 'On the other hand,' he added, 'you have to say with equal distinctness whether he died from gastro-enteritis – inflammation of the stomach. The question for you is, by what was the illness caused – was it caused by arsenic or by some other means?'

This was indeed not the question for the jury, it was noted in the gallery, but none of the learned counsel was rising to say so. Over and over again, his lordship repeated himself, but each time he seemed to ask more directly for a verdict of guilt based upon motive. 'You must decide upon the whole case,' he was again saying. 'There are three or four circumstances in the case which are circumstances of very grave suspicion indeed. And where you find a case in which this dreadful accusation is made, and is accompanied by circumstances which are likely to produce suspicion, you must consider how far they corroborate the other evidence that has been given. Gentlemen, these are really the combination of questions to which you have got to apply your minds. I do not wish to spin out the last words to you, and I accordingly will ask you to consider your verdict.'

In two days, Sir James had spoken for twelve and a half hours.

The bailiffs who would go into the jury room were sworn, and at eighteen minutes past three in the afternoon the jury retired to consider their verdict. No sound but their shuffling feet could be heard in the courtroom as they moved out of the jury box and into their room. The door closed behind them, and with proper authority one of the bailiffs dropped a dark curtain across the door.

Florence Maybrick looked anxiously around the courtroom. A matron spoke to her, and she was led down the winding stair to the basement.

A man was waiting in her detention cell. He came there, he said, as a representative of David W. Armstrong of Louisville, Kentucky. Florence

Maybrick knew Mr Armstrong. He was an attorney who represented her mother's and her interests in land in America. He was one of the many to whom the Baroness had written for help in raising money for her daughter's defence.

The gentleman reminded Florence that, nearly two years earlier, she and the Baroness had given Mr Armstrong power of attorney to settle some disputes over Holbrook property which they had jointly inherited in Virginia, Kentucky and West Virginia. Mr Armstrong had said at the time that it would be for the convenience of all concerned if the title was vested in someone who resided in the United States, and for this purpose they had conveyed title to one Harrison T. Groom.

Now, at the request of the Baroness, Mr Armstrong had arranged to sell a portion of the Kentucky land to the Kentucky Union Land Company. The company had raised, said the visitor, captious objections to a conveyance from Mr Groom, and insisted upon Mrs Maybrick's signature. Though the consideration expressed in the deed was one dollar, he assured her, the purchase price was $20,000.

Florence Elizabeth Maybrick signed the deed.

In the courtroom above, the gallery sat frozen. Not one spectator left his seat. Talk was subdued and anxious, for more than one person had confidently expected the jury to declare its verdict of acquittal without leaving the room.

Lawyers continued to compare notes. In particular, they found it hard to understand why Sir Charles Russell had absented himself from the courtroom on the first day of the judge's charge, and why he had failed to challenge the errors and mistakes and bias of the second day. However, they shrugged, the jury was certain to return a verdict of 'not guilty'.

At four minutes to four, the curtain was thrown back. A bailiff appeared. Behind him the jury filed back into the box. Word was sent to the basement and to the judge's chambers, and his lordship and the prisoner moved to bench and dock.

The stillness was overbearing. The Clerk of Arraigns, Mr Shuttleworth, called the list of the jury. He then looked at the foreman. 'Have you agreed upon a verdict, gentlemen?'

Foreman Wainwright spoke. 'We have.'

'And do you find the prisoner guilty of the murder of James Maybrick or not guilty?'

'Guilty,' said the foreman.

A long and heavy sigh went up from the gallery, almost in unison. Mrs

Maybrick, who was seated, buried her head in her hands. Her body quivered.

Mr Shuttleworth turned to the dock. 'Florence Elizabeth Maybrick, you have been found guilty of wilful murder. Have you anything to say why the court should not pronounce sentence upon you?'

Mrs Maybrick rose and clasped the rail of the dock in front of her. She trembled as she bowed to his lordship, but her voice was firm. 'My lord, everything has been against me. Although evidence has been given as to a great many circumstances in connection with Mr Brierley, much has been withheld which might have influenced the jury had it been told. I am not guilty of this crime.'

She sat down, seeming to gasp for breath, and at last sobbed like a child.

His lordship slowly put on the black silk cap reserved for this moment. 'Prisoner at the bar,' he intoned, 'I am no further able to treat you as being innocent of the dreadful crime laid to your charge. You have been convicted by a jury of this city, after a lengthy and most painful investigation, followed by a defence which was in every respect worthy of the case. The jury have convicted you, and the law leaves to me no discretion, and I must pass on you the sentence of the law. And this sentence of the law is – This court doth ordain you to be taken from hence to the place from whence you came, and from thence to the place of execution, and that you be there hanged by the neck until you are dead, and that your body be afterwards buried within the precincts of the prison in which you shall have been confined after your conviction, and may the Lord have mercy on your soul.'

PART THREE

After the Trial

XIV

'It is the most dangerous verdict
that has ever been recorded in my experience.'

Five minutes had passed since the jury returned from its deliberations. Now women sobbed openly. Men stealthily wiped flowing tears. His lordship was seen to make great use of his handkerchief. Except for the sniffling and sobbing, the hush continued over the courtroom.

Mrs Maybrick stood. She seemed to totter as she moved toward the steps. Two matrons put out their hands, but she drew back from them. The gesture of courage drew a supporting gasp from the gallery. Without help Mrs Maybrick stepped slowly down the cold steps. She seemed frail and faltering, but she went alone.

The jury remained in their seats as Mrs Maybrick's black widow's cap disappeared down the stairwell in the dock. As Mr Shuttleworth discharged the jury, loud hisses arose throughout the courtroom.

The sound was matched immediately from outdoors, for word of the verdict had reached the vast crowd in Lime Street. A few who cheered instantly regretted such open expression of opinion, for the majority groaned and hissed. The great multitude hooting and hissing its disapproval was heard deep inside St George's Hall.

In the library within the hall, four young barristers who had attended the trial discussed the verdict. Sir Charles Russell came in. His face was ashen, his demeanour grave. 'My boys,' he said, 'what is your view of this verdict?'

No one spoke.

Sir Charles looked from one to another. 'Mark what I say,' he said, his voice choking with emotion. 'It is the most dangerous verdict that has ever been recorded in my experience.'

At the door of St George's, the cook Humphreys and Cadwallader, the housemaid, escorted by a court attendant, gathered their skirts and started down through the crowd on the great stone steps. Someone cried out that they were Nurse Yapp and Bessie Brierley, and the crowd began cursing them and hooting. They were jostled and elbowed. Offensive epithets rained down on them. Their escort hurried them to a cab and helped them inside, and the driver forced his horse, with little care for shins and toes, across Lime Street to the railway station. The crowd chased after them into the station and onto the platform. Seventy policemen tried to break through the mob. To get into the station, they had to detour through the Lime Street Hotel.

At St George's Hall, those of the crowd nearest the doors of the building took charge. Anyone who came out was subjected to close scrutiny. A woman who, despite her protest, was identified as Mrs Briggs was questioned, threatened, jostled, and treated to all the verbal abuse the angry mob could offer. The police came to her aid and cleared a path. They had to struggle against the pressing, jeering throng all the way across the square to the North Western Hotel, where they took the woman inside and locked the main doors against the mob.

Now an important carriage was recognised coming toward the north end of the hall. The cry went up that it was the judge's carriage, and the crowd surged toward it, hooting and hissing incessantly. The determined driver kept his horses moving into the safety of the courtyard. There the judge, heavily guarded by policemen, climbed into the carriage. The presence of the High Sheriff, who got in to ride with the judge, did nothing to quiet the hooting and groaning, and cries of 'Shame! Shame!' were heard again and again as the carriage emerged from the courtyard with the police clearing its path. A thousand or more of the crowd, continuing their angry hooting and groaning, followed the carriage for some distance.

Florence Maybrick was kept waiting in her detention cell in the basement. When an hour had passed and the crowd had not diminished, the prison van in the courtyard was surrounded by policemen. By now, mounted officers had arrived. They blocked the entrance to the courtyard with their horses.

Inside the van, the curtains were drawn tight. Florence Maybrick sat with matrons and police, listening to the howling of the mob. She heard the command for the van to roll. The clatter of hooves was all around her as mounted police surrounded the van. But above the clatter she began to hear cheering. It swelled into a vast chorus long and loud. She could feel the van moving rapidly. The horses were cantering now, but still the cheering continued on all sides. It went on and on, and at last began to die out in the distance behind the van.

As the van disappeared and those who had chased after it came straggling back toward St George's Hall, an impromptu mass meeting began on the broad steps of the building. One speaker after another expressed his dissent from the verdict. It could be noted that all were better dressed and better spoken than the average man in the street. More than one barrister stood to identify himself, and one speaker observed that, whereas there had been a jury of twelve inside the hall, there was a jury of twelve thousand outside, and that all had read every word of the evidence and were unanimous that the case had not been proved.

At Walton Jail, Mrs Maybrick was not taken to the cell where she had previously been confined. She was led to a large room, clean and well-swept, which contained only a bed and a chair. Its windows were heavily barred. As she collapsed on the bed, two female warders were locked into the room with her.

The room and special guard were reserved for those destined for the gallows.

In London that night, a correspondent of the New York *World* found Chauncey M. Depew, a prominent New York lawyer and Republican politician. Depew was a frequent visitor in London and Paris, where his ability as a lecturer and after-dinner speaker had given him a fame even greater than that he enjoyed in America.

The correspondent asked Mr Depew what he thought of the Maybrick verdict.

'In my opinion,' he said, 'the judge's charge convicted her. Such a speech as Russell made, if made before an American jury, would have acquitted her. No American judge would have made such a charge as Judge Stephen made. The jury could not help but see that he believed the woman guilty.'

The correspondent dispatched Mr Depew's words to New York by cable.

In Mobile, Alabama, newsboys hawked the evening papers with cries of Mrs Maybrick's guilt. Old friends of the Chandler family were shocked. No one who knew her could believe her guilty of this awful crime. There seemed to be no other topic of conversation in the city of Mobile that evening.

On the streets of London, feeling was intense. Knots of people gathered to discuss the verdict. In clubs, lawyers and doctors in particular were vehement in their criticism of the outcome. Public opinion clearly was outraged.

In Richmond, a prosperous residential suburb southwest of London, a prominent barrister named Alexander W. MacDougall arrived home from Liverpool, where he had attended the trial. He went immediately to his desk and took pen in hand. He had been through this sort of thing before, and he knew what to do.

On the night of Florence Maybrick's conviction, it seemed as if all England went to bed outraged. On Thursday morning, the country rose resolved to see what could be done.

It was well known that no court of appeal existed in criminal cases. Between the verdict of the jury and the steps of the gallows stood only one resort : the Crown. Queen Victoria alone could change the fate of Florence Maybrick. However, Her Majesty would act in such a case, if she acted at all, only upon the recommendation of her Secretary of State for the Home Department, Mr Henry Matthews.

The morning papers gave their readers some hope. *The Times* expressed surprise at the verdict, and said, 'It is notable that the judge in passing sentence refrained from expressing agreement with the verdict.' The *Star* made a vehement attack on Mr Justice Stephen. The *Chronicle* and the *Standard* strongly disapproved of the verdict, and only the *Telegraph* and the *Daily News* sat on the fence.

In other cities, the majority of newspaper opinion was against the verdict. In Liverpool, the *Daily Post* denounced the disgraceful scene displayed by the mob the evening before, but published the first of many letters from outraged citizens. Written by an anonymous member of the bar, it severely criticised the judge for omitting from his summary the habits of the deceased in eating arsenic, justified the defence counsel's permitting Mrs Maybrick to make her statement, and ended, 'The whole case is about the most mysterious and extraordinary in judicial records.'

In the office of the Cleaver brothers, the morning's first delivery of mail brought hundreds of letters from all parts of the country, the writers asking to sign any petitions which might be prepared for presentation to the Home Secretary. The solicitors drafted a petition, and before noon they had it ready for the printer. They were already calling it the 'Liverpool Memorial', and it read :

> That your memorialists have read and considered the evidence adduced at the trial. That there was no direct evidence of administration of arsenic by the prisoner to the deceased. That the case against the prisoner on the general facts was unduly prejudiced by the evidence of motive, and that there is room for grave doubt whether the circumstantial evidence relied on by the prosecution was weighty enough to

justify conviction. That there was a strong body of medical testimony on behalf of the defence that death was ascribable to natural causes, and there was evidence on the part of the prosecution that it was due to arsenical poisoning. That having regard to the conflicting nature of the medical evidence and the very widespread doubt as to the propriety of the verdict on general grounds it would be in the highest degree unsafe to permit an irrevocable sentence to be carried out. Your memorialists, therefore humbly pray that you will recommend this petition to the favourable consideration of the Crown, and advise her Majesty to respite the sentence of death with a view to commutation or reprieve.

The Messrs Cleaver sent word to the press that they would supply this petition to all who sought it.

The members of the bar were busy drawing up their own petition. It read :

We, the undersigned members of the Bar of the Northern Circuit, having paid great attention to the evidence in the case of Florence Elizabeth Maybrick, humbly pray that you will recommend Her Majesty to commute the death sentence and grant a reprieve on the ground that such evidence, in view of the great conflict of medical testimony as to the cause of death, leaves so much doubt that it is inexpedient and unsafe to carry out an irrevocable sentence.

It was agreed that, after the Liverpool members had signed it, this petition would be sent to Manchester and then to London, so that members of the bar who had left Liverpool could sign it.

Still another petition was drawn up by the medical profession. Among its itemised arguments were these :

3. It was admitted by the medical testimony on behalf of the prosecution that the symptoms during life and the post mortem appearances were in themselves insufficient to justify the conclusion that death was caused by arsenic, and that it was only the discovery of traces of that poison in certain parts of the viscera which eventually led to that conclusion.

4. The arsenic so found in the viscera was less in quantity than that found in any previous case of arsenical poisoning in which arsenic has been found at all.

5. There was indisputable evidence on the part of the defence that

the deceased had been in the habit of taking arsenic, both medicinally and otherwise, for many years, and that the small quantity found in the viscera was inconsistent with the theory of a fatal dose at any time or times during the period covered by the illness of the deceased.

6. Lastly, your memorialists agree with the evidence given by Dr Tidy, Dr Macnamara, and Mr Paul on behalf of the defence, that the medical evidence on behalf of the prosecution had entirely failed to prove that the death was due to arsenical poisoning at all.

Sir Charles Russell appeared at the offices of the Cleaver brothers and spoke to the press. He made it clear that the necessary papers for a formal petition to the Home Secretary were in preparation and would shortly be filed.

The press sought those who could not be found so easily. Reporters were dispatched to Southport, Ormskirk and Bootle, to Bickerstaffe and St Helens, to Melling, Wigan and North Meols, to interview the members of the jury. They were scattered over the towns of Lancashire, for, despite the judge's so labelling them, they were not a jury of the city at all. When asked about the short time it took them to reach their decision, some said that on Tuesday night they had consulted for three and a half hours. The judge had told them, before adjournment that day, that he had nearly concluded his summing-up. All were at that point convinced of the prisoner's guilt. They felt that, though the medical evidence was contradictory, one of the medical witnesses for the defence had been so shaken in cross-examination that his testimony was not reliable. Therefore, they decided not to allow themselves to become confused by trying to reconcile the evidence of the medical experts.

Some members of the jury added that they had studied the newspaper reports of the trial each evening after court, clipping and marking the important passages.

In Walton Jail, Florence Maybrick was permitted a visit from her mother and her lawyer. The Baroness von Roques found her daughter exhausted and distraught. Two warders were on guard day and night. Florence told her mother that if it had not been for the judge's lengthy comments on her wicked immorality, the jury would certainly have acquitted her. She felt that if the medical evidence alone were placed before the Home Office authorities, they would never endorse the jury's sentence.

In the courtyard of the jail, wagons full of flowers were unloaded.

In Lime Street, a large crowd was waiting when Sir James Stephen came out after the day in court. He was again booed and hooted as he climbed into his carriage and drove away.

In Brooklyn, Dr Greggs hurriedly left for Boston. His house had been besieged by reporters for several days. Now the verdict had doubled their numbers. He left Mrs Greggs to cope with the press, and though she refused to discuss the verdict she pleaded with the reporters on another subject. 'You know my husband sometimes prescribes a face wash for the complexion, but it is not a cosmetic. I wish you would not mention the term again. The ladies don't like it.'

A *World* reporter, whose paper (mainly as a result of its comprehensive coverage of the vagaries of the human race) boasted a circulation greater than that of any two other American newspapers combined, chuckled. Two days ago, Dr Greggs himself had said, when asked if he called it a cosmetic, 'Well, you can't call it anything else. A cosmetic means a wash for the face.'

In Bar Harbour, Maine, President Benjamin Harrison was vacationing at the summer home of his Secretary of State, James G. Blaine. They refused to talk to reporters about Mrs Maybrick's fate. An assistant to Mr Blaine said that no official information had been received, and added that, as Mrs Maybrick lost her American nationality and became an Englishwoman when she married, it was difficult to see how the United States government could intervene on her behalf.

In England the evening papers universally denounced the verdict of the jury. Among those who expressed editorial opinion, no fence-sitters remained.

In Gateacre, Master James Maybrick and his sister Gladys continued to live with Mrs Janion, under the care of Nurse Yapp. Though they knew their father was dead, they had not been told the reason for their mother's long absence.

By Friday morning the excitement had increased. No case could be remembered in which the verdict had aroused more vehemence. Plans were made for public meetings at the Marble Arch in Hyde Park, London, a rallying point for soap-box orators. Such prominent lawyers as Sir Henry James, who was a member of Parliament, said they would spare no effort to have the sentence set aside. The medical profession joined the protests not only because of the conflicting nature of the medical testimony but because Mr Justice Stephen seemed to have taken pains to sneer at them with his emphasis on divergent opinion and his use of the old saying about doctors putting drugs of which they knew little into a body about which they knew less.

The Times published a number of letters to its editor. The longest came from the barrister, Alexander W. MacDougall of Richmond. He cited the Penge case twelve years earlier, in which four prisoners were sentenced to death, with the marked approval of the judge, after a trial which produced considerable conflict of medical testimony. 'I for one was not satisfied,' said MacDougall's letter, 'and I took the step of convening a public meeting at the Cannon-street Hotel.' The result was that the capital penalty was remitted in all four cases, and one of the women, who, like Mrs Maybrick, had been guilty of immorality, was unconditionally released. MacDougall now proposed a public meeting to consider the Maybrick case.

Sir Charles Russell's memorandum to the Home Secretary came to twenty printed folios. He addressed it to Mr Matthews with a strong letter that said, 'Against her there was a strong case, undoubtedly, of the means being within her reach to poison her husband; but there was no direct evidence of administration by her.' He added that 'Mrs Maybrick ought to be released at once.'

The Governor of Walton Jail was dismayed to learn that even more flowers than yesterday were arriving addressed to Mrs Maybrick. There seemed to be no end to the line of florist's delivery carts unloading bouquets in the jail courtyard.

Thomas Wainwright, plumber, gasfitter, and lately jury foreman, declared that he strongly deprecated the press's pumping the jury. He declared emphatically that the verdict was not decided until the whole of the case had been gone through.

In Liverpool and London, it was rumoured that a memorial in favour of the reprieve of Mrs Maybrick was being prepared in the House of Commons. Some held that members would refuse to sign on the ground that for the legislature to interfere with the judicature would establish a precedent of the very worst kind.

In the House itself, as quickly as members left the Chamber for the smoking room, what were expected to be tumultuous wrangles over the Irish question turned into vehement discussions of the Maybrick case.

Petitions were circulated through the Liverpool Exchange, where James Maybrick's former associates talked of nothing but the conviction. In Cardiff, merchants circulated petitions among residents, hotels offered petitions to all in their lobbies, and tables were set up in the streets for working men who wished to sign.

By the end of the day, the Cleavers' office in Liverpool had issued more than one thousand copies of their 'Liverpool Memorial' petition.

Across the Atlantic, Lawyer Macklin interrupted a vacation when he learned of the conviction of Mrs Maybrick. He telegraphed Dr Greggs in Brooklyn, asking for an affidavit that he had given Mrs Maybrick a prescription containing arsenic. He cabled an associate in Paris to visit the American Consul and try to procure a stay of proceedings until more evidence could be submitted. He cabled the Home Secretary in London, asking if he would receive additional evidence.

The fact that Mrs Maybrick was an American combined with the sensational features of the case to arouse tremendous interest in her fate. Most of the sentiment was in her favour. Countless American lawyers gave their opinions that the judge had exceeded his authority in making a charge which as much as told the jury she was guilty. But one well-known Englishman in New York disagreed. 'I cannot understand why this case has attracted so much attention in this country,' he said. 'The woman was rightfully convicted. There was no possible doubt as to her guilt. It is to the glory of British institutions that legal processes there are so prompt and just as they have been in the case of The Queen versus Maybrick.'

By Saturday, passers-by were used to seeing self-appointed orators conducting meetings on the steps of St George's Hall. The Walton Jail courtyard had become not only the unloading dock for bouquets of flowers by the hundreds, it had become the rallying place for any number of cranks who hoped to achieve Mrs Maybrick's deliverance by besieging her prison. Seven men had extended offers of marriage to Florence Maybrick, and one, observing that if an innocent person was to be hanged it might as well be himself, offered to take her place on the scaffold. Madame Tussaud's Baker Street Museum mounted a life-size wax figure of Florence Maybrick in her widow's weeds, a handkerchief in her hand. Several newspapers published a rumour that the Baroness von Roques was the niece of Jefferson Davis.

The Times editorial page contained a strong comment on the hysterical agitation 'which has made of Mrs Maybrick a species of heroine'. It repeated its surprise at the verdict, but said the jury were as competent to form an opinion as the scientific witnesses themselves. It went on to say that the wave of excitement ought to sweep away every vestige of opposition to two great reforms : the rules which prevented a prisoner from giving sworn evidence on his own behalf, and the institution of a Court of Criminal Appeal.

In Liverpool, the Cleavers issued another thousand copies of their petition, and ordered more printed. The former proprietor of the Sefton

Club and Chambers, Mr Henry Bliss, came to the Cleaver office and made a sworn deposition :

> Mr Maybrick lived in the chambers on and off for several months, and was in the habit of dosing himself. On one occasion he asked me to leave a prescription at a well-known Liverpool chemist's to be made up by the time he left 'Change. The chemist remarked : 'He ought to be very careful and not take an overdose of it.'

In London, the American ambassador, Robert Todd Lincoln, said that he could do nothing in his official capacity unless instructions came to him from Washington. There was, in fact, very little reaction among Americans in England. A few, staying in such London hotels as the Metropole, the Grand and the Victoria, got up petitions among their fellow American guests, but found little response.

Sunday sermons did not let churchgoers forget Florence Maybrick. On the Isle of Man, the Bishop of Sodor and Man, preaching to an immense congregation that included Lieutenant-Governor Walpole, urged those who felt they possessed information equal to the jury to sign the petition if they opposed the verdict.

The weekend papers brought many more letters. One, from Mr Auberon Herbert, suggested that it was unnecessary to ask what irritant may have set up gastro-enteritis in Maybrick, when the sick man's stomach had been used by his doctors as a 'druggist's waste-pipe' for an incredible succession of medicines.

Sunday readers across the Atlantic were treated to greater perspective than were those in England when they read a lengthy dispatch from the London correspondent of *The New York Times*. He wrote, 'There is candidly more acute excitement throughout the kingdom over the fact that Mrs Maybrick lies under the sentence of death than any other event has produced during the past ten years.'

> The terrible situation of the fair Alabamian, the chances for her escape, the question of her guilt – these are the sole subject of conversation everywhere, from the lobby of Parliament down to the corner pub in Whitechapel. The oldest inhabitant does not remember any case which has created a tithe of the commotion in the public mind that now exists over this young, bright, attractive American widow.
>
> What it all means is that the interesting personality of the condemned woman has acted as a spark to ignite a long accumulating store of combustible material. The state of the English law practice in

murder cases is simply shocking. Here there is no appeal from a capital conviction. A man may secure a new hearing over a case which involves sixpence, but when it is a question of his life it is rigorously denied him. The solitary avenue of possible escape lies in an appeal to the Home Secretary and all the petitions now on foot are addressed to him. But he in turn is bound in etiquette to follow the opinion of the Judge who tried the case and it is obvious that Justice Stephen would hang Mrs Maybrick with as little compunction as a gamekeeper would hang an entrapped bird of prey.

The writer expressed succinctly the tremendous influence of the judge.

The character of this Judge, as, indeed, of all English Judges, has been almost incredibly hardened by the influence of this autocratic power. As a class they are the most conceited, dogmatic, body of men probably existing in the whole English-speaking world. From habitual dealing with the whole criminal class as vermin, they come to regard jurymen as a sort of servile race. Out of this has grown a monstrous abuse of the institution known as the charge to the jury. Justice Stephen had the effrontery to harangue this Liverpool jury of artisans and small shopkeepers through a speech which took two days to deliver, and gave in detail his opinion upon every minute question of fact. In effect he devoted so much of his charge to a heated denunciation of marital infidelity that the jury practically convicted her for that offence.

The New York correspondent thought the bulk of the people seemed little occupied in their own hearts with the problem of Mrs Maybrick's guilt.

Nineteen out of every twenty persons I have talked with believe, or at least think it is probable, that she deliberately killed her husband; yet perhaps fifteen of this number would join the agitation for her free pardon, and five or six would say frankly that they don't care whether she poisoned the tiresome old fool or not.

Underlying this curious attitude and largely accounting for it is a strange moral ferment about the marriage question which is stirring under an equable surface the English social structure. The absence of an intelligent divorce law drives this corroding unrest down beneath the surface, and the inherent prudery and pretence of the English character forbid even its existence being recognised.

Meantime, the *World* sought Dr Greggs of Brooklyn. He had returned from his Boston flight, and permitted an interview. The result was a headline, 'Mrs Maybrick's Many Brooklyn Friends,' and a story that generated more sympathy for the prisoner. The doctor seemed to be a fatherly man who found the Chandlers to be people who deserved his friendship and that of his wife and daughter. There was no doubt that Florence's husband was a brute, he added, but her confession, and his forgiveness, were enough to take away any thought that she could wish to take his life. The interview could not fail to enlist sympathy for the American woman whom Dr Greggs described as 'this slight girl, with dark hair and beautiful eyes, very charming and lovable'.

The eyes of the girl in Walton Jail were dark and hollow when her mother and Mr Richard Cleaver saw her on Monday. The Baroness von Roques was now permitted free access to her daughter's cell every other day. The prisoner wore a well-washed prison dress of coarse blue homespun and a brown felt cape with a broad arrow of black, which marked her condemned status. A small white cap was on her head. She sat on a wooden chair in a cell whose walls and floor were of brick.

Mr Cleaver talked of legal expenses. Bringing witnesses from London, Dublin and the United States had been costly. He presented a deed for Mrs Maybrick to sign. It was a mortgage for $5,000 on a warehouse on land Mrs Maybrick held at 39 East Fourteenth Street in New York. The mortgage was made out to Mr Cleaver 'as security for certain debts of said Maybrick to said Cleaver, payable January 30, 1889,' with interest at five per cent half yearly. Florence Elizabeth Maybrick signed the deed.

In the prison courtyard, an assistant to the governor contradicted a statement by a reporter that Walton Jail's notorious prisoner was *enceinte*.

Alfred Brierley, who had remained in seclusion in his bachelor apartment, yielded to the newsmen who constantly pressed him for a statement. 'A most injurious misconstruction has been put upon my relations with Mrs Maybrick,' he said, 'as unjust to her as it is unfair to myself. Our meeting in London was a grave wrong, but in this trial it has been magnified greatly, and assumptions have been based upon it which are entirely unwarranted by the actual facts.' He went on to say that his intimacy with Mrs Maybrick lasted only a short time, and came to an end on 21st March. He blamed Mr Justice Stephen for assuming they had continued the relationship during Maybrick's final illness.

When the Baroness von Roques returned from her visit to Walton Jail, she wrote to a lawyer and friend, J. Treeve Edgcome. Referring to the judge's question, 'Why was the prisoner's mother not called?' she said, 'I can certainly affirm that Mrs Maybrick used arsenic as a cosmetic, and that she knew the use to which flypapers were put for eruptions of the skin and for tan and freckles.' She wished also to contradict the judge's inference that 'John' was a lover, as he was an old family friend and he was perfectly justified in taking Mrs Maybrick to dinner and the theatre and in writing to her. She had told John of her domestic un-happiness and of a visit to her solicitor with a view to a separation. Why Sir Charles Russell had not pursued the matter of the 'lady' in the case was something the Baroness could not understand, for Mrs Maybrick had strong proof of her husband's infidelity – and with such a lover to make use of, why should she poison him?

The High Sheriff of Lancashire, noting that not less than three Sundays must pass between the sentencing and the date of execution, announced that the date had been fixed for Monday, 26th August, at eight in the morning at Walton Jail. The jail governor ordered the gallows to be erected.

The Times published a letter from a prominent barrister, J. Fletcher-Moulton, Q.C. He argued that, so long as there was no appeal in criminal cases, it was natural for the results of a trial such as that of Mrs Maybrick to receive close public attention. He believed that the prosecution failed to prove that Maybrick's death was not from natural causes operating upon a system in which a long course of arsenic-taking had developed a predisposition to gastro-enteritis. This, he said, should have entitled the prisoner to acquittal. He announced a meeting to be held at the Cannon-street Hotel on Tuesday.

Other letters took up various points. 'Malaysia' argued that arsenic-eaters must maintain the habit, and that Maybrick had died because, in the course of his treatment for gastro-enteritis, his regular diet of arsenic was suddenly cut off. David Cumming wrote to say that, as a cure for eczema, he had become an arsenic-eater, and had regularly consumed, in an eight-ounce bottle of sarsaparilla, enough arsenic to kill a regiment of soldiers. 'I need hardly say,' he added, 'no one in my own home was aware of the quantity of arsenic I was putting out of sight in this way.' William Boyd wrote from Wiggonholt Rectory in Pulborough that the phrase 'sick unto death' was used to describe Hezekiah in Isaiah XXXVIII, and could be found also in Shakespeare's *Henry VIII*.

As the day ended, the clerks in the office of the Cleaver brothers counted the signatures on petitions that had been returned to them. They came to well over one hundred thousand. The flood of signed petitions and of letters requesting petitions was now more than they could cope with. Mr

Cleaver notified the press that his office simply could not supply enough forms for the entire country, and said that suitable forms published in the newspapers would be acceptable. He urged the signers, and those organising the signing of petitions, to present their memorials to their local representatives in Parliament or directly to the Home Office.

In the evening, a mass meeting was held on the steps of St George's Hall. Five thousand people crowded Lime Street to approve a motion that the Home Secretary advise her Majesty to respite the sentence of death on Mrs Maybrick. A gentleman named A. Beattie attempted to move an amendment. He was overwhelmed by the supporters of the motion. As the crowd dispersed, Beattie was attacked. He was rescued by the police and escorted to the sanctuary of the Lime Street Station.

The Liverpool Assizes had ended. Sir James Fitzjames Stephen went up to London and met on Tuesday, 13th August, with the Home Secretary. They discussed the Maybrick case throughout the better part of the morning.

At the same time, the Baroness von Roques met with a crowd of reporters. She accused Mrs Briggs and Nurse Yapp of poisoning Michael Maybrick's mind and creating suspicion. Nobody could have poisoned Maybrick with arsenic without his knowledge, she added, because he had been using the stuff for more than eleven years. She offered strong comment on Edwin Maybrick's interception of letters, on the sale of the household furnishings before the will was probated, on libellous statements published in the papers concerning the deaths of her own previous husbands, and on Nurse Yapp's resentment when her mistress chided her for lapses of duty.

That afternoon, the great hall of the Cannon-street Hotel was crowded with men and women who had responded to J. Fletcher-Moulton's invitation to consider the verdict in the Maybrick case. Elected chairman of the meeting, Alexander MacDougall announced that he had spent three nights reading the verbatim report and the summing-up. He reviewed the reasons why the public should demand that the sentence of death be remitted.

The meeting was held in an almost continuous uproar. 'Shame!' was cried at mention that the Home Secretary would not receive deputations in favour of Mrs Maybrick, 'Hear, hear!' at every point favourable to her. Loud cheers punctuated the meeting. Each mention of Mr Justice Stephen brought hissing and booing. When the resolution was at last presented, the cheering was so prolonged that the vicar of St Stephen's, Launceston, rising to second the motion, was drowned out.

A lawyer named William Hicks rose to propose an amendment. He was loudly hissed. When Mr B. C. Keevil said, 'And I have one, too,' the hall became uncontrollable. The chairman pointed out that he must ask for comment supporting the resolution before he heard amendments. Several speakers addressed the crowd in support, and Mr Hicks then rose to move his amendment. It read :

That this meeting of the citizens of London declines to be a party to a sentimental and unconstitutional attempt to interfere with the course of justice in the case of the Liverpool murderess, and desires to record its high appreciation of the painstaking care and trouble displayed by the Judge and jury in the performance of their most unpleasant duty.

Hicks got no chance to read his amendment. Copies of it had already been seen by some, who led a violent outburst of hooting, hissing, and cock-crowing. The chairman tried, above the uproar, to ask if it was the pleasure of the meeting that the amendment should be proposed. The response was, 'No, No! Turn him out!' and more hooting until Mr Hicks, howled down, resumed his seat.

Dr Forbes Winslow spoke of the twenty-one irritant poisons put into the patient's wretched insides by his doctors, and said that it was a wonder the deceased had any stomach at all to analyse. He wondered why a stomach pump had not been used when arsenic was suspected, and he wondered at the apathy of the jury.

The original resolution was now put to the meeting by the chairman, and it was carried with one dissenting vote – that of Hicks. As the meeting adjourned, the crowd turned on its lone dissenter. He escaped only with police aid.

The Times published a letter from a woman who had known English, Russian, German and American schoolgirls to soak common flypapers in Eau de Cologne to obtain a wash for the complexion. She had seen an actress of the Duke of Meiningen's troupe in Bale buy flypapers in a drugstore for the purpose. She was sorry she had become interested in the Maybrick case too late to offer this information to the defence.

It was not only the editors of newspapers who received letters about the Maybrick case. Many wrote directly to Her Majesty, as well as to the Prince and Princess of Wales. Her Majesty's ministers nearly all found their mail filled with urgent requests for help for Florence Maybrick. Most such letters strongly threatened political intimidation. The Home Secretary himself received the strongest.

In the House of Commons on Wednesday, Mr Matthews was asked to lay the twenty-folio memorandum of Sir Charles Russell on the table of the House, where it would be accessible to the members. He emphatically declined. A simple memorial was introduced, praying that the sentence of death on Mrs Maybrick might be commuted, and before the House rose at the end of the day fifty-three members, mostly Liberal and National but including a few Conservative and Unionist, had signed.

Richard Cleaver was in London that day, supervising the collection of petitions. One of many he had brought from Liverpool contained fifty-thousand names. He found that those in London ranged from a special petition of twenty-five doctors in London hospitals to a general petition of *St Stephen's Review* containing five thousand. Other petitions arrived from all parts of England.

Mrs Briggs, having read of the extensive remarks made to reporters by the Baroness von Roques, had a few things of her own to say to the *Liverpool Daily Post*. She knew nothing of the letter opened by Nurse Yapp, nor of Mrs Maybrick's intrigue with Mr Brierley, she said, until it was publicly mentioned. She searched the house after Mr Maybrick's death only in order to find the keys to the safe, as Mr Michael Maybrick wanted to find the will. 'If Mrs Maybrick had given up the keys of the safe, we should never have looked or found anything,' she added.

In Norfolk, Virginia, one of the best-known whorehouse proprietors in town, Madam Mary Hogwood, discussed the Maybrick case with two gentlemen she knew, J. A. Dalby and Barney Kahn, who was a dry-goods merchant on Main Street. When they had heard what she had to say, they advised her to go before a notary and make a statement.

Two important medical publications appeared on Thursday, 15th August. The *London Lancet* took a view unfavourable to Mrs Maybrick, based on the medical aspects of the case and on her possession of arsenic. In the *British Medical Journal* their Liverpool correspondent pointing out the irreconcilable difference of opinion among the medical witnesses, said that the striking anomalies removed it from the category of cases in which there was no room for doubt. The *Journal* also published the opinions of seven professors of medical jurisprudence, only two of whom supported the verdict.

The organisers of the Cannon-street Hotel meeting met on Thursday afternoon over a letter from a London doctor who said a Liverpool stockbroker had called on him several times while suffering from psoriasis of the feet. He had prescribed a solution of arsenic and told his patient that if he did not continue the medicine he might have paralysis. The doctor has just seen a picture of the late Mr Maybrick and had no doubt that the stockbroker he treated was that man.

One London resident, stopping by his bootmaker's shop, watched a small boy about nine years old, and his companion who admitted to thirteen, sign a Maybrick petition. The boy hesitated, then added the name of his sister, who he said was fifteen. The watcher hurried home to compose a letter to *The Times* advising the editor how the petitions were swelled to such magnificent proportions.

American newspaper stories on the Maybrick case usually mentioned lawyers Roe and Macklin in New York, and to their office at 156 Broadway came an overwhelming number of letters of encouragement and advice. Thursday's mail included a letter from a well-known Canadian barrister, Alfred Monck of Montreal. He offered to prove that Nurse Yapp had once been forced to leave Montreal to escape an indictment for perjury. 'Three years ago,' wrote Monck, 'Melvin Smith, a resident of Montreal, sued his wife for a divorce, and the witness against his wife was a woman named Yapp. She is undoubtedly the Liverpool nurse. Smith lost his case, and before Yapp could be indicted she fled from Canada. She had been an accessory along with Smith's mistress in a conspiracy to blacken the character on an honourable wife.'

At the State Department in Washington, officials were puzzled when they received several unusual letters, a deposition, and a strange object. The letters came from a number of gentlemen in Norfolk, Virginia. Each wished to say that, despite the bad character of the notorious woman whose statement was attached, she had a good reputation for telling the truth. The deposition said :

Know all men by these presents, That I, Mary Hogwood, residing in the city of Norfolk, Va., do unhesitatingly say that I knew the late James Maybrick for several years, and that up to the time of his marriage he called at my house, when in Norfolk, at least two or three times a week, and that I saw him frequently in his different moods and fancies. It was a common thing for him to take arsenic two or three times during an evening. He would always say, before taking it, 'Well, I am going to take my evening dose.' He would pull from his pocket a small vial in which he carried his arsenic, and, putting a small quantity on his tongue, he would wash it down with a sip of wine. In fact, so often did he repeat this that I became afraid that he would die suddenly in my house, and then some of us would be suspected of his murder. When drunk Mr James Maybrick would pour the powder into the palm of his hand and lick it up with his tongue. I often cautioned him, but he answered: 'Oh, I am used to it. It will not harm me.' One of the vials used by Mr Maybrick to carry arsenic was left by him in my care during his last visit here; and I shall be glad to turn it over to the authorities if it can be of any use.

I have been quite ill for a long time – so sick that I have paid little attention to the newspapers, and therefore I knew hardly anything about the facts concerning the alleged murder; but, knowing Mr Maybrick as I do and his habits, I am not surprised in the least at hearing of his death, and do not believe that his wife had any more to do with causing his death than I had. I have always believed that his habit of arsenic eating would carry him off.

Mary Hogwood

The object enclosed with the statement was what was known as a homoeopathic long dram vial.

In London that Thursday evening, Lord Fitzgerald asked in the House of Lords whether the government would consider constituting a Court of Criminal Appeal. The Lord High Chancellor, Baron Halsbury, was opposed to any discussion of the subject while the public was excited, and Baron Herschell, a former Lord High Chancellor, said that wrong decisions were rare in criminal cases. He trusted that the government would consider the matter during the Parliamentary recess.

On Friday, the 16th, the *Liverpool Daily Post* disclosed that Mrs C. E. Samuelson, who testified at the Inquest that Mrs Maybrick said she hated her husband, was not called at the trial because she had disappeared and the police were unable to serve her with a subpoena. Petitions reached the Home Office from Belfast, Wolverhampton, Leicester, Spalding, and other places, and one from Rochdale listed twelve thousand signatures. Before the House rose at the end of the day, its memorial included eighty-eight signatures. In Switzerland, British residents sent off a long petition to the Home Secretary.

The floral displays continued arriving by the cartload at Walton Jail, and on Saturday alone eleven hundred letters were delivered there for Mrs Maybrick. She was permitted to read a handful. More than one newspaper in Liverpool and London received wagonloads of letters each day. In theatres, railroad stations, and on the streets, men and women armed with petitions demanded signatures from everyone they met, and openly insulted those who refused.

At one o'clock, the Home Secretary met with Mr Justice Stephen and Lord Chancellor Halsbury and heard testimony from Dr Tidy and others. Included was a deposition from one Captain Irving, who had known Mr and Mrs Maybrick during ocean crossings and had dined at Battlecrease House on 1st May with the Maybricks and Edwin Maybrick. A short while before Maybrick's death, he had met Edwin and, knowing that Maybrick was ill, said, 'What on earth is the matter with Jim?' Edwin replied, 'Oh, he's killing himself with that damned strychnine.'

The opinion was held generally that Queen Victoria would act without hesitation on a favourable recommendation from the Home Secretary. She was said to be profoundly averse to the infliction of capital punishment on any woman. But she was strictly bound by the advice of her Home Secretary.

Mrs Maybrick's condition was decidedly better on Saturday. The hope of a respite of the death sentence, said the jail doctors, had buoyed her up greatly. The Cannon-street committee met and called a public meeting for Wednesday if no reprieve was announced in the meantime. In a Jarrow shipyard, the manager and twelve hundred workers unanimously signed a petition for the reprieve of the convict. A strong letter from Lord Esher to *The Times* brought that paper's editorial opinion that 'the Home Secretary is not a judge and has not the power of a judge. The judgment pronounced by a strong court of criminal appeal, such as Lord Esher's letter suggests, would do more to satisfy the public mind than the best efforts of the Home Secretary could possibly do.'

The New Yorker was able to learn from his *Times* of Sunday that there was 'POLITICS IN EVERYTHING.' 'The partisan line has gradually been drawn in the Maybrick agitation,' cabled the London correspondent. He went on :

Loosely speaking, the Tories are in favor of her being hanged and the Radicals and Home Rulers are against it. Of course, there are infinite subdivisions within these broadly-defined classifications. One of the most curious is that all teetotalers within the Parnelite party, who are in favor of closing the public houses in Ireland on Sunday, are to a man against Mrs Maybrick. On the other hand, the whole group of Tories who on occasion vote with Churchill are strong champions of her cause.

During the week there has been a slowly-growing conviction that the woman would be executed after all. Today it is thought here that there is a marked reaction in this feeling, apparently based on nothing more definite than the fact that the Home Secretary yesterday had a long interview with the Lord Chancellor, who is the titular keeper of the Queen's conscience.

He is a little chuckle-headed, porker-jowled man, who looks more like the custodian of the royal gin bottle than of a conscience, and is believed by lawyers who know him to be the very last man in the kingdom who would counsel the upsetting of a Judge's decision for the mere matter of a woman's neck. The agitation has grown so wide-spread that the Ministry may well fear its results in case the wretched woman is hanged.

On Monday, Henry Matthews was able for the first time since Thurs-day to set aside consideration of the Maybrick case and resume his seat as Secretary of State upon the Treasury bench in Parliament. He had been there only a few minutes when three petitions were dropped into his lap. It was an historic moment : No Secretary of State had ever before, while sitting upon the Treasury bench, had memorials forced upon his knees for the reprieve of a person condemned to death.

The number of signers of the Parliamentary Memorial rose to ninety-one. A petition in Birmingham listed forty thousand signatures.

An admitted arsenic-eater wrote to *The Times* from Paris to say that he had taken twenty drops of Fowler's Solution each day for thirteen years, and that when ill or travelling he had at times been forced to dis-continue the practice and immediately felt an extraordinary decline of physical and mental strength. He felt sure that Maybrick, deprived of his powders from the beginning of his illness, had lost the strength essential to his recovery.

In Federal Court in Louisville, Kentucky, a friendly suit was brought by Attorney David Armstrong on behalf of Florence Maybrick, her mother and her children, for the appointment of trustees for her large estate in the mountain lands of Breathitt and Pike counties. The declared object was to relieve men who were trustees for other American property of Mrs Maybrick from having to provide security in handling the Ken-tucky property.

In the courtyard of Walton Jail, carpenters began to erect a scaffold. Florence Maybrick could see and hear them a few yards beyond her cell window.

It was Yapp versus Briggs in the newspapers on Tuesday. Reporters interrupted the nurse's attentions to the Maybrick children to ask her reaction to Mrs Briggs's earlier interview. 'I never said to Mrs Briggs,' said Alice Yapp, 'that the mistress was poisoning master.' She added a story that had never been heard in inquest, inquiry or trial. A week before Mr Maybrick died, she said, the mistress sent Mary Cadwallader to the drugstore with a prescription. The chemist refused to make it up because it contained a poisonous drug but was not signed by a doctor. When she was on the witness stand, she added, she did not mention the matter because neither Mr Addison nor Sir Charles Russell asked about it.

Explaining the Kentucky lawsuit to reporters, New York lawyer W. H. Gardiner, who had once been managing clerk of Roe and Macklin's office and was one of the trustees of Florence Maybrick's property in America, said that settlers had been found on the Southern property. Lawsuits to oust them were expected to be expensive, and the trustees of her other property, seeking to avoid becoming personally liable for such expenses, sought court-appointed trustees. Gardiner's estimate of the trial expenses included Sir Charles Russell's retainer of $2,500, plus $500 a day for seven days, and well over $2,000 for the cost of sending lawyers to America and taking witnesses to Liverpool. 'Then they have had lawyers in the South hunting up evidence,' he said. 'These Southern lawyers are heavy chargers, and thousands of dollars must have been expended in this direction.' Altogether, Gardiner's interview gave New York readers the picture of a young woman who deserved great sympathy.

At the office of Roe and Macklin, a letter said that Southerners would agree that the expression 'sick unto death' was commonly used in the Gulf and adjoining states to describe any painful illness, however slight. The lawyers decided to send the letter directly to the British Home Secretary.

Wednesday, 21st August, brought the Home Secretary and the judge together again. Mr Justice Stephen now gave it as his opinion that if the prisoner was reprieved she should receive a life sentence.

The newspapers published rumour after rumour that the sentence had been commuted, that a full pardon had been granted, that the gallows would be used. Leaders of meetings in other cities, such as Birmingham, had telegraphed the Home Office for confirmation or denial of various rumours so that they could cancel or carry on their meetings. To each, the Home Office replied that no decision had been reached.

The petitions continued coming in. Estimates of the total number of signatures ranged from a half million to over a million. The *St Stephen's Review* delivered its third petition, a single paper 182 yards long and containing seventeen thousand names. The Women's Committee of the Cannon-street Committee, delivering a lengthy petition, declared that if the Home Secretary simply granted a reprieve to Mrs Maybrick it was their intention to agitate until she was set free.

On Thursday, 22nd August, Florence Maybrick was taking her daily exercise in a small yard that opened off the condemned cell. She heard a voice call her, and turned to see Captain Anderson, the governor of Walton Jail, coming into the yard with the chief matron. 'Maybrick,' he said, his voice trembling with emotion, 'no commutation of sentence has come down today, and I consider it my duty to tell you to prepare for death.'

'Thank you, governor,' she said. 'My conscience is clear. God's will be done.' She did not know what date, if any, had been set for her execution.

The governor walked away, and Mrs Maybrick soon returned to her cell. There she found tears running down the face of the female warder.

The Home Secretary received a message that day from a clergyman named Barrett Anderson. The pastor said that Captain Irving, who was now at sea, remembered that when he visited James Maybrick on 1st May, the cotton broker pulled from his breast pocket a small packet which he emptied into a glass of water, and then drank it down. The Home Secretary asked for some confirmation of the story.

Toward evening, as the steamship *Scythia* was preparing to sail from Liverpool harbour, a tall, well-built and well-dressed gentleman, suave of manner and with reddish beard pointed and close-cropped, came aboard. He was about forty years old. A somewhat younger man with him appeared to be his brother. They had scarcely boarded the ship when the older man was recognised as Alfred Brierley.

It took only a few minutes for a large crowd to gather on the pier. The younger Mr Brierley seemed flustered by the gathering of the crowd, and as soon as they had given orders about their luggage the two disappeared into their cabin. The first order from their room was for a bottle of whisky.

The *Scythia* sailed at dinner time, bound for America.

In London, Alexander MacDougall called to order a public meeting in the Olympia Theatre. The truculent crowd frequently interrupted the speakers. Some got no chance to be heard. There were both cheers and hisses for everyone.

Mr Matthews stayed late in the Home Office. At last he called for a messenger, and gave him a sealed message for the governor of Walton Jail. The messenger left London for Liverpool on the eight o'clock train.

Next, the Home Secretary sent for representatives of the newspapers. When they had gathered, he issued a statement :

After the fullest consideration, the Home Secretary advised Her Majesty to respite the capital punishment of Florence Elizabeth Maybrick and to commute the punishment to penal servitude for life; inasmuch as, although the evidence leads to the conclusion that the prisoner administered and attempted to administer arsenic to her husband with intent to murder him, yet it does not wholly exclude a reasonable doubt whether his death was in fact caused by the administration of arsenic.

Before the gentlemen of the press raced for their offices, the Home Secretary said the decision was not to imply the slightest reflection on the experienced practitioners who gave evidence, and added that the course adopted had the concurrence of the learned judge.

In the Olympia Theatre, Alexander MacDougall took the floor and asked for silence. He was greeted by an uproar. He demanded silence by remarking that the woman was now lying in the valley of the shadow of death. He achieved relative silence, then said that he had an important announcement to make. An evening paper had just announced that the Home Secretary had commuted the death sentence.

The audience came to its feet, hats flying into the air, handkerchiefs and umbrellas waving wildly. The meeting ended in uproar, moving a resolution that the Crown should never have tried the poor woman in the first place, and congratulating itself that the people were the real lawmakers of the country and that during the last fourteen days the case had been retried by a greater jury.

In Walton Jail, Florence Maybrick had said her prayers and gone to bed. She was calm but exhausted. Yet she found it difficult to get to sleep.

The Queen's messenger reached Liverpool at midnight. He took a cab for Walton Jail, more than six miles away.

It was one thirty in the morning when Mrs Maybrick heard the wheels of the cab in the courtyard beyond her cell.

The lone turnkey on duty at the gate led the Queen's messenger to the governor's residence. They roused Captain Anderson, and he read the reprieve and commutation. He called for the chaplain and hurried to Mrs Maybrick's cell.

She heard the shuffle of feet outside the cell, the click of the key in the lock. She sat up in bed as the governor came in, the chaplain and a warder behind him. 'It's well,' he said. 'It's good news.' He read her the reprieve and commutation.

XV

'How are you, Maybrick? Any complaints?
Do you want anything?'

Florence Maybrick awoke on Friday morning in the prison hospital, where she had been taken after fainting.

Alfred Brierley awoke in his cabin aboard the *Scythia* as she called at Queenstown. Word of Mrs Maybrick's reprieve ran through the ship immediately upon landing. Reporters hurried aboard to get a statement from the most conspicuous man on the ship. He would say only that he was immensely pleased with the news.

The reaction in Liverpool was one of general satisfaction. The newspapers praised the Home Secretary for the manner in which he had discharged his difficult task.

The Times was equally pleased :

It is a verdict which the jury themselves might have found if it had been suggested to them. As no such suggestion was ever made, the jury may be excused for not having evolved it out of their own brains. They took the ordinary view, that it was a case of murder or complete innocence. The Home Secretary's decision therefore justifies the jury. It makes things comfortable all round for the scientific experts. Lastly, it is to be observed that it has the concurrence of Mr Justice Stephen.

Not everyone agreed that the Home Secretary's decision made things comfortable all round for the scientific experts, or even part way round for any one else. In effect, concluded Alexander MacDougall, Mrs Maybrick had now been sentenced to penal servitude for life for an offence for which she had never been tried.

The charge for which she had been tried was that she 'feloniously, wilfully, and of her malice aforethought, killed and murdered one James Maybrick.' But here was the Home Secretary acting in the capacity of judge and jury to find that 'the evidence leads clearly to the conclusion that the prisoner administered and attempted to administer arsenic to her husband with intent to murder'. The administration or attempt to administer arsenic with intent to murder was an entirely different kind of charge, and Mrs Maybrick had never been indicted on such a charge. Outraged, Mr MacDougall knew that he could not let matters rest.

On Marylebone Road in London, the directors of Madame Tussaud's Wax Museum decided that, since Mrs Maybrick was no longer a condemned prisoner, they would have to remove her figure from the company of criminals in the Chamber of Horrors. It was a pity, for in two weeks the figure had attracted 50,000 visitors.

In New York on Friday, a letter was written to David W. Armstrong in Louisville, Kentucky, from J. S. Potter, who had once been United States Consul at Crefeld, Germany. Potter had held a power of attorney from the Baroness von Roques and her third husband some two years earlier in order to make agreements on the claims of the Baroness to Holbrook lands in Kentucky, Virginia, and West Virginia. His letter now detailed an agreement made earlier with Armstrong, in which the Baroness had been willing to accept $5,000 in full payment for her claim on the lands, but Armstrong had readily agreed to make the sum $10,000. Potter reminded Armstrong that he had said the claim would ultimately yield the Baroness a sum greatly in excess of $10,000. Potter, knowing the Baroness's intense anxiety to get a fixed amount, had finally agreed upon $10,000 as the sum Armstrong should pay.

On the high seas on Saturday, Alfred Brierley played cards, shared a drink and confided to a fellow passenger that several Liverpool cotton men had given him agencies in the United States, as his business in Liverpool had been ruined by the Maybrick case.

An American traveller in Europe, Helen Densmore, was pleased to receive on Saturday a copy of the medical testimony in the Maybrick case. Mrs Densmore's husband was a doctor who practised hygienic medicine and developed health foods. He could afford to dabble in such unprofitable ventures, for he and his brothers had developed the first successful oil wells in Oil Creek, Pennsylvania, invented the tank car for shipping oil by rail, and held British patents on the Remington typewriter. Mrs Densmore herself had attended medical school, but had not taken her degree. The Densmores were fascinated by the Maybrick case, and spent the weekend studying the testimony.

Somer B. Yume of Providence, Rhode Island, found momentary fame in New York on Monday, 26th August. He revealed to a *World* correspondent that he had taken arsenic daily in large doses for twenty years, ever since a rattlesnake bit him on the arm and he ate arsenic to hasten the death he expected. Instead of a speedy end, he obtained relief. Since then, he said, his arm swelled up once every twenty-four hours until relieved by his daily dose. His story, headlined 'EATS ARSENIC AS MAYBRICK DID', served to keep the Maybrick name on page one.

Early on Thursday morning, 29th August, Florence Maybrick was hustled out to the gate of Walton Jail. A crowd watched silently as she was escorted aboard a third-class railway coach for a long ride to Woking, Surrey. There, through woods that smelled of flowers, she was driven to the Knaphill Female Convict Prison. When she had put on her convict uniform, a warder quickly cut off her hair to the nape of the neck. With this act, a feeling of utter helplessness came over her. She was weighed and measured, and the warder noted one hundred and twelve pounds and a height of five feet three inches.

Next morning, the prison doctor found her nearly prostrate from mental strain, and ordered her removal to the infirmary until she improved.

Barrister Alexander MacDougall asked the Cleaver brothers for the indictment on which Mrs Maybrick had been tried. They wrote promptly to say they had never seen a copy of the indictment, and that the Clerk of Assize in Liverpool refused to furnish them with a copy. MacDougall wrote at once to the Home Secretary.

Arriving at Walton Jail for a last visit with her daughter, the Baroness von Roques learned that orders for her transfer had been received and promptly carried out. No visitors would be permitted until she had passed six months of her nine-month solitary confinement. The Baroness decided to return to Paris.

She stopped in at the offices of the Cleaver brothers to say goodbye, and Richard Cleaver handed her a few small articles which the Maybrick brothers had permitted him to have from Battlecrease House. One was a Bible. The Baroness said she was pleased to receive it, for it had belonged to Florence's father.

The *Scythia* steamed into Boston harbour on September first. Reporters who boarded as soon as she had passed quarantine began a game of hide and seek with Alfred Brierley, whose travelling companions had warned him of the aggressive American press. Brought to cover amidships, he said, 'Gentlemen, I have absolutely no statement to make.' He stared at them defiantly while they noted his six-foot height, his big, soulful blue eyes and his very white teeth.

One reporter suggested that a free statement now might save him a world of trouble from the interviewing corps of other cities he might visit.

'Very likely,' he said, and went to his stateroom.

Brierley's fellow passengers all voted him a capital good fellow. A Boston hotel man said, 'Brierley is one of the nicest fellows I ever met.' A young Miss Adams of Boston said he was an excellent conversationalist and altogether very attractive. Judge Oliver Wendell Holmes, son of the Autocrat of the Breakfast Table, said that he had made Brierley's acquaintance and was not ashamed of it.

Alexander MacDougall received a reply from the Home Office on Tuesday, 3rd September. He was told that the Secretary of State had no objection to MacDougall receiving a copy of the indictment, but that he had no authority to order this being done. Therefore the indictment was not enclosed.

In Europe, Helen Densmore began to write to friends, suggesting that an international association work for Mrs Maybrick's freedom. Why not call the organisation the Women's International Maybrick Association?

When Florence Maybrick was well enough to be released from the Woking prison infirmary, she was moved to a four-by-seven-foot cell with a hammock to sleep in. Her daily routine began at six, when she took a tin plate and tin mug to the cell door. A six-ounce loaf of brown bread was placed on the plate, and three-quarters of a pint of gruel were measured into the mug. The prisoner ate her few mouthfuls, then marched in line to the chapel for a twenty-minute service. The rules forbade her to speak to any other person except a warder, not to a warder unless spoken to. In her cell, she had to make five shirts a week. Obstinacy or indolence, she was told, would be rewarded with a bread and water diet.

A red cloth star on her uniform made Mrs Maybrick a member of the 'Star Class' of prisoners, who were kept separate from ordinary prisoners but enjoyed no other special treatment. It meant that she had been convicted of one crime only, committed in a moment of weakness or under irresistible pressure, that she had been educated and respectably brought up and betrayed no criminal inclinations, and that, when in the outside world, she would be socially distinct from the habitual criminal.

At ten o'clock each morning, the governor inspected her cell. 'How are you, Maybrick? Any complaints? Do you want anything?' were his only remarks, and he was gone.

Toward the end of September, Thomas and Michael Maybrick reached a decision. Michael's doctor, Charles Fuller, and his wife had offered to adopt Master James and Miss Gladys Maybrick. They would bring them up as their own, giving them their name and seeing to their education. The Baroness von Roques consented to the adoption.

In her cell, Florence Maybrick became aware that, although she was in solitary confinement, she was never alone. She knew she was watched almost constantly through the peephole in her door. The gaslight was kept burning in her cell all night.

In addition to the rules imposed upon her, she set her own rules of self-discipline. She told herself firmly that she would come out of the ordeal precisely as she had entered it, with the same good habits, manners and modes of expression her mother and friends had known when they saw her last. She kept her cell spotless, its slate floor well polished, her tin pannikins shining like silver service. She sat erect, her chin high, and never permitted herself to use fingers where good manners demanded knife, fork, or spoon.

As 1890 began, Alexander MacDougall spent almost his entire time trying to procure Mrs Maybrick's release. Rechecking the testimony of trial witnesses, he obtained a statement from Alfred Schweisso that he had been able to recognise Mrs Maybrick at the coroner's inquest only when an inspector took him into the room where she was waiting, and that he did not recognise Alfred Brierley even when he stood beside him. But MacDougall was met with obstinacy when he tried to get Edward Davies of the Royal Institution Laboratory to tell him what were the specific gravities of the meat juice he tested. 'Being perfectly satisfied of the justice of the verdict,' said Davies, 'I decline to enter upon any discussion, as that is not my duty in the matter.' MacDougall then tried to get the Home Secretary to force a reply. He refused, even though the lawyer pointed out that Mrs Maybrick's imprisonment was 'contrary to Magna Carta'.

Water froze overnight in Florence Maybrick's cell. On rainy days, since the prisoners had to exercise in all kinds of weather, Mrs Maybrick's only pair of shoes and stockings were wet through most of the day. She learned that sooner or later all inmates suffered from catarrh, influenza, bronchitis and rheumatism.

When she had completed six months of her nine-month solitary confinement, Mrs Maybrick was led by a matron to a small room. There she sat down before a grilled screen. Beyond the screen, she saw another grilled screen, and behind it she could see her mother. Sitting in the space between the screens was a prison matron.

They were allowed half an hour to visit. The Baroness spent the time telling Florence of the efforts being made in her behalf. Mr MacDougall, who headed the committee in England that believed in her innocence, was at work reviewing the evidence. The British Women's Suffrage Society was lending its support. An American woman named Helen Densmore, whose husband was a doctor, had organised the Women's International Maybrick Association. Her group was at work now winning the sympathy of the American government.

After her visit to Woking Prison, the Baroness returned to Paris. Spring was well along when she happened to leaf through the pages of Florence's Bible, which had lain on Richard Cleaver's desk all through the trial, and which the lawyer had handed her as she bade him farewell six months ago. She came across a small piece of paper. It advertised Wenck's Pharmacy, at 1200 Broadway in New York. She turned it over. Written on the back, in the hand of Dr Bay of New York, was a prescription for Florence Chandler for a face wash to be applied with a sponge twice a day. The ingredients included arsenic.

Next day, Alexander MacDougall received a visitor from Paris. The Baroness von Roques wished to show him something. It seemed too important to entrust to the mails, so she had crossed the Channel with it herself. She had found it in Florie's Bible.

The barrister examined the face-wash prescription carefully. The mark of a rubber stamp was partly legible. 'Brouant' was the name, and a prescription number seemed to have been added. Did the Baroness know a chemist named Brouant?

Why, she said, he was one of the leading apothecaries of Paris.

The Baroness took back to Paris a letter from MacDougall to Brouant asking when the prescription had been dispensed.

M. Brouant, pharmacist of Paris, sent Alexander MacDougall a certified copy of the entry in his books. Dr Bay's prescription had been filed on 17th July 1878. That would have been when Florence Chandler was a schoolgirl in Europe, three years before her marriage.

When she had completed nine months of solitary confinement, Florence Maybrick was moved to a cell twice as large as her first. She now had a narrow bedstead, with a coconut fibre mattress, two coarse sheets, two blankets, and a red counterpane. The prisoner was now in her second stage of confinement, called probation. She faced another nine-months period of absolute silence except when spoken to by the warders.

Early in 1891, trial witnesses Dr C. N. Tidy and Dr Rawdon Macnamara combined their knowledge of the effect of arsenic on the human system with the evidence in the Maybrick case and published *A Toxi-cological Study of the Maybrick Case*. 'Maybrick's symptoms', said the doctors, 'are as unlike poisoning by arsenic as it is possible for a case of dyspepsia to be. Everything distinctive of arsenic is absent.' They concluded :

(1)   That the arsenic found in Maybrick's body may have been taken in merely medicinal doses, and that probably it was so taken.

(2)   That the arsenic may have been taken a considerable time before either his death or illness, and that probably it was so taken.

(3)   That the analysis failed to find more than one-twentieth part of a fatal dose of arsenic, a quantity perfectly consistent with its medicinal ingestion.

A copy of the Tidy and Macnamara book was sent to the Home Secretary.

It was apparent to the members of the bar that the once robust mental faculties of Sir James Fitzjames Stephen had begun to be impaired. He was forced to take a long vacation, then returned to the bench, but one incident after another made all in judicial circles feel uneasy. On 23rd February 1891 his ability to continue to serve on the bench was questioned on the floor of the House of Commons.

In March, when she had completed her nine-month period of probation, Prisoner Maybrick entered the third stage of her imprisonment, hard labour. She was now permitted to converse with her neighbouring prisoners for two hours daily. After the six o'clock rising bell, she was sent to the kitchen. She and another prisoner had to carry a fourteen-quart can up several flights of stairs to the cells, while a third carried the basket containing more than thirty pounds of bread.

On 31st March, an artist and writer named Franklin George Bancroft, of Columbia, South Carolina, appeared before a notary and swore to a deposition. He said he had known James Maybrick in Norfolk between 1874 and 1876, and often saw him take from his vest pocket a packet of white powders. On several occasions, he swore, Maybrick drank such powder in Chablis, claret or champagne. Once, when Bancroft asked him what it was, he replied, 'Longevity and fair complexion, my boy.' Maybrick later informed Bancroft that the white powders consisted of arsenic and other ingredients.

Mr Justice Stephen held long talks with his colleague, Mr Justice Grantham, and with the Lord Chancellor and the Lord Chief Justice. He heard their advice, and on 7th April he made a public statement :

Not very long ago I was made acquainted, suddenly, and to my great surprise, that I was regarded by some as no longer physically capable of discharging my duties. I made every inquiry to ascertain what grounds there were for this impression, and I certainly rejoice to say that no single instance was brought to my notice in which any alleged failure of justice could be ascribed to any defect of mine. I consulted physicians of the highest eminence, and they told me that they could detect no sign whatever of decay in my faculties, and that therefore it was not a matter of immediate necessity in the public interest that I should retire.

Paradoxically, with these words the judge announced his retirement from the bench. Within a few weeks, he was admitted to an asylum for the insane.

In the summer, Alexander MacDougall published a six-hundred-page treatise, *The Maybrick Case*. The book included a number of facts and emphasised many points that had not previously been made clear. Some of these were that arsenic is quite tasteless to the ordinary person but has a strong taste to habitual arsenic eaters, so that it would be almost impossible to poison one who had the habit; that the analyst, Davies, testified in inexact language on an exact science; that Bessie Brierley noticed before Maybrick's death none of the objects found in the linen closet after his death; that the death certificate was refused because arsenic was found on the premises, although none was found until after the death; that the medical evidence contained remarkable conflicts of opinion; that Mrs Maybrick's lawyers were afraid of the truth of her statement; that Michael Maybrick had not disclosed that he saw Florence during the week of her London visit; that Home Secretary Matthews had created, in effect, a secret court of review in the parlour of the Home Office.

The middle of July produced a judgment in an action brought by Mr Cleaver and the brothers Maybrick against the Mutual Reserve Fund Life Association. The insurance company had refused to pay the balance of $11,500 it owed on James Maybrick's policy. The court decided that, as Mrs Maybrick had been convicted of murdering her husband, and as his death was caused by the person for whose benefit the action was brought, she could not recover the amount for which his life was insured.

Though it was nearly two years since the trial, the public had not exhausted its interest in the Maybrick affair. The insurance verdict brought a spate of letters asking why the benefit of the insurance policy should not pass directly to the children for whom it was provided. Why release the insurance company of its responsibilities provided by Mr Maybrick to other heirs, they asked.

In America, Helen Densmore enlisted the aid of a popular author known as Gail Hamilton, whose essays were collected in more than a dozen volumes. Mrs Maybrick's was the kind of cause Gail Hamilton liked to embrace. She would see what she could do. Since she was a cousin of the wife of Secretary of State James G. Blaine, perhaps she could help.

Soon Mrs Blaine received a flood of letters urging her to influence the Secretary of State to communicate with Lord Salisbury in the case. In August a petition prepared by Gail Hamilton was signed by Mrs Blaine and the wives of all of President Harrison's cabinet members. It then went to the White House for Mrs Harrison's signature.

There it was intercepted by the President's private secretary, 'Lige' Halford. Though Halford objected that the petition offended diplomatic proprieties, Blaine sent it to Ambassador Robert Todd Lincoln in London for presentation to the Queen.

The British minister, Sir Julian Pauncefote, sent the petition back to Blaine with a statement that the British Government had declined to receive it, and that 'no more impertinent attempt to dictate the course of internal justice within a friendly power has ever been brought to her Majesty's Government.'

The Secretary of State dropped the subject.

Florence Maybrick now spent the day from before dawn until evening in the kitchen, washing cans and dinner tins, scrubbing tables, cleaning knives, washing potatoes, serving dinners and scrubbing floors. Visitors were now permitted every two months, and the Baroness von Roques crossed the Channel faithfully to spend thirty minutes chatting with her daughter. Since the prisoner was forbidden to discuss her own treatment, the Baroness spent the time recounting the efforts being made for her on both sides of the Atlantic.

Sir Charles Russell and his colleagues continued to try to bring about a new trial. He and three other Queen's counsel asked one of England's leading law firms, Lumley and Lumley, to consider the case.

In America, Gail Hamilton learned that money was needed to retain Lumley and Lumley, and that the resources of Florence Maybrick and of the Baroness von Roques were seriously depleted. She launched a public fund-raising campaign with a letter to the New York *World*, which she said was the most relentless journal in America when it set out to accomplish any great purpose. 'What I want you to do is – immediately, tomorrow, this minute – ' she wrote, 'open a subscription fund and keep it open – blow upon the coals and kindle pity into life.'

The *World* rose to the challenge in an editorial :

> The *World* can have but one answer to make. It will gladly receive and transmit whatever sums of money Americans may contribute for the purpose of securing for Mrs Maybrick such aid as legal ability in England can furnish. Here is a cry of innocence against cruel oppression. To such a cry the *World* is never unresponsive.

Prominent American women led off with large gifts : $150 from Mrs William Walter Phelps, wife of the minister to Germany, $100 each from Mrs James G. Blaine, Dr Helen Densmore, Mrs Cyrus H. McCormick and Julia Duhrig. Dozens of small gifts came from New York and Washington, from Florida and Minnesota, Tennessee and Georgia. In New York, the popular actress, Clara Morris, offered to give a benefit matinée at the Grand Opera House for the Maybrick Fund. On 28th October, a packed house saw her, at the height of her powers, perform Sardou's *Odette*. On 9th November, the *World* sent to the Baroness von Roques a draft for $1,641.55.

In England, Albert Kenyon of Manchester announced the opening of the Maybrick Defence Fund to prepare a case inquiring into the legality of Mrs Maybrick's imprisonment. He based his argument on the thirty-ninth article of Magna Carta, which states that no subject shall be imprisoned on any charge for which he has not been indicted or tried. Under the Home Secretary's statement, he said, Mrs Maybrick was imprisoned on a charge for which she had never been indicted.

In November, following an action in the Court of Appeal in London to obtain the Maybrick insurance money, the Master of the Rolls, Lord Esher, said he did not think much of public policy if an insurance company could pocket annual payments without paying the insurance. He decided that the insurance association must pay only the Maybrick brothers, as executors, in order to pay the creditors of the estate and devote the balance to the children. It could not pay the wife's assignee, Mr Cleaver.

The Baroness von Roques had always enjoyed the theatre. But as she came through London on her way to Woking Prison in January 1892, she was not inclined to attend the Garrick Theatre. For there had opened a new play called *A Fool's Paradise*. Critic Henry Chance Newton said the playwright, Sidney Grundy, had dramatised the Maybrick Mystery in every detail. The role of Philip Selwyn, whose wife was trying to poison him in order to marry a former lover, was played by a young man named Henry B. Irving.

In February, Lumley and Lumley completed their brief. It ran to hundreds of pages setting forth the serious misdirections by the judge, and emphasising the medical disagreement in the case. It concluded that

There was no conclusive evidence that Mr Maybrick died from other than natural causes.

There was no conclusive evidence that he died from arsenical poisoning.

There was no evidence that the prisoner administered or attempted to administer arsenic to him.

There was no evidence that the prisoner, if she did administer or attempt to administer arsenic, did so with intent to murder.

The judge, while engaged in his summing-up, placed himself in a position where his mind was open to the influence of public discussion and prejudice, to which was probably attributable the evident change in his summing-up between the first and second days; and he also assumed facts against the prisoner which were not proved.

The verdict was against the weight of evidence.

The jury did not give the prisoner the benefit of the doubt suggested by the disagreement of expert witnesses on a material issue in the case.

The Home Secretary should have remitted the entire sentence by reason of his being satisfied that there existed a reasonable doubt of her guilt.

The indictment contained no specific count of felonious administration of poison, and consequently the jury found the prisoner guilty of an offence for which she was never tried.

A confidential copy of the brief crossed the Atlantic to Roe and Macklin's office in New York, where Alfred Roe went over it carefully with Gail Hamilton. Undaunted by her experience with the petition of the cabinet members' wives the summer before, Miss Hamilton took the brief to her cousin-in-law, James G. Blaine.

The Secretary of State decided to write to the American Ambassador to the Court of St James, Robert Todd Lincoln. He could not instruct Mr Lincoln officially, he wrote, since Mrs Maybrick's widowhood had not restored her American citizenship. But he could instruct him on behalf of a multitude of American citizens to investigate the case and to express the Secretary of State's deep personal interest in it.

In April, Sir Charles Russell and his committee completed an analysis of Lumley and Lumley's brief. They found that 'there is no mode by which a new trial can be obtained, nor can the prisoner be brought up on a "habeas corpus".'

We think it right to add that there are many matters stated in the case which would be matters proper for the grave consideration of a Court of Criminal Appeal, if such a tribunal existed in this country.

Gail Hamilton was disappointed by the discouraging opinion of the English Queen's counsel. If they could find no way to obtain a new trial, if Secretary of State Blaine could issue no official instructions to Ambassador Lincoln, and if an unofficial petition of wives of cabinet members had been rejected, there was at least one more recourse. A new petition must be made as official as possible by the signatures of the highest officers of the government in Washington. She wasted no time drawing up a petition to the English Home Secretary. It was signed by Levi P. Morton, Vice-President of the United States and President of the Senate, Charles T. Crisp, Speaker of the House of Representatives, Secretary of State Blaine and all of the President's cabinet, Cardinal Gibbons, and more than a dozen of the highest-ranking officers of the United States Army.

By the time the American petition reached England, Secretary of State Blaine's attention was occupied by more immediate matters. With a presidential election coming and the Republican convention about to open in Minneapolis, his name was constantly in the headlines as a possible candidate. Newspaper cartoons depicted him on the horns of the dilemma of his own ambition and his loyalty to President Harrison. In June, to make himself available for the nomination, he resigned from the cabinet, closing the door through which Gail Hamilton exerted her strong influence in the American government for Florence Maybrick.

It was now the third summer since the trial of Florence Maybrick. In America, Helen Densmore published a book on *The Maybrick Case*. In Europe, the Baroness von Roques continued to write to friends and friends of friends for help. She did not ignore the English Home Secretary. On 4th August, she sent him a long, indignant letter. Among the points on which she touched were Mrs Maybrick's family background and religious upbringing and the fact that she held proof of cause for divorce from Maybrick had she desired it. Her daughter had no more access to arsenic than anyone else at Battlecrease House, she said, and the police did not find the bottles and other items, they were simply shown where they were found. There was evidence, she added, that Mrs Maybrick's will, her private papers, and a compromising packet of letters from other women to James Maybrick had been abstracted by Mrs Briggs and Mrs Hughes within one hour of Maybrick's death. The letter revealed the affidavit from George Bancroft, and reminded the Home Secretary that the prescription for the face-wash containing arsenic had recently been found and a copy sent to him.

'I must draw your attention to the apparent motives of others,' she went on. 'Certainly this would be so in France and America. The only persons who have been benefitted by James Maybrick's death are his brothers, and they lived at feud with him and were seldom with him.'

Mr Matthews acknowledged receipt of the communication from the Baroness and, within a few days, left office. He was succeeded by Herbert Asquith.

On the last day of August, Messrs Lumley and Lumley submitted their brief, paid for partly by the New York *World*'s subscription fund, to the new Home Secretary. Ten days later, he announced that he had reviewed the brief and could take no action.

In Woking Prison, Mrs Maybrick completed the third year of her sentence. Until now, she had not been permitted to see her own face. With the anniversary, a mirror three inches long was placed in her cell.

In 1893, Florence Maybrick learned that it was usual in the case of a life convict who had earned good marks to have her sentence reviewed after she had served fifteen years. A life sentence usually meant twenty years, and as a reward for good behaviour three months were taken off each year. She went about her work hoping that nearly one third of her sentence had already passed.

The Baroness von Roques learned from friends in America that David W. Armstrong had sold some of her Kentucky land for $85,000, and some of her Virginia land for $25,000 and for $250,000. Hadn't the purchase price quoted by Armstrong's agent, while Florence waited for the verdict of the jury, been $20,000 for the Kentucky land, she wondered? They had all been so excited that day, and the man had appeared at such an inopportune time. Armstrong had later forwarded only $3,000, retaining the balance for services and expenses, he said. Shortly, in Richmond, Virginia, Attorney Samuel V. Hayden of Washington, representing the Baroness, brought suit against Armstrong.

In the spring, Sir James Fitzjames Stephen was reported to have died where he had lived for the past three years – in a home in Ipswich, Suffolk.

Sir Charles Russell quit the bar in May. He accepted the appointment

as a Lord of Appeal in the House of Lords and a life peerage as Lord
Russell of Killowen. Within a month, he was elevated to the highest
judicial office in the land, Lord Chief Justice of England. Almost immediately he met with Herbert Stephen, son of the late judge. The Lord
Chief Justice explained that he thought Mrs Maybrick ought to be
released, and that he was about to lay the case before Mr Asquith. Since
Herbert had acted as marshal to his father during the trial, said Lord
Russell, he wanted to know everything that his father had said to him in
private about it, and asked the judge's son to put what he told him in
writing.

As they stood up to say goodbye, Herbert Stephen said, 'Do you really
mean to tell me that you think she didn't do it?'

Lord Russell looked at his visitor for several seconds. Then he said, 'I
don't think she ought to have been convicted on that evidence.'

In the prison kitchen, Mrs Maybrick watched a succession of dukes, peers,
judges, magistrates, authors, philanthropists, and other privileged visitors
tour through the prison. She heard one benevolent-looking old lady, after
close inspection of the cells, say, 'Everything is so nice and homelike.'

She wondered what the lady's home was like.

Valentine Blake read in a newspaper that Mr Jonathan E. Harris of
London was now acting for Mrs James Maybrick and her mother. He
remembered that he had never received an answer to his letter, written
at the time of the trial, telling Richard Cleaver about giving Maybrick
arsenic after their discussion of the ramie fibre. He went to see Mr Harris
and told him the story.

A long and detailed affidavit related in full the cotton broker's offer to
do his best with the ramie grass product if Blake would make him a
present of his arsenic. Said Blake's deposition :

> I handed him all the arsenic I had, amounting to about 150 grains,
> some of the 'white' and some of the two kinds of 'black' arsenic, in
> three separate paper packets. I told him to be careful, as he had 'almost
> enough to poison a regiment.' When we separated the said James
> Maybrick took away the said arsenic with him.

Another man of the sea turned up. Master Mariner John Fleming, of
Halifax, Nova Scotia, deposed that he had been in the Dutch East Indies
during the trial, but that he had known Maybrick in Norfolk between
1882 and 1884. He had seen the broker put grey powder into food he

was cooking in his office. 'You would be horrified, I dare say,' Maybrick had remarked, 'if you knew what this is – it is arsenic.'

When Fleming expressed his astonishment, Maybrick went on, 'We all take some poison more or less. For instance, I am now taking arsenic enough to kill you. I take this arsenic once in a while because I find it strengthens me.'

When the government of England again changed, in 1885, Lord Russell of Killowen wrote to Mrs Maybrick on 27th June :

I beg to assure you that I have never relaxed my efforts to urge your release. I feel as strongly as I have felt from the first that you ought never to have been convicted, and this opinion I have very clearly expressed to Mr Asquith, but I am sorry to say hitherto without effect.

Rest assured that I shall renew my representations to the incoming Home Secretary, whoever he may be, as soon as the Government is formed and the Home Secretary is in a position to deal with such matters.

Sir Matthew White-Ridley was the new Home Secretary. Lord Russell pointed out to him that for more than six years Mrs Maybrick had been suffering imprisonment on the assumption of Mr Matthews that she committed an offence for which she had never been tried and of which she had never been found guilty. 'I have honestly tried to judge the case,' he said, 'and I now say that if I was called upon as head of the Criminal Judicature of this country, I should advise you that Florence Maybrick ought to be allowed to go free.'

In 1895, Mrs Maybrick was deeply hurt by someone she had not seen since the day before her husband died. Each year, Thomas Maybrick had sent pictures of James and Gladys, but now his usual letter was months overdue. Mrs Maybrick sent word to Richard Cleaver to ask Michael Maybrick to send recent photographs of her children. Thomas Maybrick replied that Michael Maybrick refused. Mrs Maybrick applied to the prison governor for help. Michael answered that young James, who had reached an age at which he could be told about the case, did not wish either his own or his sister's photograph sent to his mother. The news of her son's attitude had a devastating effect upon the prisoner, almost as if she had learned that he had died.

The new Home Secretary was in no hurry to answer Lord Russell's letter. It was March 1896, before he announced that after careful consideration he had decided not to interfere with the sentence.

Alexander MacDougall would not leave the Home Secretary alone. By summertime, he had published his second long treatise, *The Maybrick Case, a statement of the case as a whole. Being three letters addressed to Sir Matthew White-Ridley, bart., MP, HM Secretary of State for the Home Department, etc.* It brought the Home Secretary under questioning on the floor of the House of Commons. He said that he was still most strongly opposed to the release of the prisoner.

In September 1896, handcuffed to a chain of nine other Star Class prisoners, Mrs Maybrick was taken on a five-hour railroad trip to Aylesbury Prison. This new prison near London was now to be England's only national prison for females.

No chapel had yet been built. Divine service was held in one of the halls each morning. Florence Maybrick missed the spiritual atmosphere of a real place of worship. She was soon relieved to hear that the Duchess of Bedford, a member of the Board of Visitors, had offered to provide the prison with a chapel. The prisoners were amused when the Home Office 'graciously' accepted the offer.

In the new prison there was an enlightened approach to penal conditions. By the spring of 1897, any prisoner who had a complaint to make, or who wanted advice, could have an appointment with the governor. The women now slept in nightshirts instead of in their clothes, and were allowed a small mat for the stone floor, a wooden stool, toothbrushes (a luxury never known in Woking Prison), and wide-brimmed hats for protection from the glare reflected into the courtyards by the stone walls.

One day a few months later, Mrs Maybrick found a matron and several warders inspecting her cell. Particular attention was called to the polish of the floor, the orderliness of the shelves, the shine of the tinware. She learned that Aylesbury was the training school for female warders for all county prisons. Her cell was shown as the model on which all others should be patterned.

It was the year of Queen Victoria's Diamond Jubilee. In the expectation that she would grant a number of pardons in celebration, President McKinley was advised to ask for a pardon for Mrs Maybrick. Ambassador John Hay told the British Government that the President would regard it as a friendly act if the Queen would release Mrs Maybrick. He was refused. There were some who said no pardons were given because the Irish refused to participate in the Jubilee.

Mrs Maybrick had by now earned the respect not only of the female warders and higher authorities, but of her fellow prisoners as well. When one became morbidly depressed, the prison chaplain gave her permission to visit Mrs Maybrick. A quiet talk with Florence Maybrick left her brighter, and for several days she seemed improved. Then she asked to see Mrs Maybrick again. Since none of the authorities were in the building at the time, the matron refused. When supper was served, the woman was found to have hanged herself in her cell.

Next morning, when the cells were unlocked for breakfast, the prisoners came out shouting that the suicide had been driven to it. The uproar was getting out of control when one of the ringleaders saw Mrs Maybrick and shouted, 'Mrs Maybrick, is it true she was driven to it?' The matron permitted Mrs Maybrick to talk to the prisoners for a few minutes, explaining the conversation she had had with the suicide. They quietened and returned to their cells.

Early in 1898, the supporters of Florence Maybrick announced that they had abandoned their efforts to secure her release on technical grounds. From now on, they said, they would argue that her punishment was disproportionate to the sentence usually imposed for the crime of attempted poisoning.

The Baroness von Roques drew a discouraging picture of Mrs Maybrick's physical condition for newspaper reporters. 'My daughter is merely existing,' she said. 'She is still in the infirmary, where she has spent six of the eight years. She has grown so thin it would be hard to recognise her. There are great black rings under her eyes, and she can barely drag herself about. The prison fare, which is repulsive to a well person, has entirely ruined her digestion. She is unable to do any work whatever, even to taking care of her cell.' She went on to say that Florence had been given drugs for insomnia, but they were taken away because they were so injurious to her system, and that her sight was failing and she could no longer read.

While her mother was providing this description, Mrs Maybrick was given a privileged assignment in the officers' mess. She did all scullery chores, washing the crockery, glass, tableware, pots and pans needed for breakfast, lunch, dinner, tea and supper. The work was endless. Because the staff of twenty-five came in by turns from their duties, one meal scarcely ended before the next began.

Lord Russell wrote to the Home Secretary that Mrs Maybrick had now served four times as long as the minimum punishment fixed by law for the commission of a crime for which she had never been convicted. His protest had no effect.

One of the most active supporters of the Women's International Maybrick Association in America was a writer named Laura Dayton Fessenden. A resident of Highland Park, Illinois, Mrs Fessenden had published a number of flowery and sentimental books and children's stories. Her Mayflower ancestry, her indignation at injustice, and her high patriotism had all contributed to her earnestness in speaking, writing, and circulating petitions for the cause of Mrs Maybrick. 1898 saw the publication of her new novel, *Bonnie Mackirby*, subtitled 'An International Episode'. Maybrick partisans quickly recognised the anagram in the last name, and realised that the story was a fictional and sentimental version of the Maybrick case. Sale of the book was banned in England and in Canada.

In the next year, the strain of her years in prison and her hard work in the officers' mess at last broke the health of Florence Maybrick. She was admitted to the infirmary of Aylesbury Prison. She had been living there for a year when, early in 1900, she heard visitors approaching. Among them, she realised at once, was a voice she had not heard in almost eleven years – a voice she could never forget.

The prison governor himself opened the cell door, and the Lord Chief Justice of England stepped in. While the governor waited outside, Lord Russell chatted for half an hour. As he rose to leave, he saw tears in Mrs Maybrick's eyes. 'Be brave,' he said. 'Be strong. I believe you to be an innocent woman. I have done and will continue to do all I can for you.'

When he left, he wrote to the Home Secretary. 'I have seen the wretched woman, looking wretched,' he said, 'although I believe she is not ill in the ordinary sense.' He repeated his objections to Mr Matthew's original decision.

When friends of Mrs Maybrick pressed the Lord Chief Justice for a statement, he said,

I will make no public statement of what my personal belief is as to Mrs Maybrick's guilt or innocence, but I will tell you that I took an unusual step : I went to see her in prison before her trial, and questioned her for the purpose of getting the truth out of her. During the trial I made careful observation of her demeanour, and since her imprisonment I have availed myself of my judicial right to visit her at Aylesbury Prison; I decided in my own mind that it never for a moment entered her mind to do any bodily injury to her husband.

In August, after a brief illness, Lord Russell died.

The *Liverpool Daily Post*, which had led the clamour for Mrs Maybrick's conviction before her trial and had been among the last newspapers to change its opinion when the evidence in her defence was presented, offered eloquent comment :

The death of the Lord Chief Justice recalled a sad and sordid tragedy enacted eleven years ago, in which he was a principal performer. To those who were there, a vivid recollection still persists of that bright July morning when a thronged court, hushed in expectancy, awaited the beginning of the Maybrick trial. In fancy one still hears the distant fanfare as the judges with quaint pageantry passed down the hall, and still with the mind's eye sees the stately crimson-clad figure of the great mad judge as he sat down to try his last case.

Few who looked upon the strong square head can have suspected that the light of reason was burning very low within; yet as the days dragged by – days that must have been as terrible to the judge as to the prisoner – men began to nod at him, to wonder, and to whisper. Nothing more painful was ever seen in court than the proud old man's desperate struggle to control his failing faculties. But it was clear that the growing volume of facts was unassorted in his mind; that his judgement swayed in the conflict of testimony; that his memory failed to grip the most salient features of the case for many minutes together. It was shocking to think that a human life depended upon the direction of this wreck of what was once a great judge.

In the Autumn of 1900, the prison doctors decided that Florence Maybrick was well enough to be given light work in the library. She was now the only convict in the prison who had served earlier in Woking, and the only one in Aylesbury who had served more than ten years. Her work included selecting the books to be taken through the cells, binding damaged books, cataloguing new books, entering borrowers' slips.

She was on duty in the library when a visitor touring the prison noticed the 'L', for 'Life Prisoner', on her sleeve. 'How long a time have you to do?' asked the woman.

'I have just completed ten years,' said Mrs Maybrick.

'Oh, well,' said the visitor. 'You've done half your time, haven't you? The remaining ten years will soon slip by.'

In the summer of 1902, the governor of Aylesbury Prison permitted a New York newspaperwoman named Harriet Hubbard Ayer to visit Mrs Maybrick in her cell. Only the Lord Chief Justice and Dr Clark Bell of the Medico-Legal Society of New York had previously been so privileged.

When she returned to America, Mrs Ayer reported that she had seen dumb anguish in Mrs Maybrick's face. The frail little woman's hair was luxuriant, she wrote, her face waxen from lack of sunlight, her eyes large and blue, her teeth beautifully white. They had spoken of Mrs Maybrick's work, of her meals and prison routine, of her chidren. As Mrs Ayer learned that for seven years no photographs had been sent to their mother, tears welled in Mrs Maybrick's eyes. It was, wrote Mrs Ayer, the first sign of real feeling she showed.

After reading Mrs Ayer's story, clubs and associations all over the United States asked her to come tell them about her visit with Mrs Maybrick. New sympathy was aroused, and further efforts to secure Mrs Maybrick's release were pledged.

A February morning in 1903 brought the sound of footsteps to the door of Florence Maybrick's cell. She looked up to see the governor himself ushering in three men. One, who was tall and stern, talked with her about her work, while the others stood by and observed the conversation. A week later, she was summoned to the governor's office. From a sheet of paper on his desk, the governor read: 'The prisoner, Florence E. Maybrick, is to be informed that the Secretary of State has decided to grant her discharge from prison when she has completed fifteen years of her sentence, conditional upon her conduct.'

Mrs Maybrick was overwhelmed. For a few minutes, feeling in a daze, she stayed in the governor's office, and learned that her visitors the week before had included the Secretary of State, who was the tall gentleman who conversed with her, and the chairman of England's Prison Committee.

The public announcement came on 24th March, 1903. Mrs Maybrick would be released, said the Home Office, in July 1904. Her Washington lawyer, Samuel V. Hayden, was authorised by the Home Secretary to use the announcement to secure postponement of the trial of lawsuits on the Holbrook lands in Kentucky, Virginia and West Virginia until Mrs Maybrick could be present to testify.

Adeline Marie, Duchess of Bedford, who had developed her friendship with Mrs Maybrick over the years since she donated the chapel to Aylesbury Prison, asked about her plans for her release. She had connections with a convent retreat at Truro, in Cornwall, where Mrs Maybrick could have quiet and privacy during a six-month probationary period which she would have to spend in England, beginning in January. Would Mrs Maybrick like her to speak to the Mother Superior?

The Baroness von Roques paid her last call at the prison on Saturday, 23rd January 1904. Mrs Maybrick spent Sunday in a dream, trying to make herself realise she would be free the next day. In the evening, the governor said a kind 'goodbye'. Only he, the chief matron, and a matron who was to travel with her knew that she was leaving. She had asked the governor to request the Home Office to keep her destination secret.

There were warders, some of whom she had known since her earliest days at Woking, and prisoners to whom she wanted to say goodbye. But she thought it best to slip away from the prison as quietly as possible. She said no farewells.

Early next morning, she dressed in new clothes and walked quietly down to the courtyard. The chief matron and her escort walked out with her through the great iron gates of Aylesbury Prison. No one spoke. They waited in silence until a cab drove up. The escorting matron and Florence Maybrick climbed silently in.

It was six-thirty in the morning of Monday, 25th January, 1904.

XVI

'That's Bartholdi's Statue of Liberty'

Mrs Maybrick had been at the Home of the Community of the Epiphany for a week before an Associated Press correspondent traced her there. His announcement brought crowds to the little town of Truro. The famous guest at the convent went out only when the road was clear, walking shady country lanes as spring came to the Cornish coast and the fresh sea air brought some colour back to her cheeks.

Early on the morning of 20th July, 1904, she put on a new light grey gown with a white boa and smart grey hat to match, sent from Rouen by her mother. After breakfast, she strolled alone through Truro, met a gentleman from the American embassy, and boarded the express for London. A fellow passenger said that evening, 'I noticed particularly the drawn features of the closely veiled lady dressed in grey,' but no one knew her.

The embassy official escorted Florence Maybrick safely to her mother in Rouen. There, after several days, the members of the press became so annoying that the Baroness asked the United States consul to have them withdrawn.

Samuel V. Hayden, the Washington attorney who was handling the long-delayed suit of the Baroness and her daughter against David W. Armstrong of Richmond, was finishing a European tour with his wife. The Haydens invited Mrs Maybrick to return to America with them, and booked passage for her under the pseudonym, Rose Ingraham. When she reached the gangplank of the liner *Vaderland* at Antwerp, half a dozen newspaper correspondents paid no attention as Rose Ingraham's name was checked.

Though it was Rose Ingraham's first trans-Atlantic voyage, it was Florence Elizabeth Chandler Maybrick's twenty-fourth. Ship's officers knew her identity and had been sworn to secrecy, and it was four days out before the passengers learned that the pale-faced woman who protected her eyes with smoked glasses was Mrs Maybrick. Two women who had been seated at her table refused to continue dining with her.

On 22nd August, it was disclosed that the chief reason for Mrs Maybrick's coming home was to prosecute in the Supreme Court of the United States her claim to property in New York valued at $40,000 and in the South worth several millions. Mrs Maybrick's claim would be that immediately after her conviction she was persuaded by her lawyer, under false pretences, to sign a paper which surrendered her rights in the property.

With Mrs Maybrick safely out of prison and on the high seas coming to America, David Armstrong felt that he could at last tell his side of the story. He met the press and said that, while searching a title in Kentucky many years earlier, he had found a deed conveying a tract to Darius B. Holbrook. Armstrong began a search for Holbrook or his heirs. Eventually, he obtained the address of Holbrook's daughter, the Baroness von Roques. He was warned that the Baroness defrauded all who dealt with her.

Ignoring the warning, said Armstrong, he made a contract with the Baroness whereby he was to try to obtain title to the property on her behalf. He was to pay all expenses and share half of the proceeds. In 1884, through United States Consul J. S. Potter, of Crefield, Germany, an old friend of Holbrook, the Baroness began urging Armstrong to buy out her entire claim for $5,000. For three years, Armstrong refused. Finally, he voluntarily offered her $10,000 in cash. Potter, who held her power of attorney, agreed in writing on 14th September, 1887, yielding to Armstrong all claims of the Baroness to any land situated in Kentucky, Virginia and West Virginia.

To secure his position, Armstrong got both Mrs Maybrick and her husband to sign papers conveying the property to him. The Baroness wrote to Armstrong on 10th March, 1889, that she would always sustain whatever contract had passed between him and Potter. On 23rd August, 1889, the day after Mrs Maybrick's death sentence was commuted, Potter confirmed the agreement. Armstrong added that the signature obtained on 7th August, while Mrs Maybrick was awaiting the verdict of the jury, merely ratified the previous transaction.

On Wednesday morning, one passenger aboard the *Vaderland* awoke, as usual, before dawn. She was on deck with the sunrise. Mrs Hayden, hearing Mrs Maybrick stirring, dressed quickly. She arrived on deck in time to hear Mrs Maybrick, as she pointed to a mass of purple bronze shining in the rising sunlight, ask a deckhand, 'What is that?'

'That's Bartholdi's Statue of Liberty,' said the sailor.

Mrs Maybrick shielded her eyes and stared at the statue as Mrs Hayden moved to her side. 'This is the happiest moment of my life,' she said.

The gangplank was lowered into a packed crowd. Mrs Maybrick waited in the first-class saloon until the other passengers had gone ashore. Then, moving a step ahead of Samuel Hayden, she crossed the deck to the top of the gangplank.

Those on the pier saw a slight woman walk toward them with her head held high. From a flat, broad-brimmed straw hat fell a fine veil. Through it, the sunlight fell on a face that was pale but had a touch of rosiness. Her simple silk dress of shepherd's plaid had a wide waistband of velvet and a short cape which fell just below the shoulders. As her foot touched the pier, the *Vaderland*'s band, standing on deck, struck up 'Home, Sweet Home'. Mrs Maybrick stopped, took Mr Hayden's arm, and burst into tears. For a minute or two she stood laughing and sobbing.

When she recovered, they started down the long pier. The crowd followed. Customs inspectors abandoned their work and went tumbling and sprawling over trunks and bags to glimpse the notorious Mrs Maybrick. At the pier entrance, thousands of people blocked the stairs. The police had to clear the way to an elevator. A stampede tried to follow, but at the street Mrs Maybrick was whisked into Dr Emmet Densmore's carriage. He immediately urged the driver to move on. A little girl tossed a bouquet into the carriage as it started to move. Smiling through her tears, Mrs Maybrick leaned from the window and called, 'Thank you, thank you.'

They raced to the Holland House. The driver, asked afterward what route he had taken, said, 'Faith, and I dunno. We just kept a'comin', and here we are.'

Those who had seen Mrs Maybrick arrive wondered how she could look so young. Though she was forty-three, no one would guess her age at more than thirty-five. Her step was so light that she seemed to have danced along the pier. The low voice that had been heard was scarcely audible a few feet away, but when Mrs Maybrick laughed – as her shipboard companions remarked – the sound was hearty and musical.

By late afternoon, letters and telegrams were piling up at the Holland House. A large number of publishers wanted Mrs Maybrick to write a book about her experiences. Other proposals ranged from editing a magazine to writing songs to appearing on the lecture platform.

Next morning, Mrs Maybrick and Dr Densmore travelled to Cragsmoor, a colony of artists and writers in the Shawangunk Mountains near

Ellenville, in New York state, where the Densmores maintained a summer home. There Florence Maybrick received a warm welcome from a friend of many years' standing whom she had never met – seventy-one-year-old Helen Densmore, who was suffering from heart disease.

In the Hudson Valley uplands, Mrs Maybrick relaxed in complete seclusion. Soon she permitted Samuel Hayden to announce that she was at work on a book. He also announced that she had been offered $500 a week to appear on the lecture platform. This, he said, she would turn down.

Helen Densmore worked closely with Florence Maybrick on the book, and they became devoted friends. When the Cragsmoor house was closed for the season, Mrs Maybrick moved with the Densmores to their home in Brooklyn. Early in the morning of Saturday, 26th November, Dr Densmore realised that his wife was having another heart attack. He summoned his neighbour, Dr Hugh Blackmar. Helen Densmore died soon after Dr Blackmar arrived. In her room, Mrs Maybrick, who until she joined the hygienic Densmore household three months earlier had been an insomniac, slept soundly through the excitement.

When the will of Helen Densmore was probated, it provided a small income quarterly to the Baroness von Roques and Mrs Maybrick.

Mrs Maybrick's Own Story: My Lost Fifteen Years was published in December. It told the story of the trial and of Mrs Maybrick's years in prison, set forth her views on needed prison reforms, and devoted more than one hundred pages to a summary of the Lumley and Lumley brief. Though the book mentioned neither Alfred Brierley nor the trip to Flatman's, it did discuss the letter opened by Nurse Yapp, for Mrs Maybrick wanted to make it clear that the phrase 'sick unto death' was an American colloquialism commonly used in the South with reference to any illness at all serious.

Publication of the book brought invitations to visit American prisons. Mrs Maybrick toured the prisons of New York state, and went through the city's notorious Tombs Prison. There she told Warden Flynn that, compared with English prisons, his was a paradise.

Mrs Maybrick's book and the publicity on her prison visits drew the attention of a New Jersey philanthropist, Alden Freeman, who had had the good fortune to choose a parent who had helped William Rockefeller organise both the Standard Oil Company of Ohio and Standard Oil of New York. As a result, Freeman himself had been able to retire from business at 27, and for ten years had pursued interests in architecture and horse-breeding. Recently he had turned to political reform and developed a course of free public lectures. He had often battled an aroused citizenry to give a platform to such controversial speakers as the anarchist, Emma Goldman.

Freeman invited Mrs Maybrick to East Orange to lecture on her experiences. Although the mayor and other citizens by no means approved of a former convict taking the platform, the lecture was an immense success. Mrs Maybrick's intelligence made as strong an impression as did her plea, 'I swear to you I am innocent.' She was self-possessed and articulate. The public welcomed her.

The appearance in New Jersey launched Mrs Maybrick on a nation-wide tour, visiting prisons and lecturing. Audiences seeing the woman for whose release they had signed petitions over a fifteen-year period were charmed by her sweet voice and the plea, repeated wherever she went, 'I swear to you I am innocent.' They were moved by her description of penal conditions. In Oklahoma, she discovered and exposed the fact that the State of Oklahoma, by contract, furnished convict labourers to coal mine operators in Kansas. Through her efforts, the water cure, the ducking pool and other disciplinary atrocities enforced among the Oklahoma convicts were abolished.

For four years, Florence Maybrick filled every hall in which she spoke, earning more than enough to live comfortably. Particularly exciting was her visit to Mobile in 1908. There, cousins, aunts and uncles gathered to meet Cousin Florence at the home of her father's sister, Sallie Chandler Stanard. In the evening she appeared at the Battle House Hotel, an emporium compared to which 'nothing else counted', as one Mobile woman put it. The Battle House was packed. Mrs Maybrick was introduced by John C. O'Connell, editor of the *Mobile Register*. O'Connell was especially well qualified to introduce the speaker. He was a Liverpool native who, as a nineteen-year-old reporter for the *Liverpool Post*, had attended her trial and written cable dispatches on it to the United States.

December 1908 brought the end of litigation over the disputed tracts. The Chancery Court in Richmond awarded Mrs Maybrick papers which clearly showed her title to more than two and a half million acres, including all of Buchanan County, in Virginia.

In Highland Park, Illinois, a suburb of Chicago, the Hotel Moraine was owned by Fred Cushing. Its well-to-do clientele included many permanent guests. One Saturday morning in the summer of 1910, F. E. Maybrick telegrammed for accommodations. When F. E. Maybrick checked in, Cushing recognised Mrs Maybrick. He found her French excellent, her conversation lively. She found a friend in Highland Park's Laura Dayton Fessenden, who had published the novel *Bonnie Mac-*

Kirby, based on the Maybrick case, more than ten years earlier. Soon she told Cushing she would make his hotel her headquarters.

The elderly Baroness von Roques came for a long visit with her daughter at the Hotel Moraine in 1910. By the time she returned to France, her health was declining. She died there within a few months.

In Rossland, British Columbia, a small town some 250 miles east of Vancouver, Jim Fuller, a young man of twenty-nine, was chief engineer of the Le Roi Mining Company. On 10th April, 1911, he was working alone on an assay in the laboratory. At about two o'clock, just after telephoning his fiancée to make plans for the evening, he decided to eat a sandwich he had brought with him in the morning. As he had often done, he filled a small beaker with water to drink with his sandwich.

Shortly, in another office, the telephone of the mine foreman rang. A voice said, 'Oh, Peters !' then was silent.

The foreman recognised Fuller's voice. He rang him up again, got no answer, and hurried toward the assay office.

He found the chief engineer lying at the foot of the steps outside the office. He wore an asbestos mitt, and in his hand was a sandwich. Peters phoned a doctor and, with another employee, carried Fuller into his office. He died on the way.

They found several beakers on the laboratory table. One contained water. Another contained potassium cyanide, a clear liquid that looked like water.

They notified the mine manager and the young lady to whom Fuller was engaged. The manager and the girl and her family revealed a secret known only to themselves : James C. M. Fuller was James Chandler Maybrick, son of the notorious Mrs Maybrick. A graduate of the Camborne School of Mines in Cornwall, he had come to Rossland in 1904 and had proved himself to be bright, capable, and popular. Devoted to the parents of his fiancée, he had told them, as well as his employer, the story of his mother's life.

Fuller was buried in his fiancée's family plot in Vancouver. The name of the doctor who was summoned as he lay dying was Chandler.

Fuller's fiancée sent pictures of Jim to Mrs Maybrick in Highland Park, and to his sister, Gladys, in England. She received no reply from Mrs Maybrick. She and Gladys Fuller became lifetime correspondents.

It was not until a month later that word of her son's death was brought to Mrs Maybrick by the members of the fourth estate. 'The past is dead,' said Mrs Maybrick. 'This boy has been dead to me for more than twenty years. Since I entered the English prison life I have never seen my children.'

More than two years had passed since Mrs Maybrick's last public lecture. Fred Cushing knew his guest's funds had dwindled. He was beginning to wonder what her plans were when she told him she had a claim to more than two and a half million acres. Cushing examined the papers from the settlement of the Virginia lawsuit. They proved that her grandfather, Darius Holbrook, had bought land grants from the Commonwealth of Virginia in 1797, covering all of Buchanan County in Virginia and Pike County in Kentucky. Though Holbrook had not known it, the territory was almost entirely the great Pocahontas coal field, which had been partly responsible for James Maybrick's decision, in 1883, to move from Norfolk to Liverpool. Mrs Maybrick asked Fred Cushing if he would try to get something for her out of her vast claim.

Cushing had had his successes and failures in speculative investments. Years earlier, he had helped a friend, Elisha Gray, who had patented telegraph equipment and was rigging it to carry sound. Through Gray's equipment, Cushing had talked over telegraph wires between Chicago and New York. He had shared in the claim that Gray's and Alexander Graham Bell's patent applications had reached the patent office on the same day and that the patent official, who was in debt to Bell, had favoured him with preferential treatment and with a look at Gray's ideas.

Cushing thought there was a fair chance of getting at least some of Mrs Maybrick's land for her. He travelled to Washington and to Virginia to see her lawyers. Soon he was paying legal fees and court costs. He knew he was taking a long-shot chance, but that if he succeeded he would be well rewarded with a commission.

After two years of investigation, Fred Cushing told Mrs Maybrick she could expect nothing from her properties. Neither she nor her mother had ever paid taxes or taken possession. Settlers had long squatted on the land. Certainly there was little chance of moving the great coal companies which had been operating for almost thirty years.

Mrs Maybrick answered that she would disappear from the world. She would use her maiden name, Chandler, she said. There would be no more Mrs Maybrick.

Between maintaining her as a non-paying guest and pursuing her claims, the hotel owner estimated that he had now spent nearly ten thousand dollars on Florence Maybrick. He could not continue indefinitely, but he was too kindhearted to ask her to leave. He was relieved when she answered an advertisement and took a position with a publishing firm, selling books throughout the state.

Within a few months, Cushing learned that Mrs Maybrick's poor health had forced her to give up the bookselling job. She had pawned her effects, returned to Chicago as a hobo, regained her health in the hands of the Salvation Army, and started out again. Next came a postcard in French, saying she would make one more effort to establish herself. If she succeeded, she would write. If she died, she said, he would probably hear of it.

Nothing is known of where or how Mrs Maybrick lived for the next three years. But in 1918 she wrote to Miss Cora Griffin, a playwright who had befriended her some years earlier. Did Cora know of anyone who might have employment for her?

Cora Griffin's friend Miss Henrietta Banwell, of Gaylordsville, Connecticut, was looking for a housekeeper who could help generally around her poultry farm. The arrangements were quickly made.

Mrs Maybrick stopped in New York on her way to Gaylordsville. She went to see a lawyer named Julian Gregory, whom she had met years earlier through Alden Freeman. She told Gregory she was going to settle in Gaylordsville. She and Cora Griffin had agreed that she would be known as Mrs Chandler.

Within a few days, Julian Gregory told his client, Alden Freeman, about Mrs Maybrick's plans to live in Connecticut under her maiden name. It was Freeman's observation that Mrs Maybrick could not have chosen a more circumspect confidant than Julian Gregory. So far as they were concerned, they agreed, if anyone asked about Florence Maybrick, they would say she had vanished.

XVII

'She has fleas, mother'

Mrs Chandler's cultured way of speaking, her outdated clothing, her inept ways of planning meals and handling the household budget did not fulfil Miss Henrietta Banwell's ideas of a housekeeper. Within a few weeks, the ladies agreed that perhaps a mistake had been made.

But in the anonymity of her new name and among the Yankee farmers who minded their own business, Mrs Chandler found that she had escaped from her past. She wanted to continue living along the quiet dirt road that meandered through the narrow valley between Gaylordsville and South Kent, Connecticut. She wrote to her friend Cora Griffin for advice.

Soon Cora Griffin had made arrangements with a friend who would see that Florence had a house built. Neighbours sold Mrs Chandler three quarters of an acre for sixty dollars, and the C. M. Beach Company in New Milford built a small house for $1200 in the spring of 1919. It was just twelve by twenty feet, with a six-foot porch looking several miles southward down the Housatonic Valley. Though the kitchen had a sink, the house was without running water. Heat came from a pot-bellied stove in the living room, and for cooking Mrs Chandler had a kerosene stove in the kitchen. Kerosene would provide light, too, for no power lines came near.

Mrs Chandler asked the Beach carpenters to provide three cat-sized portals: one to admit the cat to a three-foot-long boxed tunnel through the wood bin outside the shed at the kitchen door, another a guillotine-like sliding door to control cat entrances and exits between the wood bin tunnel and the shed, and the third a hinged door from the shed into the kitchen.

In the summer of 1920, Mrs Chandler met Louise Watter, a young native of Czechoslovakia who had come to visit a Gaylordsville family. Soon she heard that Louise planned to marry Martin Tomasovski, a native of Poland who worked on the Straight Farm, north of Mrs Chandler's house. One day not long before the wedding, Mrs Chandler presented Louise with a beautifully embroidered white nightgown. As Louise thanked her for it, Mrs Chandler said, 'I hope you have better luck than I did.'

Soon, Louise Watter Tomasovski visited Mrs Chandler. She noticed a picture of a young girl with long curls. 'Who is this, Mrs Chandler?' she asked.

Mrs Chandler tossed her head and said, 'Oh, that's the daughter of a friend of mine.' She did not tell Louise that it was the last picture of her daughter Gladys that she had received in prison, nor that she had long since destroyed the last picture of her son.

In Paris in 1922, Sylvia Beach published the first edition of James Joyce's *Ulysses*. Readers who made their way seven pages into Molly Bloom's soliloquy found her saying:

. . . take that Mrs Maybrick that poisoned her husband for what I wonder in love with some other man yes it was found out on her wasnt she the downright villain to go and do a thing like that of course some men can be dreadfully aggravating drive you mad and always the worst word in the world what do they ask us to marry them for if were so bad as all that comes to yes because they cant get on without us white Arsenic she put in his tea off flypaper wasnt it I wonder why they call it that if I asked him hed say its from the Greek leave us as wise as we were before she must have been madly in love with the other fellow to run the chance of being hanged O she didnt care if that was her nature what could she do besides theyre not brutes enough to go and hang a woman surely are they

In 1923, two young men, Samuel S. Bartlett and Richard M. Cuyler, bought the Straight farm and opened the South Kent School for boys. It emulated the pattern of their alma mater, the unique Kent School, founded in 1906 by an Episcopal monk of the Order of the Holy Cross, the Reverend Frederick H. Sill. Father Sill himself bought them a team of horses for $200 and, in the bluff way that was one of his charms, declared that Martin and Louise Tomasovski came with the team. Martin (whose name was always pronounced, Old World fashion, 'Marteen') was the school farmer from then on.

One day, a Buick automobile stopped in front of Mrs Chandler's cottage and attorney Julian Gregory came in. He revealed that it was Alden Freeman who had paid for the cottage and who had been sending her cheques through Cora Griffin. Now he would undertake to provide $150 a month anonymously through Julian Gregory.

Though the demands of his law practice had been supplemented by his appointment to the Port of New York Authority, where he was leading the planning of the West Side Highway, the George Washington Bridge, and the tunnels connecting New York and New Jersey, Gregory found time as often as he could to drive to Gaylordsville and deliver Mrs Chandler's cheque in person. He regarded his visits to her as a joy. Utterly lacking in bitterness at her present condition, she never mentioned the past. Once he found her carrying water from the spring 75 yards away. He was impressed by the strength and agility she showed at her age.

She had other visitors. Genevieve Austin and her sister-in-law, Alvie, were just leaving once when Mrs Chandler handed Genevieve a box containing a black lace dress. She insisted that her friend take it.

At home, Mrs Austin took the dress out of the box. A dry cleaner's tag fell from the sleeve. It read, 'Mrs Florence E. Maybrick, The Moraine.' The ladies were mystified by the name. They wrote to a niece who was a librarian in New York City. A prompt reply reminded them of all the excitement the name Maybrick had stirred thirty years earlier.

Genevieve and Alvie Austin told Genevieve's husband, Tom, and they told his cousin, Mrs Connie Kissam, who lived in Kent, about the tag. As long as the old lady said nothing about her past, they all swore, they would say nothing.

By 1926, Mrs Chandler had begun to charge her groceries and staples at E. A. Honan's General Store in Gaylordsville. There her unpaid balance mounted. Neighbours had begun to notice that Mrs Chandler no longer invited them in. She had taken to avoiding her visitors' eyes.

Early the same year, England was supplied with sensational new evidence of Mrs Maybrick's guilt. The *Weekly Dispatch* published extracts from *Fifty-Two Years A Policeman*, the autobiography of Sir William Nott-Bower, recently retired commissioner of London Police, who had been chief constable of Liverpool at the time of the Maybrick trial. His revelation said:

> Some time after the Home Secretary announced Mrs Maybrick's reprieve, a highly respectable Liverpool chemist came to the police. He said that in the Spring of 1889 Mrs Maybrick drove up to his shop in a dogcart and asked for powdered arsenic to kill rats or cats, and that he supplied her with a large quantity which she took away. A week or two later she again drove up to the shop and told him she had lost the

arsenic she had previously bought and asked for more, which he supplied to her.

He said that he was afraid to tell the police at the time, as he feared that being mixed up in such a case would injure his business, and also he had made no entry of the transaction in his books, as required by law.

I repeated the statement to the Home Office, but, of course, it was useless for any practical purpose. If given as evidence at the trial, it would have been of supreme importance.

One day, in the mood for a visit with Louise Tomasovski, Mrs Chandler walked northward to find her old friend at the boys' school on the Straight place. There she met Miss Clara G. Dulon, who was the school dietician and housemother. Miss Dulon had a compassionate strength of character that touched Florence Chandler in a way that no hand of friendship had reached her across the rocking chairs of the Hotel Moraine or the dusty roads of Gaylordsville. She had found a dear friend. Mrs Chandler began to be seen near the school campus. Headmaster Sam Bartlett became aware of her as an eccentric-looking old lady who wore a battered straw hat. Her long black skirts reached the dusty road, and she always faced away when he passed her in an automobile. When he met her on foot, he found that, if spoken to, she usually kept on going. Occasionally, on the other hand, she stopped to talk at length. He decided she was just one of those people one left alone.

By the end of 1926, Mrs Chandler's unpaid bill at Honan's store had reached $638.96. But in 1927, though the unpaid bill remained, she began to pay cash again. In March she had the Beach company add a screened porch, with a cat portal, to the house. It now had five doors for her and four for cats.

On a grander scale, Alden Freeman was building expensive homes on the resort seacoasts at Miami, Florida, and at Santa Barbara, California. With friends to help him spend money in both places, he was now imposing a major drain on his inherited wealth.

Friends rescued Mrs Chandler from her money problems. Miss Mabel Mountsier, a New York schoolteacher whom she had met at Miss Banwell's, regularly sent her cheques and urged other teachers who had never met Mrs Chandler to contribute. By summertime, the account at Honan's was paid up.

In October, the Earl of Birkenhead, England's foremost criminologist, published *More Famous Trials*. The book ranked Mrs Maybrick with

Marie Antoinette, Joan of Arc, and Charles I. In considering what Lord
Russell might have thought about her guilt, Lord Birkenhead said,

> I feel certain that he was convinced that, whatever the evidence
> might indicate, she was in truth and in fact an innocent woman, and
> in that belief thought it his duty to aid her as a man, when as Counsel
> he had no longer any opportunity to help.

A prompt reaction came from Sir Herbert Stephen, son of the late
judge in the case. He remembered Lord Russell saying, 'I don't think she
ought to have been convicted on the evidence.' Cyril Asquith wrote that
Lord Russell said the same thing to his father, Herbert Asquith, former
Home Secretary. An extensive debate was held in letters to editors.

It was all too much for Lord Birkenhead. On 7th November he wrote,

> I find myself unable to resist the weight of authority reinforced by
> the culminating testimony of Lord Justice Russell. This evidence was
> not available to me when I wrote. In the next edition of *More Famous
> Trials* I will modify the expression of opinion.

Mrs Chandler walked back and forth to see her friend Miss Dulon
through all kinds of weather. She got to know Mrs Sam Bartlett and Mrs
Samuel A. Woodward, and the wives of other faculty members. Students
Court Mulford and Alexander Hamilton frequently carried her bundles
– not knowing they were weighted with cat food – from Rob Boyd's
Acorn Store in South Kent, which she had discovered at the crossroads
there. But they were almost never invited inside.

In January 1931, Mrs Amy Lyon arrived at the South Kent School
to serve as nurse. A widow who was a native of England, she soon met
Miss Dulon's friend, Mrs Chandler. She was struck with the delicate
build, the musical voice, the rough yet beautiful little hands, the unkempt
hair, the dirty, threadbare little navy blue jacket.

Mrs Chandler occasionally walked up the road on Sunday morning
to attend chapel with Miss Dulon and Mrs Lyon. Sometimes she wept.
As she trudged home, she often carried a slice or two of cake or a few
cookies saved for her from a Saturday night birthday party of one of the
schoolboys.

In the spring, Julian Gregory received a visitor. Alden Freeman was
concerned about his financial situation. He had lost money in the stock
market crash, and his fortune had been depleted by years of largesse to

stranger and sycophant. His support of Florence Chandler Maybrick would have to cease.

Soon Mrs Chandler was again charging her groceries at Honan's store. In October, when her account had reached more than $100, E. A. Honan asked if she would sign a mortgage on her house to cover the indebtedness. She would not. Deciding to avoid Honan's store, she asked Cora Griffin and her few other correspondents to address her mail to the South Kent post office, located in Rob Boyd's store.

The infant Charles Lindbergh had been kidnapped on the first day of March 1932. For a month Mrs Chandler's *New York Times* had brought her every detail of the story. By 2nd April, the ransom had been paid but the baby had not been returned.

Dick Cuyler ran into Mrs Chandler and remarked that he was off on his spring holiday, headed for his native Princeton, New Jersey. She knew Princeton was near the kidnap scene. Shortly, she came back to him. She had found a pigeon in her yard, she said. A capsule on its leg contained a cryptic message about the Lindbergh baby. Cuyler wrote down the message and drove to Princeton, where he reached New Jersey state police. They decided against pursuing a wild goose chase. Neither the investigators nor the South Kent School teachers who smiled at Mrs Chandler's eccentricities realised that the kidnapping had triggered a reaction in the mind of a mother whose own children had been taken from her without so much as a farewell.

Miss Dulon died of cancer in June 1933. From then on, Mrs Chandler came only rarely to Sunday morning chapel. When she did, a strong odour accompanied her. At last during one service, when it was time for communion, Mrs Lyon whispered, 'Now, Mrs Chandler, we'll go take our sacrament,' and found the old lady weeping. She remained in her seat, the tears streaming down her wrinkled cheeks, while Mrs Lyon went to the altar rail. She never came to the service again.

The changing seasons were hard on Mrs Chandler. Some winters, she was snowed in for long periods and Mrs Lyon, Mrs Tomasovski, and students struggled through knee-deep snow for nearly a mile to carry wood and water to her. A neighbour, Howard Conkrite, who was known as 'Pop' and who kept cows and sold milk to neighbours, began to leave milk for her and take notes to Honan's store. Tom Honan pushed through the snowdrifts with her orders. The store's books still carried the large balance due from 1931. When the weather improved and Mrs Chandler emerged, she seemed to have put on weight. One teacher wondered if she didn't sew herself into several layers of bulky clothes for the winter.

In the summer, Mrs Lyon often found Mrs Chandler sitting on the steps of the Infirmary, sometimes holding a few wildflowers and a dilapidated gold parasol with a fringe. She always invited her into her house next door. Before the old lady could reach the house, Mrs Lyon's son, Dickie, hurried to remove an upholstered chair and replace it with a straight wooden chair.

'She has fleas, mother,' he said.

When Mrs Chandler said she was not hungry, Mrs Lyon put a good meal before her anyway. It was always consumed. Often the nurse said, 'Would you like to take a nice hot bath, Mrs Chandler?' but the old lady declined.

When a summer thunderstorm rumbled in the twilight, Mrs Lyon offered Mrs Chandler a bed for the night. It was refused. The nurse, watching her guest hurry off into the gathering darkness as the rain began to pelt her, knew she was going home only to feed her cats.

More than bad weather and illness plagued her. The tax collector for the Town of New Milford proposed that she sign a lien on her house, for since 1933 she had failed to pay her taxes, which totalled $11.90 a year. The lien would deed the house and lot to the town, but she could live there undisturbed through her lifetime.

Florence Chandler refused. But the proposal gave her an idea. She went to Headmaster Bartlett and asked if the school would help her with expenses if she deeded her property to it.

The headmaster talked with Samuel Woodward. They arranged a pension for Mrs Chandler, under Connecticut's Old Age Assistance Act, but a lien on the property was inevitable. Mrs Chandler held off from the autumn of 1935 until the summer of 1937, accepting baskets of staples from the school and worn clothing from Mrs Lyon and adding cat food and condensed milk every few days to her mounting account at Rob Boyd's store (Honan's remained unpaid), before she agreed to sign Connecticut's reimbursement agreement and lien on her property. Once she had signed, in return for a pension of $6 a week, the State of Connecticut held first claim on the estate of Florence Elizabeth Chandler after the payment of probate fees, taxes, and the costs of final illness and funeral.

Meantime, she had written to the headmaster:

August 3rd, 1935

My dear Mr Bartlett,

I wish to give you full authority herewith, to take charge of my property and person, in the event of death, incapacitating illness or accident, and to act on your own judgment in each case.

With deepest appreciation of your kind interest and friendly services,

I am

Very sincerely yours,

Florence E. Chandler

Gaylordsville, Conn.

Next time she saw Mr Bartlett, she told him that, when the time came, she would like to be buried beside her friend Miss Dulon on the school grounds uphill behind the chapel.

The summer storms in 1938 were hard on the tiny house. Mrs Chandler wrote to Mrs Lyon :

I ran up to see Mr Woodward about the damage. The place was almost blown to pieces and I need help to have things straightened out. Hammy [Alexander Hamilton] says I will get it sometime when school work has a lull. The torrents of rain recently ruined all the strawberry crop on the farms, and I have begged the soft broken berries to make jam. It will be a messy job but with sugar the berries will harden up. I saw Miss Bull [Mr Bartlett's secretary] too and asked for something that she knows of that will kill black ants. I am almost eaten up with insects. The long grass so close to the house lets them in when the wind blows. It does not seem as though the place will ever dry out.

The attempt to preserve fruit was disastrous. Mrs Chandler got word to Mrs Lyon that she was ill, and the nurse and Hamilton found her lying on a cot in her living room, overcome with food poisoning. In the tiny bedroom, Mrs Lyon discovered enough canned cat food to last all winter, while Hamilton found the mattress crawling with maggots. He took it out and burned it.

Florence Chandler had not had a visit from Julian Gregory for more than two years. In March 1939, she learned why. *The New York Times* announced the death of the former head of the Port of New York Authority. The news, combined with the fact that she felt tired and weak, added to her loneliness.

Now she kept close to her cottage even in summer. A rare walk took her to Boyd's store. Gaylordsville schoolchildren, who knew her as a friendly old lady who turned her back on grownups but paused to chat with children, called her 'the cat woman'. The South Kent schoolboys, who saw her detour abruptly into the underbrush when she encountered them, called her 'the witch of the woods'. Though Sam Bartlett had long since had the school provide her with a telephone, she had it taken out, re-installed, taken out again. She ignored more tax bills, and the collector again warned of a lien. In February, her three burner stove gave out during a blizzard. E. A. Honan replaced it on credit. Amy Lyon took her a winter coat and found several cats sleeping on a new blanket she had recently given her. When the tax collector and the telephone company sent overdue notices, Mrs Chandler put them away unopened.

Pop Conkrite's ten-year-old granddaughter helped her grandfather deliver milk on summer mornings. When she put two quarts on the shelf outside Mrs Chandler's window, she saw cats scattering into the heavy underbrush. When she did not see the shadowy figure of Mrs Chandler through the window, she felt her presence in the house. Sometimes a note for her grandfather asked him to bring wood from the shed out back. As he carried the wood to the front door, he told Doris, he could see the old lady standing far back across the room.

In October, Mrs Chandler received mail from E. A. Honan. Remembering Mr Honan's suggestion, nearly ten years earlier, that she sign a mortgage to cover her debt, she sent the envelope unopened to Mr Woodward at the South Kent School. 'His purpose in bringing up the matter,' she said, 'is no doubt due to the recent sale of the Thorpe farm below me for $500 and his wish to secure this claim in the event of my property being sold.' She never knew that the envelope from Honan contained a statement for the fifteen-dollar stove purchased back in February and a few groceries charged in March, with a gentle note :

Dear Mrs Chandler –
    Perhaps you can arrange a small weekly payment on this account.
Sincerely,
E. A. Honan

Among the new boys at the South Kent School in the fall of 1940 was Charles F. Wreaks. With the school's system of 'jobs', adapted by its founders from the unique Kent School, by which the students themselves performed all housekeeping chores, Wreaks was assigned to work in the Infirmary. There one day Nurse Lyon asked him to take a 'blickie' to Mrs Chandler. Blickies were stacks of enamelled metal pans, six or eight atop each other, held together by a handle. This name, origin unknown, was said to date back to their use by the English army in World War I. In them the faculty members carried cooked food home from the school kitchen to their families.

At the cottage, Wreaks found the door opened only widely enough for him to pass the blickie through. Extremely dirty and gnarled hands took the hands as an attractive voice thanked him. He carried the blickie often to the cottage, noticing large numbers of unfriendly cats. In time, Mrs Chandler began to converse with him, holding the door open only two or three inches and talking in a cultivated accent that made him wonder, young as he was, how a person of such quality could be in such dire straits.

Another summer brought more tall grass and insects and greater physical decline. Mrs Bartlett and Mrs Lyon noted that Mrs Chandler seemed unsteady on her feet as she stood in her yard. Henry Smithwick, a power company linesman, found the old lady prostrate in the path across her overgrown yard. She refused help, insisting that he send for Mrs Lyon. The nurse summoned Dr Josephine Evarts, who had recently become the school physician. Mrs Chandler admitted she had had a number of fainting spells.

In September, she turned 79. In October, Alexander Hamilton stopped to see her during a weekend visit to the school. Because he had always been one of her favourites, he was invited to enter the cottage. He found the smell of cats overpowering. He and Mrs Chandler talked about the war, and he was impressed with her concern for the dim prospects for the winter ahead. It seemed to Hamilton that the old lady was just wearing out.

Next day, she wrote to Samuel Woodward.

Monday

My dear Mr Woodward

I am feeling sick. I do not know how I will pull through. Mrs Lyon will tell you the emergency things that I have ordered. Perhaps the faculty ladies will help pay for them. In case I cannot write again please continue to care for the interest of the property in conformity with the interest of the school according to the terms of my will which Mr Bartlett has. A small legacy will be coming to me sometime. I have this information from Mr Gregory – before he died.

Much gratitude and appreciation of your friendly aid.

Florence E. Chandler

By the end of the week, she asked Pop Conkrite to call Dr Josephine Evarts. The doctor found her patient in the tiny kitchen, surrounded by cats. She realised in a moment that the strong odour she had smelled all the way out at the roadside came from a combination of the countless cats, the oil stove, the kerosene lamps, and unwashed humanity. Noticing that Mrs Chandler's feet and legs were swollen, she surmised that she had a bad heart. She suggested that Mrs Chandler go to the hospital. Under no conditions, the old woman said, would she consider such a thing.

The doctor ordered foods that Mrs Chandler should have, and sent the visiting nurse, Miss Louise Hanson, to cook some of the new food and see that the emaciated woman ate. The nurse was impressed with the number of tins of cat food on the shelves. For the next ten days, Mrs Chandler seemed to welcome Miss Hanson's calls. She did not know, as Dr Evarts knew, that after each visit the nurse went straight home, washed her hair and took a bath.

On Tuesday evening, 21st October, Pop Conkrite stopped with his granddaughter at Mrs Chandler's. The old lady raised the window a few inches and said she was feeling no better. Early next morning, delivering milk, they stopped again. Conkrite went to the cottage himself. He put the bottles on the shelf and rapped on the window. He heard the cats scrambling around inside the house, but Mrs Chandler did not answer. He tried to peer in the window but could see nothing.

He went back to the truck and got Doris. He lifted her up to the living room window. Through the sooty windowpane, the eleven-year-old girl made out the figure of Mrs Chandler lying awkwardly half on her cot and half on the floor.

Conkrite told Doris to wait while he walked around to the door and went in. Florence Elizabeth Chandler was dead.

XVIII

'Aren't you interested in getting
this thing written up in the paper?'

When Conkrite phoned the school, Samuel Woodward asked Martin Tomasovski to take Mrs Lyon to the cottage. Miss Hanson came along, and together they scraped the caked dirt from Mrs Chandler's hands and arms. When they had finished, though she was beginning to feel ill from working in the strong odour in the cottage, Mrs Lyon was pleased to see how beautiful the remains of her elderly friend looked.

News of Mrs Chandler's death spread quickly through the South Kent School. After lunch, fourth former Charlie Wreaks hurried to the cottage, for he had wanted to get a look inside it for more than a year. He found stacks of newspapers everywhere. On a table in the centre of the room he saw a number of yellowed clippings, a photograph album, and some scrapbooks. They seemed to have been carefully placed there. Within minutes, he was driven away by the odour.

By afternoon, Tom and Genevieve Austin had told their friends how they learned Mrs Chandler's real identity years earlier. In the evening, someone called the *New Milford Times* and told the editor about Mrs Maybrick. No one thought of calling anyone at the South Kent School to reveal the Austins' secret.

Headmaster Sam Bartlett was asleep when his wife woke him with a call from the New York *Herald Tribune*.

'Look, fellow,' said Bartlett. 'I'm half asleep. Call me up in the morning.'

'Aren't you interested in getting this thing written up in the paper?' said the voice.

'No,' said Bartlett. 'I don't give a particular darn. Call me up in the morning.' He went back to bed.

Only in the morning did he learn why the reporter had called. Mrs

Maybrick's name was front-page news all over America for the last time. On page one of *The New York Times*, the headlines read:

Mrs Maybrick Dies a Recluse;
Her Case Stirred World in 1889

Clamor in England and America Saved Her
From Death as Poisoner of Husband –
Scrapbook in Cottage Reveals Identity

In Sam Bartlett's office, the phone rang continuously for two days and two nights with calls from newspapers and press services across the United States and in Canada, England and Australia. The headmaster, Sam Woodward and Dick Cuyler took turns saying that they had nothing to contribute, for they had never heard of Mrs Maybrick.

In one call, John C. O'Connell, of the editorial board of *The New York Times*, explained that as a youth of nineteen he had covered the trial of Mrs Maybrick for a Liverpool paper. Would Mr Bartlett mind if he attended the funeral?

On Saturday morning, at Mr Bartlett's request, state police closed the South Kent School grounds. They held at bay a fleet of reporters' cars, letting only John O'Connell and a representative of the *New Milford Times* climb the long hill to the chapel.

The day was balmy and spring-like. Mrs Lyon and Mrs Tomasovski decorated the chapel with the last of the autumn wildflowers from along the Chandler Road. Some forty students and all the Gaylordsville and South Kent neighbours heard Father Wood read the Order for the Burial of the Dead, then followed six schoolboys, including Charlie Wreaks, as they carried the casket up the slope behind the chapel and lowered it into a grave beside that of Miss Clara Dulon.

As they strolled down the hill, Sam Bartlett and Sam Woodward asked the elderly editor, John O'Connell, about the Maybrick case. He told them how he had introduced Mrs Maybrick when she spoke in Mobile, and he said that he had always thought, from the evidence he had heard at the trial, that she was guilty.

Bartlett remarked that it was quite inconceivable to him that Mrs Chandler, as he knew her, could or would commit murder.

John O'Connell walked on a few steps. Then he paused. Far down the hill, at the gate of the school grounds, waited the swarm of reporters barricaded by the state police. It was Mrs Maybrick's last crowd.

He turned, looking first at Bartlett, then at Woodward. 'You know,' he said quietly, 'at the time of the trial she was considered the most beautiful woman in Liverpool.'

Appendix

The Law is changed – too late for Mrs Maybrick

by

THE RT HON. THE LORD HAVERS, QC, MP

It is difficult for the layman and indeed for the lawyer to realise that some of the accepted rights which now exist for accused persons in criminal courts are of recent origin. The right to give evidence on your own behalf when charged with a criminal offence and the right to ask a Court of Appeal to review your trial are accepted without question as fundamental rights and widely assumed always to have existed. Indeed Lord Loreburn, the Lord Chancellor speaking in the debate in 1907 on the Criminal Appeal Bill described the fact that a man before 1898 could not in every case, and especially in a trial for murder, give evidence on his own behalf in a criminal court as 'scarcely credible'. The development of our present system of humane justice is much more recent than is usually supposed. In 1832 Lord Eldon in the House of Lords spoke against the Bill which abolished capital punishment for the theft of a horse or of £5 in a dwelling house on the grounds it was based on sentimental ideas.

The trial of Mrs Maybrick demonstrates how recently these rights have become part of our law. In 1898 the obvious injustice that could arise from the rule that in certain cases an accused person could not give evidence was removed by the Criminal Evidence Act and was one of a number of changes in the rules of evidence which take up just over two pages of the Statute book. Its existence stemmed from the increasing number of judicial comments about the unfairness of the procedure and finally persuaded Parliament after a number of unsuccessful attempts to remedy this curious anomaly. In the 25 years before 1898 there had been 26 Acts of Parliament which created exceptions to this rule which led to the ridiculous situation where a man charged with a bombing offence or entering a dwelling house and committing rape could give evidence in his own defence but if charged with murder, was limited to a statement from the Dock.

The proposal was met, in Parliament, with long speeches deploring the risk that the change would cause to defendants who would be helpless at the hands of professional cross-examiners, or that the change would double or treble the length of trials or that 'the impartial and ever friendly attitude of the judges to prisoners' would be affected. One MP quoted Mrs Maybrick's case as an example against allowing those charged with murder to give evidence. The lawyers in Parliament were divided, for example Edward Carson (who was to become Solicitor-General and later Attorney-General and, finally, as Baron Carson, a Lord of Appeal in the House of Lords) was against the Bill and for it Sir Edward Clarke (who had been Solicitor-General from 1886 to 1892 and had appeared in many famous trials, and whose grandson is a judge at the Old Bailey). Finally it was passed by a very substantial majority on second reading in the House of Commons and its third reading took only a few minutes.

The creation of the Court of Criminal Appeal only took place in 1907 after some 30 attempts to provide this obviously just remedy had been defeated in Parliament over the previous half-century. Until 1907 there was no power for a man convicted by a jury to ask to have his case reviewed by a Court. If the trial judge was uncertain about any question of law that arose during the case he could, if he chose to do so, refer it to the Court for Crown Cases Reserved which had developed from an informal practice of the Assize judges of discussing different points between themselves before giving a final decision. This practice received Parliamentary approval in 1848 by the Crown Cases Reserved Act, which gave power to a judge presiding over a trial by jury to reserve any question of law which arose during the trial for consideration by the judges of the High Court and, in the meantime, if he chose to do so, to postpone judgment.

The trial judge then set out a document containing a brief account of the facts and the point of law; this was sent to the High Court in London where it was considered by as many judges as were available, usually four or five.

After consideration, the judges would reverse, affirm or amend the trial judge's decision and affirm or quash the conviction. A copy of their ruling signed by the presiding judge would be sent to the Court of trial and entered into the record of the Court. If the conviction had been quashed in respect of a prisoner who had been sentenced to imprisonment, a copy was also sent to the Governor of the jail so that he could be released.

The Court for Crown Cases Reserved sat in public and its decisions were reported in the Law Reports. Cases were argued by counsel in the same way as would happen nowadays in a Court of Appeal, except that only points of law could be argued. Usually the prosecution was represented by counsel and, in many cases, the prisoner's case was argued by the counsel who had appeared for him at the trial. A considerable number of convictions were quashed on points of law. However, this practice did not provide any remedy for the prisoner who believed that he had received an unfair trial or where the jury's verdict might have been perverse. In particular, there was no remedy against the unfair judge or the judge who influenced the jury to convict by means of a biased summing-up.

It has not always been the case that the judges command the undoubted respect and trust of the public which they now enjoy. In the same debate in 1907, the member for Cambridge, Stanley Buckmaster (later Lord Chancellor) said : 'It was no use disguising the fact that the judgment of our judges had ceased to command the confidence of the public and of the profession. The reason was plain, and the cause might be removed. Judicial offices, from the highest to the lowest, had been tossed to this man and to that as a reward for Party service, or, still worse, for personal favour. The Lord Chancellor said he wanted to keep these promotions outside the pestilential atmosphere of Party service.

'It ought to be an improper thing for a Government to appoint a man who was notoriously unfit, he did not say by reason of his character, but by reason of disposition or temper, of the lack of learning and experience, to discharge the duties he was called upon to fulfil. If steps were taken to ensure that every man who administered the law was a man fit to administer it, the main cause for this Bill would have disappeared, and there would be removed from the great profession to which he belonged the taint which had always clung to it – the taint of time service.'

F. E. Smith, later Lord Birkenhead, Lord Chancellor, intervened to say that while he did not 'dissent from the view that judges should be appointed without regard to political considerations, or rather that incompetent persons should be appointed merely because they were politicians, statistics showed that appeals during the last ten years were not substantially fewer from the decisions of those judges who had formerly taken no part in Party politics than from the decisions of those who before being raised to the bench were active politicians.'

Buckmaster replied, 'I cannot agree; but in any case that is not the question. The question is – Who are the judges who command the confidence of the public and of the profession? I unhesitatingly say the men who enjoy that confidence to the least degree are the men who have been the subject of political appointments, who ought never to have been made judges.'

I do not know how justified these criticisms were but it certainly improved one's chances of a judicial appointment to have been in the House of Commons during the first half of this century. Nowadays it is the exception rather than the rule for a politician to be made a judge and thus the 'taint of time service' or, in other words, the reward of a judicial appointment for those who have served their time in Parliament is now not heard about judicial appointments.

Lord Buckmaster when Lord Chancellor in 1915–16 may have remembered the words he used when he discharged his duty of appointing both High Court and County Court judges.

The other safeguard, if it could be described as such, was provided by the power of the Home Secretary to review criminal trials, both on conviction and sentence.

It was the mishandling of this power in the Maybrick case which caused such public outcry and anxiety and which was still remembered 18 years later when E. H. Pickersgill, the member for Bethnal Green, and who was a barrister, said in the debate in the House of Commons :

'The mischief of the present system was that the Home Secretary had to use a kind of machinery which might be appropriate to the prerogative of mercy, while he was really discharging the functions of a Court of Criminal Appeal. In recent years there had been several cases where the unsatisfactory nature of the present system had been brought to the public attention. In the Maybrick case the capital penalty was remitted by the Crown, and the Home Secretary of the day declared that there was the most grave and serious doubt as to whether any act of Mrs Maybrick had brought about the death of her husband, but that he was convinced that Mrs Maybrick intended to murder her husband; and so during all those years she had been imprisoned for a crime for which she had never been tried, and a crime of which she could not have been found guilty on the indictment of which she was tried and on an issue which was not strictly raised upon the trial. But the case did not end there. The then Lord Chief Justice, speaking as the head of the English Judiciary, declared his opinion that Mrs Maybrick ought to be released. He submitted his reasons to the Home Secretary of the day, who declined to act upon his recommendation, and Mrs Maybrick remained in prison.'

This speech by Pickersgill demonstrated dramatically the difference between the intervention by the Home Secretary and what would have been bound to happen if a Court of Criminal Appeal had been in existence. If an Appeal Court had come to the conclusion that there was 'grave and serious doubt as to whether any act of Mrs Maybrick had brought about the death of her husband' (the Home Secretary had, in fact, used the words 'does not wholly exclude a reasonable doubt') it would, in either event, have quashed the conviction for murder, and set her free. I share the surprise that greeted the Home Secretary's decision to keep her in prison at all, let alone for nearly 15 years.

Lord Halsbury put an opposite view when he said 'Speaking of a recent reprieve in a murder case, I agree that dissatisfaction with the decisions of the Home Office has increased; and I do not wonder at it, when it is found that the only mitigating circumstances in a case of murder is that the murderer thought his victim was his father and shot him.'

The memories of the Maybrick trial did not seem to extend to the judge who tried the case. One MP said that Lord Justice Fitzjames Stephen (an inaccurate promotion) 'than whom no greater authority on criminal matters ever existed, expressed his conviction that legislation of this kind would be the death blow of the trial by jury.' This interesting opinion was contradicted by another Member who reminded the House that Mr Justice Stephen had been one of a Committee of four judges who reported in 1878 in favour of a Court of Criminal Appeal. In fact neither was right, unless the judge had changed his mind after the Maybrick trial, because his Committee did no more than to recommend that the Home Secretary should be given power to refer cases of difficulty to the judges, the Court having power to deal with all the circumstances on the same principles as those on which the Home Secretary then acted.

The difficulties facing the Home Secretary were emphatically expressed by H. J. Gladstone (son of the former Prime Minister) who occupied that office at that time:

'Let me show precisely the disadvantages to which Home Office jurisdiction stands exposed as compared with a Court of Criminal Appeal. A Court of Criminal Appeal, if dissatisfied with a conviction, has the power of quashing it. There is no power of that kind in the Home Office. If, after full inquiry, the case is doubtful, it would sometimes advise the granting of a pardon to the prisoner, or it can grant a remission of imprisonment. But it can give no definite and final judicial finding, such as a Court of law can give, and a case, because of that, might remain in doubt. In the second place, the Court decides after hearing both sides. On a petition to the Home Office the prisoner's case only is before it. The result of that is that the Home Office has to discover the case against the prisoner, to test his conviction and his guilt, in order to establish, if possible, his innocence. But in doing so, the Home Office is open to misconception, and is often bitterly represented as being hostile to the prisoner, for whom, as a matter of fact, the Department is really acting. In the third place, the decision of a Court of law is final. There is no legal finality in the position of the Home Secretary. The consequence of that is that, although he might come to a clear and definite decision, he is always exposed to pressure to reconsider that decision. Questions may be asked in the House of Commons, and letters written to the Press. A newspaper may appoint a commissioner, who starts with absolutely no knowledge of the case, to put a particular case, that of the prisoner, and then, because the Home Secretary adheres to the decision at which he has arrived on the fullest information that anybody could have he is exposed not only to criticism, but to censure and abuse.

'In the fourth place, the Court, as its decision is final, is enabled to state its reasons for that decision. The Home Office cannot state its reasons as a general rule. The cases that come before the Home Secretary necessarily include those which are of special difficulty. There is, in these cases, much to be said on both sides, and if the reasons were stated, obviously those reasons would be debated in the Press and in Parliament by those who could not know all the facts and who are not in a position to arrive at anything like a judicial opinion. But that is not the only reason for reticence. In the interests of the prisoner, inquiries are continually made which are of a confidential character, and information is given only because it is confidential. A statement of reasons would involve the disclosure of confidential communications. That is undesirable, and, I maintain, impossible. It would preclude the Home Secretary from making confidential inquiries; that would be absolutely against the interests of the prisoner and would have the most unfortunate results.

'In the fifth place, the Court may think it necessary to take fresh evidence on oath and to cross-examine witnesses. The Home Office has no such power, and, in fact, it is or it ought to be generally known that the prerogative of mercy was never intended to be used for the purpose of a Court of Appeal or a Court of Revision. If that were the practice or the effect, obviously the Executive Government would have the direct power given to it to interfere with the judicial independence which is one of the glories of the British Constitution, and yet I am constantly pressed from all sorts of quarters, as my predecessors have been pressed, from the executive point of view, to interfere with the decisions of the Courts.

'There are three aspects which criminal cases on examination by the Home Office may take. First of all, it may be perfectly clear that there is no case for interference. Secondly, the original conviction may appear unsatisfactory, either because the evidence before the Court at the time of the trial was unsatisfactory or insufficient, or because of subsequent information which may have come to knowledge. In any of these circumstances the principle which would guide a Scottish Court of Law to a decision would be "Not proven". In the third place, there may be a clear establishment of the innocence of the person who has been convicted. The first and the last aspects are simple. The second aspect is where the real difficulty comes in, and it is, I regret to say, a common case. There may be grave suspicion, such as makes it most undesirable to give a free pardon, and yet sufficient doubt to make it unsafe to maintain the conviction. If the man is in prison he can be released, and he sometimes thinks himself lucky to get out. Occasionally it may happen that in the desire to do the utmost for a possibly innocent man – especially if he has served his sentence – a free pardon is given, even though his innocence is not established.'

Some of Gladstone's comments are particularly interesting in the light of the exercise of the prerogative in the recent cases of George Davis and Patrick Meehan. Davis was convicted of armed robbery, a conviction generally based on identification. He and his friends and family waged a vehement campaign for his release and the Home Secretary ordered an Inquiry. Eventually the Home Secretary released him from prison but did not grant him a free pardon, on the grounds that there was no evidence to justify his innocence, but doubts about the identification evidence were such as to make it right to release him from prison.

Patrick Meehan was convicted of murder and a campaign to reverse the verdict was maintained for some years in Scotland. Finally, a confession by another man exonerating Meehan, and a review of the evidence at the trial led the Secretary of State for Scotland, who exercises similar powers in Scotland as the Home Secretary does in England and Wales, to advise the Queen to grant a Royal pardon. The Secretary of State described this to mean that the conviction was wiped out and Meehan was to be regarded as if he had been acquitted at his trial. This view has led to considerable argument as to the actual effect of a Royal pardon, an argument which, at the time of writing (1976), has yet to be resolved.

By 1907 the public clamour for a Court of Criminal Appeal was at its height. The case of Adolf Beck had shocked and angered the public who felt that the Home Office had failed to act in circumstances which cried out for action. Beck had been granted free pardons in 1904 in respect of convictions in 1896 and 1904 for frauds on women after it had been established following a most careful enquiry that the identifications both of the man and his handwriting by an established handwriting expert were false. He served a sentence of 7 years penal servitude after the conviction in 1896 and was only pardoned when another man was found to have committed the offences.

Thus, in 1907 the Government introduced the Criminal Appeal Bill. Although this was the last of many attempts to remedy an obvious injustice, strong opposition was again mounted in both the Commons and the Lords. No less than 180 columns of Hansard (Parliamentary Reports) are taken up with the Bill which on one occasion was debated through the night. The objections ranged from the cost of three extra judges (£15,000) to the risk of swamping the new Court with the prospect of thousands of appeals each year. A sophisticated argument was based on the risk of jurors not bothering to try the case properly because the Court of Criminal Appeal would deal with it better. It was said time after time that the existence of an Appeal Court would diminish the sense of responsibility of the judge and jury.

Alfred Lyttelton, a KC and later Secretary of State for the Colonies, who was fortunate enough to represent the comfortable safe seat of St George's, Hanover Square said :

'Nobody with knowledge of human nature, who had had the experience of criminal trials, would deny that at the close of a long sitting and at the end of a complicated case, if this Bill were passed there would not be that shrinking from finding a connection between the prisoner and the crime where there was an element of doubt that there now was, as there would be the knowledge that the decision would be open to revision.'

Finally, the view that this was 'an obvious and great piece of justice', as one MP described it, prevailed probably because the fact that England was the only civilised country which did not have some system of appeal in criminal cases persuaded those who took pride in our legal system in other respects that their previous opposition could not be maintained.

When I recently read the debates which took place in 1907 I found the most puzzling aspect of the long discussions was the almost total lack of interest shown in the fact that there was already in existence a Court of Appeal dealing with appeals in civil cases, a number of which would have been decided by juries. However, it may be that members of the House of Commons read the Speech of the Lord Chancellor during a debate in which only four other Peers spoke. He said :

'Everybody agrees that on questions of law there should be an appeal, but questions of law are very rare in criminal cases. It is nearly always a question of fact, either as the sole element or as the main ingredient in it. The reason for wishing to have an appeal on the question of fact is derived, in the first place, from the antecedent probability that human nature will make mistakes, or is liable to make mistakes, and that there ought to be some means of obtaining a skilled review in appropriate cases. It is a terrible thing for a man to be convicted. It ruins his future; his character is gone, and it causes infinite pain and anguish and misery to all who belong to him.

'But apart from the antecedent probability of error there is the acknowledged fact that error exists. We are constantly investigating in this House and in the Court of Appeal cases in which juries have gone wrong on questions of fact; and we are often unable to agree with the views of judges on points of law and on directions of law upon the question of fact and their treatment of questions of fact. If men are liable to go wrong with their judgments in civil causes, why are they not under similar liability in criminal cases? In a civil cause any one can appeal down to £50; but that a man should have no right of appeal against a conviction which may involve penal servitude and a career and character blasted for life is most extraordinary, and in this position this country is unique among nations. I do not believe there is any country that has not some form of appeal.'

The reference to 'in this House' was to the power given to the Appellate Committee of the House of Lords to review, in certain cases, decisions in civil appeals by the Court of Appeal.

Such an appeal to the highest court in the land was also included in the Court of Criminal Appeal Act 1907 subject to the requirement that the unsuccessful party in the Court of Criminal Appeal, whether prosecutor or defendant, obtained the consent of the Attorney-General on the ground that the decision of the Court of Criminal Appeal involved a point of exceptional public importance and that it was in the public interest that a further appeal should be brought. Since 1968 the duty to consent no longer lies upon the Attorney-General and an appeal can only be heard in the House of Lords with the leave of the Court of Criminal Appeal or the House of Lords.

The law providing for criminal appeals has now been established for longer than the experience of anybody still practising in the Courts. Its value is unquestioned and the major changes made in 1968 have been to increase the powers of the Court of Appeal (Criminal Division), as it is now called, to ensure that justice is done and to remove the deterrent effect of the risk of an increased sentence. It is not surprising that these two major changes were the subject of heated debate in 1907.

The first change was designed to remove what was believed to be an unintended and artificial restriction placed upon the Court that the appeal should be allowed if the verdict of the jury was unreasonable or could not be supported by the evidence. This was questioned by F. E. Smith during the debate in 1907 when he suggested that the test should be whether the verdict was under all the circumstances unsafe or unsatisfactory. This amendment was treated with scorn by the Attorney-General who wondered where F. E. Smith had got the words since he would not have got them from a lawyer. Sadly, Smith (later Lord Birkenhead) did not live long enough to see Parliament in 1968 adopt without alteration the words he had earlier suggested.

The other change was to give power to the Court to order a retrial in a very limited class of case, such as where certain important evidence for the accused was not available at the trial. I would be very surprised if the law as it exists now had applied at the time of the Maybrick trial that any Court of Appeal would not have held that the verdict of the jury in her case was unsafe or unsatisfactory.

Every person now charged with a criminal offence has the right to give evidence in his own defence. If convicted, the absolute right to have his case reviewed by the Court of Appeal on any question of law, and with the leave of the Court on any ground which involves a question of fact or on any other ground which appears to the Court of Appeal to be a sufficient ground of appeal. Any epitaph to Mrs Maybrick should include our gratitude for the part she, unwittingly, played in two such important reforms in our law.

In the Criminal Justice Bill 1988 two major alterations have been made to the existing provisions when I wrote the appendix in 1977:

1 The Court of Appeal can now order a re-trial much more generally.
2 The power of the Court of Appeal to increase sentences has been restored.

Acknowledgements

To rank those who have been helpful according to the extent of their helpfulness is impossible. The only fair ranking is alphabetical. But certain individuals deserve a particular word of thanks.

Two linen closets played important parts in Mrs Maybrick's story. The first was in Battlecrease House. The second was at the South Kent School. In it a number of Mrs Chandler's letters and bills, her address book, and three photographs reproduced in this book lay untouched from soon after her death in 1941 until the spring of 1967, when Mrs Martin Tomasovski remembered seeing them there.

The memories of the late Mrs Amy F. Lyon, Samuel A. Woodward, and Alexander Hamilton, and their continuing interest in the Mrs Chandler they knew, have added much detail to the South Kent period of her life.

Mrs E. A. Small, daughter of the late Fred Cushing, and Mrs Darland L. Crosman, daughter of his late daughter, Katharine Cushing Tremble, graciously consented to the use of information contained in Mr Cushing's unpublished autobiography. Miss Margaret Merryweather led the way to the Cushing manuscript and heirs.

Libraries and librarians can never be adequately thanked. The following helped answer many background questions: the excellent public libraries of Wilton and of Westport, Connecticut; John B. Birley, reference librarian, The G. W. Blunt Library, Mystic Seaport, Mystic, Connecticut; Mrs Theodore Davis, librarian, The Joyce Memorial Library, Brookfield Centre, Connecticut; John B. Lochhead, librarian, The Mariners Museum, Newport News, Virginia; Mrs Frank C. Pinkerton, Kirn Memorial Library, Norfolk, Virginia; Elizabeth R. Wood, librarian, South Kent School, South Kent, Connecticut. And the New York Public Library's Newspaper Annex on West Forty-third Street, its Typing Room in the Central Building at Fifth Avenue and Forty-second

Street and its Central Reading Room were host to the author through many a long day.

The alphabetical ranking remains. These have been willing to be interviewed in person, over the telephone, or by mail, or have helped find others to be interviewed : the late Samuel S. Bartlett, Mrs Rob Boyd, Mrs Charlotte Brody, Richard M. Cuyler, Dr Josephine Evarts, Julian A. Gregory, Miss Louise Hanson, Mrs Sinclair Hatch, Martin A. Henry, C. John Herkert, Thomas Honan, Mrs George D. Hopper, Mrs Lucy Hubbell, John S. Jenkins, Jr, Charles Jones, Mrs W. R. Kissam, the late Mrs William Robert Knapp, Miss Ella C. Levis, John Merryweather, Randolph Montgomery, Miss Mabel Mountsier, Mrs Samuel S. Murphy, Miss Elizabeth Parmelee, Mrs Robert G. Peck, J. Trevor Peirce, Jr, Foster Richards, William Sivec, Henry Smithwick, George Strid, Mrs Robert Terhune, Mrs Martin Tomasovski, Mrs Marion Martin Tuck, Mrs Clinton Van De Water, Mrs Thomas Whitney, the Reverend Alonzo L. Wood, Charles F. Wreaks III.

Without exception, those approached have responded with interest and enthusiasm to the request for assistance or information. They have given the author much detail of Mrs Maybrick's life and much to be thankful for in his own.

B.R.

Bibliography

Newspapers and Periodicals

The Times (England), *The New York Times*, the New York *World*, throughout the period from the first news story on 'The Aigburth Poisoning Case' in May, 1889, through Mrs Maybrick's obituaries in October 1941. Also specific issues of the *Isle of Wight County Press*, the *Mobile Register*, the *New Milford* (Connecticut) *Times*, the *Norfolk Pilot*, the *American Weekly*, *Time*, *Newsweek*, and *Pageant* magazines, and the *Norfolk Museum Bulletin*.

Books and Pamphlets

Warren Armstrong (pseud. for William E. Burnett), *Atlantic Highway*. New York: John Day Co., 1962.

F. Lawrence Babcock, *Spanning the Atlantic*. New York: Alfred Knopf, 1931.

The Earl of Birkenhead (Frederick Edwin Smith), *Famous Trials of History*, Vol. II. New York: Clark Boardman, Ltd., 1929.

Charles Boswell and Lewis Thompson, *The Girl With the Scarlet Brand*. New York: Fawcett Publications, Inc., Gold Medal Books, 1954.

Paul Brown, *Aintree – Grand Nationals Past and Present*. New York: Derrydale Press, 1930.

Lamont Buchanan, *Ships of Steam*. New York: McGraw-Hill, 1956.

Anne Buck, *Victorian Costumes and Costume Accessories*. New York: Thomas Nelson and Sons, 1961.

C. F. Carter, *Wedding Day in Art and Literature*. New York: Dodd, Mead and Co., 1900.

Carl C. Cutler, *Queens of the Western Ocean*. Annapolis; U.S. Naval Institute, 1961.

Emmet Densmore, *How Nature Cures*. New York: Stillman and Co., 1892.

– – – *Sex Equality*, New York: Funk and Wagnalls, 1907.

James Dugan, *The Great Iron Ship*. New York : Harper and Bros., 1953.

Lady Elizabeth Eliot, *Portrait of a Sport* : The Story of Steeplechasing in Great Britain and the United States. Woodstock, Vermont : The Countryman Press, 1957.

C. Hamilton Ellis, *Ships*. New York : Macmillan, 1957.

Laura Dayton Fessenden, *Bonnie Mackirby*. Chicago and New York : Rand, McNally and Co., 1898.

Alden Freeman, (pamphlets) *The Abbey Memorial,* 1916; *A Year in Politics,* 1916; *The Fight for Free Speech,* 1909; *Memorial of Capt. Thomas Abbey,* 1917; *The Quest of Ancestors,* 1905; *Seven Years as a Lecture Manager* (undated); *The Suppression of Free Speech in New York and in New Jersey* (undated).

Walter Phelps Hall and Robert Greenhalgh Albion, *A History of England and the British Empire*. New York : Ginn and Company, 1937.

Henry Harald Hansen, *Costumes and Styles*. New York : E. P. Dutton and Co., Inc., 1956.

W. T. Harries, *Landmarks in Liverpool History*. Liverpool : Philip, Son and Nephew, Ltd., 1934.

James J. Hodge, *Famous Trials* (third series). Harmondsworth, Middlesex : Penguin Books, 1950.

Angus Holden, *Elegant Modes in the Nineteenth Century*. New York : Greenberg, 1936.

Ronald Hope, *Ships*. New York : Macmillan, 1958.

Hester E. Hosford, *The Forerunners of Woodrow Wilson*. East Orange, New Jersey : East Orange Record Print, 1914.

H. B. Irving, *Trial of Mrs Maybrick*. Edinburgh and London : William Hodge and Co., 1912 (rev. 1922).

George Gibbard Jackson, *The Romance of the Sea*. New York : Fred A. Stokes Co., (undated).

James Joyce, *Ulysses*. New York : Random House (Modern Library), 1934.

James Laver, *English Costume of the Nineteenth Century*. London : A. & C. Beach, Ltd., 1929.

– – – *English Children's Costume Since 1775*. London : A. & C. Beach, Ltd., 1930 (rev. 1958).

Edgar Lustgarten, *Verdict in Dispute*. New York : Charles Scribner's Sons, 1950.

Alexander William MacDougall, *The Maybrick Case*. London : Bailliere, Tindall and Cox, 1891.

C. F. Dendy Marshall, *100 Years of Railways*. London : LMS Railway Co., 1930.

Florence Elizabeth Maybrick, *Mrs Maybrick's Own Story* : My Fifteen Lost Years. New York : Funk and Wagnalls Co., 1905.

Nigel Morland, *This Friendless Lady*. London : Frederick Muller, Ltd., 1957.

Joseph Shearing, *Airing in a Closed Carriage*. New York : Harper and Bros., 1943.

Eugene W. Smith, *Trans-Atlantic Passenger Ships Past and Present*. Boston : George H. Dean Co., 1947.

J. F. Smith, *Liverpool – Past, Present and Future*. Liverpool : The Northern Publishing Company, 1948.

J. B. Snell, *Early Railroads*. New York : G. P. Putnam's Sons, 1964.

D. C. Somervell, *English Thought in the Nineteenth Century*. New York : Longmans, Green and Co., 1938.

Stevens and Pendlebury, *Sea Lanes*. New York : Minton, Balch and Co., 1935.

J. Stopford Taylor, *Report of the Health of Liverpool, 1886–1887*. Liverpool : Public Health Report.

Warren Tute, *Atlantic Conquest*. Boston : Little, Brown and Co., 1962.

Hudson Tuttle, *Arcana of Nature*. New York : Stillman Publishing Co., 1909.

Alan Villiers, *Wild Ocean*. New York : McGraw-Hill, 1957.

Thomas Jefferson Wertenbaker, *Norfolk: Historic Southern Port*. Durham : Duke University Press, 1931 (rev. 1962).

Reese Wolfe, *Yankee Ships*. New York : Bobbs-Merrill Co., 1953.

Raymond F. and Marguerite W. Yates, *A Guide to Victorian Antiques*. New York : Harper and Bros., 1949.

H. S. and H. E. Young, *Bygone Liverpool*. Liverpool : H. Young and Sons, 1913.

(author unknown), *Household Work – Or, the Duties of Female Servants*. London : Joseph Masters, 187–?

(author unknown), *The Management of Servants*. London : Frederick Warne and Co., 188–?

(author unknown), *129 Views of Liverpool*. Liverpool : Bunneys, Ltd., 1910.

The Dictionary of American Biography.

The Encyclopedia Americana.

The National Cyclopedia of American Biography.

The Oxford Companion to English Literature.

Who's Who in America, 1899 through 1937.

Index

FOR THE BEST IN PAPERBACKS, LOOK FOR THE

In every corner of the world, on every subject under the sun, Penguin represents quality and variety – the very best in publishing today.

For complete information about books available from Penguin – including Pelicans, Puffins, Peregrines and Penguin Classics – and how to order them, write to us at the appropriate address below. Please note that for copyright reasons the selection of books varies from country to country.

In the United Kingdom: Please write to *Dept E.P., Penguin Books Ltd, Harmondsworth, Middlesex, UB7 0DA*

If you have any difficulty in obtaining a title, please send your order with the correct money, plus ten per cent for postage and packaging, to *PO Box No 11, West Drayton, Middlesex*

In the United States: Please write to *Dept BA, Penguin, 299 Murray Hill Parkway, East Rutherford, New Jersey 07073*

In Canada: Please write to *Penguin Books Canada Ltd, 2801 John Street, Markham, Ontario L3R 1B4*

In Australia: Please write to the *Marketing Department, Penguin Books Australia Ltd, P.O. Box 257, Ringwood, Victoria 3134*

In New Zealand: Please write to the *Marketing Department, Penguin Books (NZ) Ltd, Private Bag, Takapuna, Auckland 9*

In India: Please write to *Penguin Overseas Ltd, 706 Eros Apartments, 56 Nehru Place, New Delhi, 110019*

In Holland: Please write to *Penguin Books Nederland B.V., Postbus 195, NL–1380AD Weesp, Netherlands*

In Germany: Please write to *Penguin Books Ltd, Friedrichstrasse 10–12, D–6000 Frankfurt Main 1, Federal Republic of Germany*

In Spain: Please write to *Longman Penguin España, Calle San Nicolas 15, E–28013 Madrid, Spain*

In France: Please write to *Penguin Books Ltd, 39 Rue de Montmorency, F-75003, Paris, France*

In Japan: Please write to *Longman Penguin Japan Co Ltd, Yamaguchi Building, 2–12–9 Kanda Jimbocho, Chiyoda-Ku, Tokyo 101, Japan*

FOR THE BEST IN PAPERBACKS, LOOK FOR THE

PENGUIN BESTSELLERS

Oscar Wilde   Richard Ellmann

'Exquisite critical sense, wide and deep learning, and profound humanity
. . . a great subject and a great book' – Anthony Burgess in the *Observer*
'The witty subject has found a witty biographer who is also distinguished
for his erudition and humanity' – Clare Tomalin in the *Independent*

Presumed Innocent   Scott Turow
The No I International Bestseller

'One of the most enthralling novels I have read in a long, long time' – Pat
Conroy. 'If you start *Presumed Innocent* you will finish it . . . it grips like
an octopus' – *Sunday Times*

Spring of the Ram   Dorothy Dunnett
Volume 2 in the *House of Niccolò* series

Niccolò has now travelled as far as the frontier of Islam in order to
establish the Silk Route for the Charetty empire. Beset by illness, feuds
and the machinations of his rivals, he must use his most Machiavellian
schemes to survive . . .

A Time of Gifts   Patrick Leigh Fermor

'More than just a Super-travel book . . . it is a reminder that the English
language is still a superb instrument in the hands of a writer who has a
virtuoso skill with words' – Philip Toynbee in the *Observer* 'I know of no
other account of pre-war Europe which conveys so much so powerfully'
– Peter Levi

A Fatal Inversion   Barbara Vine

Ten years after the young people camped at Wyvis Hall, the bodies of a
woman and child are found in the animal cemetery. Which woman?
Whose child? 'Impossible to put down . . . she is a very remarkable writer'
– Anita Brookner. 'I defy anyone to guess the conclusion, but looking
back, the clues are seen to be there, unobtrusively but cunningly planted,
so that it seems one should have known all along' – *Daily Telegraph*

FOR THE BEST IN PAPERBACKS, LOOK FOR THE

PENGUIN BESTSELLERS

Is That It? Bob Geldof with Paul Vallely

The autobiography of one of today's most controversial figures. 'He has become a folk hero whom politicians cannot afford to ignore. And he has shown that simple moral outrage can be a force for good' – *Daily Telegraph*. 'It's terrific . . . everyone over thirteen should read it' – *Standard*

Niccolò Rising Dorothy Dunnett

The first of a new series of historical novels by the author of the world-famous *Lymond* series. Adventure, high romance and the dangerous glitter of fifteenth-century Europe abound in this magnificent story of the House of Charetty and the disarming, mysterious genius who exploits all its members.

The World, the Flesh and the Devil Reay Tannahill

'A bewitching blend of history and passion. A MUST' – *Daily Mail*. A superb novel in a great tradition. 'Excellent' – *The Times*

Perfume: The Story of a Murderer Patrick Süskind

It was after his first murder that Grenouille knew he was a genius. He was to become the greatest perfumer of all time, for he possessed the power to distil the very essence of love itself. 'Witty, stylish and ferociously absorbing . . . menace conveyed with all the power of the writer's elegant unease' – *Observer*

The Old Devils Kingsley Amis

Winner of the 1986 Booker Prize
'Vintage Kingsley Amis, 50 per cent pure alcohol with splashes of sad savagery' – *The Times*. The highly comic novel about Alun Weaver and his wife's return to their Celtic roots. 'Crackling with marvellous Taff comedy . . . this is probably Mr Amis's best book since *Lucky Jim*' – *Guardian*

FOR THE BEST IN PAPERBACKS, LOOK FOR THE

PENGUIN OMNIBUSES

The Penguin Book of Ghost Stories

An anthology to set the spine tingling, including stories by Zola, Kleist, Sir Walter Scott, M. R. James and A. S. Byatt.

The Penguin Book of Horror Stories

Including stories by Maupassant, Poe, Gautier, Conan Doyle, L. P. Hartley and Ray Bradbury, in a selection of the most horrifying horror from the eighteenth century to the present day.

The Penguin Complete Sherlock Holmes   Sir Arthur Conan Doyle

With the fifty-six classic short stories, plays *A Study in Scarlet*, *The Sign of Four*, *The Hound of the Baskervilles* and *The Valley of Fear*, this volume is a must for any fan of Baker Street's most famous resident.

Victorian Villainies

Fraud, murder, political intrigue and horror are the ingredients of these four Victorian thrillers, selected by Hugh Greene and Graham Greene.

Maigret and the Ghost   Georges Simenon

Three stories by the writer who blends, *par excellence*, the light and the shadow, cynicism and compassion. This volume contains *Maigret and the Hotel Majestic*, *Three Beds in Manhattan* and, the title story, *Maigret and the Ghost*.

The Julian Symons Omnibus

Three novels of cynical humour and cliff-hanging suspense: *The Man Who Killed Himself*, *The Man Whose Dreams Came True* and *The Man Who Lost His Wife*. 'Exciting and compulsively readable' – *Observer*

PENGUIN CLASSIC CRIME

The Big Knockover and Other Stories Dashiell Hammett

With these sharp, spare, laconic stories, Hammett invented a new folk hero – the private eye. 'Dashiell Hammett gave murder back to the kind of people that commit it for reasons, not just to provide a corpse; and with the means at hand, not with handwrought duelling pistols, curare, and tropical fish' – Raymond Chandler

Death of a Ghost Margery Allingham

A picture painted by a dead artist leads to murder . . . and Albert Campion has to face his dearest enemy. With the skill we have come to expect from one of the great crime writers of all time, Margery Allingham weaves an enthralling web of murder, intrigue and suspense.

Fen Country Edmund Crispin

Dandelions and hearing aids, a bloodstained cat, a Leonardo drawing, a corpse with an alibi, a truly poisonous letter . . . these are just some of the unusual clues that Oxford don/detective Gervase Fen is confronted with in this sparkling collection of short mystery stories by one of the great masters of detective fiction. 'The mystery fan's ideal bedside book' – *Kirkus Reviews*

The Wisdom of Father Brown G. K. Chesterton

Twelve delightful stories featuring the world's most beloved amateur sleuth. Here Father Brown's adventures take him from London to Cornwall, from Italy to France. He becomes involved with bandits, treason, murder, curses, and an American crime-detection machine.

Five Roundabouts to Heaven John Bingham

At the heart of this novel is a conflict of human relationships ending in death. Centred around crime, the book is remarkable for its humanity, irony and insight into the motives and weaknesses of men and women, as well as for a tensely exciting plot with a surprise ending. One of the characters, considering reasons for killing, wonders whether the steps of his argument are *Five Roundabouts to Heaven*. Or do they lead to Hell? . . .'

FOR THE BEST IN PAPERBACKS, LOOK FOR THE 🐧

PENGUIN CLASSIC CRIME

Ride the Pink Horse   Dorothy B. Hughes

The tense, taut story of fear and revenge south of the border. It's fiesta time in Mexico but Sailor has his mind on other things – like revenge. Among the gaudy crowd, the twanging guitars and the tawdry carnival lights are three desperate men fighting over a dark and bloody secret.

The Narrowing Circle   Julian Symons

The editor's job at Gross Enterprises' new crime magazine is 'in the bag' for Dave Nelson. Or so he thinks, until the surprising appointment of Willie Strayte. When Strayte is found dead Nelson must struggle to prove his innocence and solve the elaborate puzzle. 'One of our most ingenious and stylish home-grown crime novelists' – *Spectator*

Maigret at the Crossroads   Georges Simenon

Someone has shot Goldberg at the Three Widows Crossroads and Maigret is carrying out a thorough investigation, getting to know the lives of the small community at Three Widows. Although he is suspicious of everyone, he has a hunch about the murder – and that means the case is as good as wrapped up.

The Mind Readers   Margery Allingham

When rumours of a mind-reading device first came out of Godley's research station, Albert Campion found it difficult to take them seriously. Especially as the secret seemed to rest exclusively with two small boys, who were irritatingly stubborn about disclosing their sources . . .

The Daughter of Time   Josephine Tey

Josephine Tey's brilliant reconstruction of the life of Richard III, now known to us as a monster and murderer, is one of the most original pieces of historical fiction ever written, casting new light on one of history's most enduring myths.

CRIME AND MYSTERY IN PENGUINS

Deep Water   Patricia Highsmith

Her chilling portrait of a psychopath, from the first faint outline to the full horrors of schizophrenia. 'If you read crime stories at all, or perhaps especially if you don't, you should read *Deep Water*' – Julian Symons in the *Sunday Times*

Farewell, My Lovely   Raymond Chandler

Moose Malloy was a big man but not more than six feet five inches tall and not wider than a beer truck. He looked about as inconspicuous as a tarantula on a slice of angel food. Marlowe's greatest case. Chandler's greatest book.

God Save the Child   Robert B. Parker

When young Kevin Bartlett disappears, everyone assumes he's run away . . . until the comic strip ransom note arrives . . . 'In classic wisecracking and handfighting tradition, Spenser sorts out the case and wins the love of a fine-boned Jewish Lady . . . who even shares his taste for iced red wine' – Francis Goff in the *Sunday Telegraph*

The Daughter of Time   Josephine Tey

Josephine Tey again delves into history to reconstruct a crime. This time it is a crime committed in the tumultuous fifteenth century. 'Most people will find *The Daughter of Time* as interesting and enjoyable a book as they will meet in a month of Sundays' – Marghanita Laski in the *Observer*

The Michael Innes Omnibus

Three tensely exhilarating novels. 'A master – he constructs a plot that twists and turns like an electric eel: it gives you shock upon shock and you cannot let go' – *The Times Literary Supplement*

Killer's Choice   Ed McBain

Who killed Annie Boone? Employer, lover, ex-husband, girlfriend? This is a tense, terrifying and tautly written novel from the author of *The Mugger*, *The Pusher*, *Lady Killer* and a dozen other first class thrillers.

FOR THE BEST IN PAPERBACKS, LOOK FOR THE

CRIME AND MYSTERY IN PENGUINS

Call for the Dead   John Le Carré

The classic work of espionage which introduced the world to George Smiley. 'Brilliant . . . highly intelligent, realistic. Constant suspense. Excellent writing' – *Observer*

Swag   Elmore Leonard

From the bestselling author of *Stick* and *La Brava* comes this wallbanger of a book in which 100,000 dollars' worth of nicely spendable swag sets off a slick, fast-moving chain of events. 'Brilliant' – *The New York Times*

Beast in View   Margaret Millar

'On one level, *Beast in View* is a dazzling conjuring trick. On another it offers a glimpse of bright-eyed madness as disquieting as a shriek in the night. In the whole of Crime Fiction's distinguished sisterhood there is no one quite like Margaret Millar' – *Guardian*

The Julian Symons Omnibus

The Man Who Killed Himself, *The Man Whose Dreams Came True*, *The Man Who Lost His Wife:* three novels of cynical humour and cliff-hanging suspense from a master of his craft. 'Exciting and compulsively readable' – *Observer*

Love in Amsterdam   Nicolas Freeling

Inspector Van der Valk's first case involves him in an elaborate cat-and-mouse game with a very wily suspect. 'Has the sinister, spellbinding perfection of a cobra uncoiling. It is a masterpiece of the genre' – Stanley Ellis

Maigret's Pipe   Georges Simenon

Eighteen intriguing cases of mystery and murder to which the pipe-smoking Maigret applies his wit and intuition, his genius for detection and a certain *je ne sais quoi* . . .

PENGUIN TRUE CRIME

Titles published and forthcoming:

Who Killed Hanratty?   Paul Foot

An investigation into the notorious A6 murder.

Norman Birkett   H. Montgomery Hyde

The biography of one of Britain's most humane and respected judges.

The Complete Jack the Ripper   Donald Rumbelow

An investigation into the identity of the most elusive murderer of all time

The Riddle of Birdhurst Rise   R. Whittington-Egan

The Croydon Poisoning Mystery of 1928–9.

Suddenly at the Priory   John Williams

Who poisoned the Victorian barrister Charles Bravo?

Stinie: Murder on the Common   Andrew Rose

The truth behind the Clapham Common murder.

The Poisoned Life of Mrs Maybrick   Bernard Ryan

Mr Maybrick died of arsenic poisoning – how?

The Gatton Mystery   J. and D. Gibney

The great unsolved Australian triple murder.

Earth to Earth   John Cornwell

Who killed the Luxtons in their remote mid-Devon farmhouse?

The Ordeal of Philip Yale Drew   R. Whittington-Egan

A real life murder melodrama in three acts.